STUDIES ON MODERN ASIA
AND AFRICA

Volume 7

POLITICS AND SOCIETY
IN INDIA

POLITICS AND SOCIETY IN INDIA

Edited by
C. H. PHILIPS

Routledge
Taylor & Francis Group

LONDON AND NEW YORK

First published in 1963 by George Allen & Unwin Ltd

This edition first published in 2022
by Routledge
2 Park Square, Milton Park, Abingdon, Oxon OX14 4RN

and by Routledge
605 Third Avenue, New York, NY 10158

Routledge is an imprint of the Taylor & Francis Group, an informa business

© 1963 George Allen & Unwin Ltd

British Library Cataloguing in Publication Data
A catalogue record for this book is available from the British Library

ISBN: 978-1-03-215171-7 (Set)
ISBN: 978-1-00-324754-8 (Set) (ebk)
ISBN: 978-1-03-215398-8 (Volume 7) (hbk)
ISBN: 978-1-03-215412-1 (Volume 7) (pbk)
ISBN: 978-1-00-324404-2 (Volume 7) (ebk)

DOI: 10.4324/9781003244042

Publisher's Note
The publisher has gone to great lengths to ensure the quality of this reprint but points out that some imperfections in the original copies may be apparent.

Disclaimer
The publisher has made every effort to trace copyright holders and would welcome correspondence from those they have been unable to trace.

POLITICS AND SOCIETY
IN INDIA

EDITED BY

C. H. PHILIPS

*Professor of Oriental History and Director of the School of Oriental
and African Studies, University of London*

LONDON
GEORGE ALLEN & UNWIN LTD
RUSKIN HOUSE   MUSEUM STREET

PRINTED IN GREAT BRITAIN
in 11 point Fournier type
BY UNWIN BROTHERS LTD
WOKING AND LONDON

INTRODUCTION

The act of independence of 1947 brought to the surface in the Indian sub-continent political forces which had previously been obscured by the struggle for independence. The British Government had been able to conduct its political conversations with the Indian middle classes, but since 1947, its successors, the Indian middle-class leaders, have had to come to terms with the implications of a universal franchise in the context of the indigenous social order. New relationships between the middle classes and the masses, between the central governments and local agencies, between the modern parliamentary system and the traditional social systems are therefore fast emerging.

It is feasible to describe contemporary Indian politics solely in terms of the parliamentary system, and some western political scientists have tended to do this. It is feasible, too, to begin with the study of the nature of Indian society, and to interpret the political process solely in terms of caste interests and struggles. Each of these explanations is patently unsatisfactory, and incomplete. The papers printed here were presented to a seminar which came together at the School of Oriental and African Studies in order to explore the emerging relationships between the indigenous, traditional systems and the new-style democratic concepts and parliamentary forms of government. The seminar consisted mainly of historians, anthropologists and political scientists, and it is from these viewpoints that the following papers were presented. No attempt was or has yet been made to make a comprehensive study of the whole range of the problems indicated.

In the first three papers Professors Basham and Cantwell Smith and Dr Hardy give some indication of the nature of the Indian political heritage from the remote past. They emphasize the gulf that exists between traditional Indian, Hindu and Muslim, theories of government and politics and those of the modern world. In ancient India the lack of a single, consistent body of political doctrine is stressed. In India under Muslim rule, Islamic theology accepted the Muslim *umma* as the ideal human community, whose purpose was to pay obedience to God in the ways indicated by the Muslim ruler in terms of Holy Law. In the interpretation of this Law classical Muslim jurists necessarily played an important part. From them descended the *ulama*, and Professor Cantwell Smith has traced their gradual emergence into a clear-cut class in the nineteenth century.

In an analysis of the political background to the British declaration

7

of the policy of promoting Indian self-government, Dr Mehrotra brings out the contrasts that are implicit between these traditional attitudes and the pragmatic exchanges of British and Indian middle-class political leaders in 1917.

The remaining papers place their emphasis on Indian political practices and emergent forms of government since 1947. Professor Haimendorf, Dr Bailey and Dr Mayer consider the extent to which the indigenous social order in different parts of India has influenced and been influenced by the working of a representative system. Caste is seen to vary in its degree of influence and political importance from place to place and from time to time. They demonstrate that explanations of the political process cannot rest satisfactorily on a simple juxtaposition of the indigenous social order with a western-type representative system. Professor Morris-Jones finds a similar complexity under the superficial appearance of normal western parliamentary practices in the main centres of government. The influence of the indigenous social system is pervading politics at all levels of activity, and the idiom of modern parliamentary practice penetrates the social order. The Indian National Congress itself provides a perfect example of this intermingling of the 'different languages of politics'.

In such a complex process, it was hardly likely that British-instituted forms of local government would long persist in India, and Dr Tinker therefore analyses the decay of those institutions, and the recent attempts to replace them in India by a system of *panchayat raj*, which sets out to use the social group, not the individual, as the basis of the democratic system.

*   *   *

In the spelling of Indian words I have not attempted to impose a uniform system of transliteration. The editor and the contributors are indebted to Miss Nora Shane and Dr S. R. Mehrotra for checking the proofs, and to Dr Mehrotra for preparing the index.

C. H. PHILIPS

CONTENTS

SOME FUNDAMENTAL POLITICAL IDEAS
OF ANCIENT INDIA

A. L. BASHAM

*Professor of the History of South Asia
in the University of London*

In any study of ancient India it must be borne in mind that we are
dealing with a very long period of time and a very large area. Some
of the most important ideas on kingship arose in India among semi-
tribal monarchies in the days before the Buddha. The centralizing
bureaucratic Mauryan Empire produced a political atmosphere very
different from that which was to be found in the quasi-feudal kingdoms
of later times. Speculations from all these periods have become part
of the common Indian heritage. Racial and cultural differences must
also be allowed for. It is often forgotten that the political climate of
the Dravidian South was appreciably different from that of the Aryan
North.

Moreover, ancient India allowed considerable freedom of specula-
tion. It is hardly necessary to point out that, as well as the six orthodox
philosophical systems, schismatic and heterodox schools of thought
flourished freely, and differences in metaphysics and theology were to
some extent reflected in the realm of political ideas. Thus the Buddhist
and Jaina doctrines on the origin and basis of kingship were by no
means the same as those of orthodox Hinduism. Most of the views
described in this brief survey might have been heard in a typical
Hindu court of the first millennium AD, but it must be recognized that
within any such kingdom differences of opinion existed. A single
consistent body of doctrine, universally accepted, was probably never
to be found anywhere in ancient India.

Though the ancient Indian loved controversy in the field of metaphysics and in certain other branches of study, there is not much
evidence of serious discussion on problems of political philosophy.
We have records of vigorous and sometimes acrimonious debates on
matters of religion, often taking place under royal patronage before
large and interested audiences; no discussions on such themes as the
origin of kingship or the nature of political obligation are recorded.

Several well-known textbooks on polity, such as the *Kauṭilīya Arthaśāstra*, the *Kāmandaka Nītisāra*, and the *Nītivākyāmṛta* have survived from our period. These treat of the conduct of state affairs in considerable detail, and often refer to differences of opinion on specific questions, such as the ideal constitution of the king's ministerial council. But they contain no lengthy discussions on the fundamental questions of political philosophy. The student can find answers to these questions, but they are often tucked away in texts dealing with other matters, where they are put forward as categorical statements of ancient truths, substantiated only by myths and legendary instances.

The three chief religio-philosophical schools of ancient India— Brahmanical Hinduism, Buddhism, and Jainism—differed considerably, not only in their theology and metaphysics, but also in their attitude to social life and politics; but they had certain fundamental ideas in common. One of these, and a very important one, was the doctrine of the cyclic universe, on which the cosmologies of all three systems, though differing in many respects, were in full agreement. It seems that everyone in ancient India, without exception, believed that the universe passed through an interminable series of immensely long cycles, and that it was at present passing through a phase of decline, which would culminate in a state of utter wretchedness, until the next cycle commenced. Again there would be general agreement that government is an unfortunate necessity in an age of universal decay. In former times, when the world was closer to perfection, society functioned without the need of government; but as the world degenerated evil and crime became rife among men, and government appeared, whether on divine initiative, through a corporate act of human will, or in the natural course of events, in order to preserve the social order as far as possible, and to arrest for a while the inevitable ruin of all things.

In twentieth-century terms the corollary of this is that society is prior to government and that government is the servant of society, which it exists to preserve. Though the Hindu king was often thought of as divine, the monistic tendencies of much Indian thought never strongly affected political thinking, and political mysticism of the Hegelian type is quite foreign to the Indian tradition.

There are three immediate aims in the life of man, *dharma*, *artha*, and *kāma*, which may be roughly paraphrased as piety, profit and pleasure. All are perfectly legitimate, but the claims of the first override those of the second, while the third is subordinate to the two others. The ideal layman achieves in his daily life a harmonious

balance of the three aims, thus contributing to the ultimate achievement of a fourth aim, salvation (*mokṣa, mukti*). This is too remote to
be pursued directly by the ordinary man, but the ascetic puts aside
all other considerations in its favour. Ancient India generally had a
healthy realization that most men were not temperamentally suited to
asceticism, and her systems of society and government, while making
room for the *sannyāsī*, did not generally envisage an extremely
puritanical order, where the layman was forced to conform to the
ascetic's standards as far as possible. To this generalization some
Jaina writers form something of an exception, for they would have
kings enforce vegetarianism by law, and ban the distilling of liquor,
cock-fighting, and other popular practices which infringed the
principle of *ahiṃsā* or were otherwise reprehensible. Aśoka too seems
to have been something of a puritan, and to have attempted to enforce
his own high standard of morality by legislation. But in general the
king was not the arbiter of morals; he merely enforced the existing
moral codes of the classes and castes in his kingdom, as interpreted
for him by the learned brahmans of his court.

The doctrine of the three aims is closely linked with the all pervading concept of *Dharma*. Each class or caste has its own divinely
ordained norm of conduct—this is its *dharma*. There is also a *dharma*
appropriate to each stage in a man's life. The rights and duties of a
brahman are not those of a *śūdra*, while those of the schoolboy are
not those of the paterfamilias. The *dharma* of all classes and ages,
taken collectively, was known as *varṇāśrama-dharma*, 'the *dharma* of
class and stage of life'. *Varṇāśrama-dharma* was in fact the traditional
order of Aryan society, a society which by virtue of this very *dharma*
formed a unity, though composed of diverse ethnic and social groups
and of men and women of all ages and characters. Only within the
framework of *varṇāśrama-dharma* might men achieve the three aims.
In lands where it was strictly observed they would increase in virtue,
wealth and happiness, and draw nearer to the ultimate goal, the
salvation of the soul from the bonds of transmigration.

Thus as a *sine qua non* of human welfare the preservation of
varṇāśrama-dharma was one of the first duties of government. But
at this degenerate stage in the cosmic cycle the *dharma* of Aryan
society is also degenerating. Long ago, in the days of the legendary
Kṛta-yuga, the age of gold, men followed it automatically in its com-
pleteness; with the decline of all things the eternal norms became
more and more infringed; now, in this benighted *Kali-yuga* the
maintenance of *varṇāśrama-dharma* is at best precarious, for it is

attacked from within by heterodoxies such as Buddhism and Jainism, by unbelief, and by the evil propensities of the human nature of the age; while from without it suffers the assaults of hordes of barbarians, knowing nothing of the eternal laws of the Aryans. Some of these, known as *mlecchas*, were in theory quite beyond the pale of Aryan society, but others were redeemable, and might be incorporated into the Aryan order if they accepted the spiritual authority of the brahmans and adopted the Aryan way of life. The series of invasions from the North-west, beginning with that of the Yavanas or Bactrian Greeks at the end of the Mauryan period (*c.* 200 BC), on the one hand brought new features into Indian culture and society, and thus served as a stimulating force, but on the other hand it seems to have encouraged a certain social pessimism, which increased with the years, and which, after the Hūṇa occupation of western India (*c.* AD 500–30), became more and more rigid and conservative.

The Turks in the twelfth and thirteenth centuries repeated on an even larger scale the feats of the Yavanas, Śakas, Kuṣāṇas and Hūṇas of earlier times, and drove Hindu society even further back upon itself. The rigidity of social norms was intensified by alien occupation. The social system had always been compartmentalized and more or less static, except perhaps in the proto-historic period of the *Ṛg-veda*. Centuries of attack certainly strengthened its rigidity, and throughout the first millennium AD the political atmosphere was increasingly affected by the uncompromising system of class and caste. The culmination of the process was the ossified Hindu social system found by the European traders in the seventeenth and eighteenth centuries.

In the present century much has been made by Indian scholars and propagandists of the presence of republics and democracies in ancient India. There can be no doubt that such forms of government did exist in several parts of northern India down to the fourth or fifth century AD; but they were rarely, if ever, a significant factor in the politics of India as a whole, and most of the texts on polity do not even mention their existence. Monarchy, in fact, was always the normal system of government.

There are significant differences between the Hindu view of government on the one hand and those of the Buddhists and Jains on the other, but, as we have seen, all schools of thought had the doctrine in common that government is an unfortunate necessity of the age of decline. There are, however, certain differences in the interpretation of this belief. According to most Hindu tradition, in the period of anarchy before government was instituted men had become so evil that the strong destroyed the weak and all creatures 'in fear scattered in all directions',[1] until kingship was instituted by divine decree. In some stories the first king was appointed by the High God at the behest of men, in others he was a divine being himself, sent down to earth in answer to men's petitions in order to restore and maintain the social order. Nearly all Hindu legends on the origin of kingship depict men in a state of anarchy as praying to the gods to save them.

The old Buddhist legend, devised, it would seem, as a sort of counterblast to the brahmanic one, tells of the slow decline of the cosmos as the result, rather than the cause, of men's increasing greed. When mutual agreements became ineffectual in protecting private property men met together and chose one of their number to preserve law and order by enforcing punishment, in return for a share of their produce. Thus for the Buddhist kingship is dependent on consent, and is a purely human institution, based on a sort of social contract. The Jainas also believed that kingship evolved naturally, though not by an act of popular will but by an almost automatic process. When this age of decline began men did not need to work for food and clothing, which were provided by wonderful 'wishing trees'. Gradually these disappeared, and life became correspondingly more complicated. People looked at first to a series of natural leaders, the patriarchs (kulakāra), men naturally wiser than their fellows who taught to humanity the arts and crafts of civilization and organized society without coercion, their authority enforced purely by moral suasion. But ultimately, with the continued cosmic decline and growing human wickedness, moral suasion was not enough. The last patriarch, Ṛṣabha, appointed his son Bhārata as the first king and himself took to a life of asceticism, becoming the first great teacher (tīrthaṅkara) of Jainism.

The traditions of orthodoxy and those of heterodoxy betray an implicit difference of attitude. For the Hindu kingship saves the world from the most terrible anarchy, in some degree halts the cosmic decline, and restores some semblance of the age of gold. On the lowest estimate the Hindu king is a charismatic figure, divinely appointed; at the most he is a great divinity himself. For the Buddhist and Jain, on the other hand, kingship is a necessary evil in an evil age, and the king is nothing but a mere human being. The relevant heterodox sources contain no positively anti-monarchical sentiments, but they

[1] Manu, vii, 3.

give no support to exaggerated claims on the part of the king, or to the idea of royal divinity.

The orthodox conception of kingship was certainly the more influential in the thought of pre-Muslim India, and we find even Buddhist and Jain kings laying claim to divinity. In its finished state the doctrine of royal divinity is explicit and categorical. The king contains immortal particles of the eight *Lokapālas*, the great gods who guard the world; he is a great divinity in human form. But it must be borne in mind that the Hindu conception of divinity differs greatly from that of the West, which has largely inherited the transcendent and unitary God of early Jewish theology. For Hinduism the divine inheres in some measure in everything, but especially in beings and objects which are powerful, or otherwise wonderful or impressive. 'Whatever is fortunate, splendid, or strong', says Kṛṣṇa in the *Bhagavad-gītā*,[1] 'springs from a portion of my glory.' Thus divinity is almost commonplace, the property not only of the great gods, but also of brahmans, ascetics, husbands, wives, parents, teachers, cows, snakes, *tulasī*-plants, *pīpal* and banyan trees, and many other things too numerous to mention. So, though he was regularly addressed as *deva* or god, the king did not always receive in ancient India the abject and obsequious adoration accorded to emperors in some other ancient civilizations. In drama and story we read of kings being roundly abused by their wives, boldly criticized by their ministers, and scathingly condemned by their subjects, usually with complete impunity. Bāṇa, the court poet of Harṣavardhana, denounced in no uncertain terms the sycophants who persuaded foolish kings that they were more than mortal; such kings, in their attempts to act like the four-armed Viṣṇu or the three-eyed Śiva, merely made themselves look ridiculous.[2]

In nearly all sources the first duty of the king is said to be Protection (*pālana*). The term covers a wide range of activity, including the protection of life and property by the enforcement of law, and the protection of the kingdom from invasion, but first and foremost the king's protective function should be exercised in respect of the divine social order, the *varṇāśrama-dharma*, thereby giving the optimum chance of spiritual progress to as many individuals as possible. The king is the guardian of something greater than himself, his subjects, and his realm put together—the eternal and holy laws of a society which is itself part of the eternal cosmic order. In many sources the king is explicitly encouraged to act unscrupulously, or

[1] X, 41. [2] *Kādambarī*, tr. Ridding, pp. 177-8.

with extreme ruthlessness, in times of emergency, but only because of the overriding necessity of maintaining society, the end of all statecraft, to be achieved by any means whatever. Only a few unorthodox sources, such as the *Arthaśāstra* ascribed to Kauṭalya, notable for its secular and machiavellian approach to politics, would justify the king in resorting to fraud or tyranny for motives of power alone.

The *Dharma* which the king protects is primarily the general *Dharma* of Aryan society, but it also includes the many lesser *dharmas* of the tribes, castes, clans, and trade associations and guilds within his kingdom—their traditional customs and rules of behaviour. He is not himself the arbiter of what constitutes *Dharma*, and theoretically he has no power to alter *Dharma* in any way. The ideal king accepts the interpretation of *Dharma* given by the paṇḍits attached to his court, and enforces it ruthlessly and impartially by means of coercion (*daṇḍa*). Some sources make much of this principle, which is personified as a divinity in its own right. In this decadent age the sacred order hangs precariously in the balance, and men are naturally evil, selfish, and prone to sin; so the king must be stern in the administration of justice, for otherwise *Dharma* will perish. Only where fierce and red-eyed *Daṇḍa* stalks the land, like the death-god himself, punishing the evil-doer, will the kingdom be happy and prosperous.

It is often said that in contrast to the political thought of the West, that of India lays much stress on duties and obligations, but says little or nothing about rights. Such statements are hardly justified—in fact rights are often mentioned in many contexts. But in any case no obligation or duty can exist without a complementary and corresponding right or claim. Implicit in the doctrine of the king's duty of protection is the right of the Aryan to enjoy his legally acquired property without hindrance, and to live according to the traditional ways of his forefathers. The royal duty of protection is interpreted to include the protection of his subjects from injustice and oppression of all kinds, and much stress is laid on the protection of the honour of women, and of widows, orphans, the diseased, and the indigent. As might be expected, in the legal texts, which were the work of brahmans, the priestly order is particularly commended as the object of the king's care.

Among the official activities of the king 'Pleasing the People' is almost as strongly stressed as Protection. The ideal king is not only the grim punisher of evil-doers, but also the genial and gracious benefactor of his law-abiding subjects. 'He should not look on as good whatever pleases himself, but whatever pleases his subjects', says the *Arthaśāstra*.[1] The benevolent aspect of monarchy is clear from the false etymology given in several sources to the word *rājā*, which is wrongly derived from the verb *rañjayati* 'he pleases'. The king's paternal aspect is evident also from the usual word for 'subjects', *prajā*; this is derived from the root *jan* 'to be born', and its first meaning is 'progeny'.

Not only because it is his duty to please his subjects, but also for the sake of his own welfare and security, the king is advised always to be sensitive to public opinion. This seems to have been fairly vocal, and an organized corps of secret agents reported it to the palace. The emphasis placed in all the textbooks on the organized secret service has often received adverse criticism from democratic twentieth-century critics, but it must be remembered that among the most important functions of the spies was that of keeping the royal finger on the public pulse.

The duty of satisfying his subjects involved many positive responsibilities, some of them also connected with his primary duty of protection. These included the enforcement of law and order, the speedy and just settlement of disputes, fair taxation, the care of the indigent, the provision of utilities such as irrigation works, the distribution of largesse on festive occasions, and the patronage of temples, religious institutions, learned men, and poets.

As we have seen, ancient India recognized rights as well as duties, and after fulfilling his duties of protecting and pleasing his subjects the king had the right to comfort and pleasure. He is often referred to as the 'eater' or 'enjoyer' (*bhoktā*) of his kingdom, and his relationship with it is conceived on the analogy of that of husband and wife. This comparison rarely occurs in the *Dharmaśāstra* literature, but is common enough in courtly panegyrics, where even petty monarchs are said to have 'gained the sea-girt earth as a bride'. The implication of the simile is evident. As the husband, who provides for her care and maintenance, has the right to the obedience of his wife, and to the physical and other satisfactions which she can provide, so the king enjoys by right the proceeds of the taxes and services rendered by his obedient subjects, and the tribute and homage of conquered kings and vassals. In accordance with the doctrine of the three aims, moreover, the king is fully entitled to a life of great luxury and comfort, after fulfilling his duties. As far as can be gathered from literature the private life of the king was one of refined and tasteful

[1] i, 19.

luxury. Though on the battlefield he was expected to show great powers of endurance, though poets might describe him as adorned with the scars of a hundred wounds received in righteous warfare, the ideal Hindu king was not merely a tough warrior, but, in his leisure time, also a cultured pleasure-seeker, fastidious in his tastes. The famous murals of Ajanta, the court scenes of which are reflected in much secular literature, give a very vivid impression of the graceful and charming private life of the Indian king.

As a corollary of the king's status as the 'husband' of his kingdom he was generally thought of as the ultimate owner of the land. This question, however, is one of the most disputed topics in the field of ancient Indian polity. Texts can be found which appear to reject the royal ownership of arable land, and it is clear that custom limited this in many respects. Though the lord of the land, the king was expected to abide by certain norms in his treatment of it, just as the husband, who was the lord of his wife, had not, according to the Aryan *dharma*, complete rights of life and death over her. Thus it does not appear to have been considered legitimate for the king to confiscate arbitrarily the land of a peasant who paid his taxes and was otherwise a good citizen. Certain theorists of the *Mīmāṃsā* school, basing their views on the *Brāhmaṇa* literature, which for them was completely authoritative, never accepted the doctrine of royal ownership.

Connected with the idea of the king as the father of his people and the husband of his realm was the concept of the organic relationship of the king and his kingdom. The king, the land, the people, the flora and fauna, and even the weather, were mystically interlinked. As the lord, husband and father of his realm the king formed a sort of microcosm of it, and the interrelation of the king's conduct and the kingdom's welfare was believed to be a much deeper one than was obvious and rational. Not only did the careless or oppressive king ruin the kingdom by his neglect or cruelty, but his private virtues or vices were thought to have an unseen effect on the whole order of nature in the kingdom. Bad conduct on the part of the king, even though it might have no obvious ill effects on his realm, might lead to inadequate or superabundant rainfall, crop-failure, famine, plague, and other calamities. His righteousness, on the other hand, protected the land from all misfortunes, whether due to natural causes or human agency. This doctrine, which is also to be found in ancient China, seems to be a moralized refinement of the widespread belief among primitive peoples that the welfare of the tribe is magically connected with the vitality or virility of the chief.

As we have seen already, Indian political thought was much concerned with moral obligations on the part of both king and subject, each of which implicitly involved corresponding moral rights. It must be emphasized that these are in both cases moral only. In no ancient Indian kingdom was there any constitutional machinery for enforcing them, and in practice their effectiveness must always have depended on the consciences of the king and his ministers and vassals, and on the initiative and political awareness of his subjects.

The king is morally obliged to govern according to the principles of Protection and 'Pleasing the People'. They in turn are morally obliged to pay their taxes and dues and otherwise to obey the king's commands, where these do not conflict with *Dharma*. If they refuse to obey him the king is morally obliged to compel them to do so and to punish them for their recalcitrance, in order that society may be preserved.

There are varied views on the rights of the people, or of certain sections of them, against a king who rules inefficiently or unjustly, and on the obligation to resist injustice. Certain passages here and there suggest a doctrine of passive obedience, but some rights are almost universally conceded. Ministers have the right, and indeed the moral duty, to speak their minds freely to the king, and to criticize his policy if they deem it necessary; the king is morally obliged to respect their right of free speech, though not necessarily to act on their advice. Nowhere, to my knowledge, is it stated that mild and respectful criticism of royal policy is contrary to *Dharma*, and it would seem that there was often a good deal of such criticism. From the evidence of the *Rājataraṅgiṇī* and other sources it appears that much influence was exerted by pressure groups of varying strength, mainly consisting of caste associations and guilds. Associations of brahmans, as might be expected, were often very influential.

It would seem that the right of free movement from place to place was generally recognized. In several sources the king is warned that if he oppresses his subjects they will leave the kingdom, and the texts do not appear to conceive of the possibility of the king's forcibly preventing them from doing so. The tendency for the Indian peasant to migrate from an anarchic or despotically governed district to one where there are stable conditions and benevolent rule can be traced from the time of the Buddha down to the early days of the East India Company. The early Indian king encouraged such immigrants, for, except in times of famine, there seems to have been no question of under-employment or serious pressure on the land in ancient India, and manpower was a source of strength and prosperity.

Here and there passages may be found advocating complete and passive obedience even to a wicked king, because the effects of anarchy are so terrible that any king is better than none. But nearly all sources admit, either explicitly or implicitly, the moral justification of revolt against a king who blatantly infringes the Sacred Law. The doctrine of royal divinity did not carry with it the corollary that the king was infallible or incapable of sin, for even the great gods may err. Doctrines similar to Mencius' conditional Mandate of Heaven are to be found here and there, the most famous of which, made much of by modern Indian democrats, is in the *Mahābhārata*.[1] The king is a divine being, and should not be resisted by his subjects. But by definition he pleases and protects the people. If he fails in this function, therefore, he is not really a king at all, but a mere mortal, in no sense divine, and no more worthy of obedience than a common man. So 'the people should take up arms and kill the king who plunders their wealth and fails to protect them . . . They should combine to slay him like a mad dog.' This explicit justification of revolt does not, however, seem to have had much effect in practice, for no example of a successful popular revolt is to be found in the history of pre-Muslim India; but there is little doubt that the support of the populace gave strength to the plotters of palace revolutions, which were quite frequent.

Many modern scholars, perhaps motivated by the idea that the concept of the state is a *sine qua non* of a civilized system of political thought, have tried to find evidence of such a concept in ancient Indian political writings. Though they have usually succeeded to their own satisfaction, it seems doubtful whether there was any clear idea of the state in pre-Muslim times. As used in the West the term seems to imply a corporate entity controlling a definite territory, which maintains its identity and continues to exist, irrespective of changes in the governing personnel. In the writings of the more doctrinaire theorists the state seems to take on the character of a living entity, greater than the sum of its parts. In India such political mysticism was discouraged by the doctrine of *Dharma*, which concerned society and not the state, and by the fundamental individualism of all the metaphysical systems. The ultimate aim of all valid and worthy human activity is salvation, which cannot be achieved by corporate entities such as peoples, castes, and families, but only by

[1] xiii, 61, 31–3.

individual human beings. Government exists to serve society, and, on final analysis, society exists to serve the individual. This latter proposition is hardly to be found in implicit form, but it is a necessary corollary of the fundamental presuppositions on which all Hindu thought was based. Buddhism was quite categorical in its rejection of the doctrine that the whole is more than the sum of its parts, and provided a very unfavourable soil for political mysticism of the Hegelian type. The same may be said of Jainism, with its doctrine of an infinite number of discrete monadic souls.

Rājya, the term generally translated 'state' and used in that sense in modern Indian languages, is a secondary nominal formation from the word *rājā*, and etymologically implies 'that which pertains to the king'. In early sources it is best translated 'kingdom'. The nearest approach to a developed concept of the state is to be found in the stock list of the seven constituents (*prakṛti*) or members (*aṅga*) of the *rājya*, a rather illogical formula which is repeated in numerous sources: king (*svāmī*), ministers (*amātya*), the land (*janapada*), fortifications (*durga*), armed forces (*bala*), treasure (*kośa*) and allies (*mitra*). These *aṅgas* are occasionally compared to the limbs of the human body, but only in the *Śukranīti*, a nineteenth-century text,[1] is the comparison made at all forcibly. It is significant that in some manuscripts of the *Arthaśāstra* the list is augmented by the addition of an eighth element, the enemy (*amitra*); in the mind of the scribe responsible for this interpolation the series of the seven members of the *rājya* could not have corresponded to anything like the modern state. Moreover as it stands the list does not include the subjects, without which no state can exist. The scholars who believe that the seven members represent the state of modern political thought claim that the subjects are subsumed in the third element, the land, and point to the *Arthaśāstra*[2] in justification of this. Here Kauṭilya, in a list of the distinctive features of the ideal land, states that its peasants should be industrious and its inhabitants loyal and of good character, but this comes at the end of a long list of other characteristics of the territory of the ideal realm, in no way connected with the subjects of the king. The seven factors of sovereignty, it seems, are merely a conventional and not very accurate formulation of the main elements which must be taken into account for the successful conduct of government.

We conclude, therefore, that ancient Indian political theorists had no very clear idea of the state, in the sense in which that word is used in western political thought. There might be a case for the view that

[1] Lallanji Gopal, *BSOAS* 25, pp. 524–56.　　　　　　[2] vi, 1.

they are deserving rather of praise than of blame on that account, because 'the state' has no real existence except as an abstraction in the minds of political theorists and as a rather more portentous synonym of 'government' in the speeches of politicians. Perhaps Europe has gone astray too often in the past by attributing an illusory reality to such abstract entities.

In this brief paper we have tried to give a rapid summary of certain basic ideas and attitudes in the political thought and life of pre-Muslim India. For reasons of time and space we have confined ourselves to those aspects of political thought which chiefly relate to the internal polity of the kingdom, and have written nothing about the ideas of India concerning international relations and warfare, which form a subject in themselves, and which, though of much interest, have little significance as pointers to a national policy in the atomic age. In so far as any ancient Indian thought on international relations still has any effect on policy it is that of Aśoka, whose ideas of non-aggrandizement and conquest by moral suasion were completely at variance with those of the textbooks.

It is debatable how far the ideas which we have discussed are still influential in Indian polity. Certainly all the reformers and political leaders of Hindu India, from Ram Mohan Roy onwards, knew something about them, but in most cases their efforts were directed rather at finding prototypes of modern western ideas in ancient India than at interpreting basic ancient Indian concepts in terms suitable to contemporary conditions. Whether such an interpretation would serve any useful purpose in meeting the political needs of twentieth-century India is very debatable, but certain principles may still have some validity, when expressed in modern terms to suit a secular state. The subordination of government to the needs of the social order is perhaps one such principle; another is the doctrine that the king's duty is not only to protect but also to please his subjects, which might perhaps be taken to foreshadow the Welfare State. The government envisaged by the political theorists of ancient India is a rather stern paternalistic one, but one which provides for the welfare, both moral and material, of all its subjects. It is in no sense a democracy, but it allows freedom of speech and freedom of movement, and the idea of government by discussion is not wholly absent from it. And, finally, government is not an end in itself. There is only one final end to which all valid human activity should serve as means—the achievement of inner peace (if we may thus interpret *mokṣa* in secular terms) by each individual.

TRADITIONAL MUSLIM VIEWS
OF THE NATURE OF POLITICS

P. HARDY

*Reader in the History of Islam in South Asia
in the University of London*

My object is to expound the dominant assumptions which Muslims
of recognized religious authority, living before any major segment
of the Muslim community came under the political authority or the
cultural influence of non-Muslims, made about the nature and ends
of political activity. This account aims at being a study of theory not
of practice, of the ideas and pre-suppositions of academicians rather
than of the working assumptions of practising rulers and administrators. It should be taken broadly to refer to the assumptions being
made among Muslim scholars at the beginning of the fifth/twelfth
century, by which time the doctrines of the four *Sunnī* schools of
jurisprudence had been formulated in great detail, dogmatic theology
or *kalām* had been cast in the mould which it was to retain for centuries
and the challenge of Greek philosophy had been contained and sealed
off, if not repulsed.

It is true that the 'Abbāsid Caliphate had yet to be destroyed by
the Mongol Hūlāgū, but long before 1258, Muslim theories of government had been adjusted to a situation in which the *Khalīfa* was no
longer the effective head of a politically united Muslim community.
What had been conceived as the ideal functions of the *Khalīfa* had
become the ideal functions of the sultan, or of the *de facto* holder of
military power; what should have been the character of political life
in the Muslim community as a whole should now become the character
of political life in a segment of that community.[1] Nor, in assessing
traditional Muslim ideas of politics should the doctrines of the *Shī'a*

---

[1] On this development see H. A. R. Gibb, 'Some Considerations on the
Sunni Theory of the Caliphate', *Archives d'Histoire du droit oriental*, III,
1947.

Illustrations of the process in Indo-Muslim thinking are given in *Sources of
Indian Tradition*, ed. Wm. Theodore de Bary and others (1958), pp. 478–95,
503–4.

or of the *falāsifa* be taken to require three separate accounts of three quite different phenomena. *Sunnī* and *Shī'a* disagree over the question of who should rule and how the ruler is designated; they do not disagree over the nature of the ideal body politic, the qualifications for membership of it, the decisions it is proper for rulers to take or the relations which should obtain between rulers and ruled. As for the Muslim philosophers, al-Fārābī, Ibn Sīnā and Ibn Rushd, in their general conceptions of the proper ends of politics, they had converted Plato and Aristotle to Islam.[1] In general, however, what follows represents the views of the '*ulamā*' and of the jurists whose works are referred to in the exhaustive footnotes given by D. Santillana in his *Istituzioni di Diretto Musulmano Malichita*, Rome, 1926, *Libro primo*, pp. 1–24. The ideas of the *sūfīs* have not been considered.

It is a measure of the intellectual value of comparative political studies embracing a wide diversity of civilizations and periods that they forbid the settling of problems of definition of terms by appeal to the conventional usages and the restricted language of one particular society or indeed of one particular civilization. What 'politics' means cannot now be settled by an appeal to what the Greeks of classical antiquity or European thinkers of the eighteenth or nineteenth centuries meant by the term. We have to find a definition applicable equally to the experience, say, of Arab tribes of the seventh century AD, of Mongol hordes under Chengiz Khān, of scholar bureaucrats of classical China, or of modern Congress politicians of present-day rural Orissa. That is, we must find the denominator common to loosely-knit nomadic empires with slow communications, to decentralized agricultural states, to ruthless dictatorships armed with all the modern means of controlling not only deeds but words and sometimes thoughts as well, and to states possessing representative institutions on the model of Westminster. It is necessary also to arrive at a definition which would be intelligible, if not acceptable, to those societies where the rulers and the laws are considered divine as equally to those where they are not.

It would, it is presumed, be universally accepted that in form, politics is a manner of social activity, that a solitary individual is not engaged in politics and that the manipulation of things, without the help of other human beings, is not a political activity. The decision of an individual to spend money on tobacco rather than food could not be called a political decision. It would also, it is presumed, be accepted that politics has, in some way, to do with government, the

[1] See E. I. J. Rosenthal, *Political Thought in Medieval Islam* (1958), pp. 113 ff.

activity of doing something to, through and with a society taken as a whole and as distinct from other societies. The essential activity of government is to decide and to act—about and toward men and not about and toward things.

But, surely, it may be objected, government is an end-product not the ground of political activity, that government is not possible except as a consequence of politics. There must be recognition, sufficient to the purpose, of who constitutes the government. Logically, the activity of persuading or inducing some men to accept the authority of others is a necessary prelude to the establishment of government and indeed to the activity of forcing some men to accept the will of others. The formation of groups or aggregates of men bound together by loyalty and acceptance of a common allegiance is of the essence of politics. No doubt many political groups in history have been created by force; but first there was, and indeed must have been, consent by some men to follow others.[1] Every Samson has his Delilah. The rallying of wills[2] for the achievement of purposes the individual will, acting on its own, finds it impossible to achieve, may be regarded as political activity.

But not the whole of that activity and not the peculiar *differentia* of that activity is political. No doubt decision and persuasion, the rallying of wills, occur in such groups and associations as tennis clubs, Imperial Chemical Industries, not to speak of the simplest of all human groups and associations, the family. And this is not merely or indeed mainly because such associations are for limited, specified and often transitory purposes, whereas political associations are often thought to have more general purposes and more enduring lives. It is because a body politic is endowed with the authority to issue commands which shall be obeyed by all who are members, whether by consent or habit or duress, of that body politic. It is endowed with the power to enforce law, whether that law be of its own devising or not. There is no escaping the authority of a political association merely by an expression of disagreement with its decisions. That is not to say that constraint and the ability to constrain is the heart of politics; it does however enable us to distinguish Politics from politics.

[1] The history of the bomb plot against Hitler on July 20, 1944, is a significant illustration of the necessity of some consent and respect for constituted authority even in modern totalitarian dictatorships. The voice of Hitler on the telephone swung Von Remer and hence his vital Berlin troops against accepting the orders of Colonel von Stauffenberg and the conspirators in Berlin.

[2] With acknowledgements to Bertrand de Jouvenal, *Sovereignty: an inquiry into the political good* (1957), Chapter I.

This definition of Politics as the activity of forming human aggregates and of reaching decisions within those aggregates which are enforced by penalties generally applicable throughout the aggregate in question, in short by coercion, has it is hoped, the advantage of general application whether the society in question be eastern or western, northern or southern, ancient, medieval or modern. It does not reject as un-political societies where the element of coercion is dominant and the area of consent, minimal; nor does it reject as non-political the life of those societies where the ambit of decision is narrow and the origin of law, divine. All societies in history have known human aggregates formed by the rallying of human wills by whatever means; they have known authorities endowed with the right of decision, albeit only over issues of peace and war; they have known an apparatus of enforcement.

The examination of traditional Muslim views of the nature of Politics which follows will concentrate on the nature of the ideal human association, the Muslim *umma*, and of authority therein, the ends that the association should pursue, how those ends are to be known by man and how far joint activity is a feature of the traditional Muslim conceptions of politics, together with such explanations by reference to other spheres of Muslim thought as appear necessary.

For the classical Muslim jurists,[1] social and political relationships and the authority of men over men can exist only as a consequence of a right relationship between individual men and an entity outside human society, namely, Allāh. Left to themselves, men will not learn to co-operate, they will tear each other to pieces.[2] It is true that human needs drive men together—but equally true that human instincts drive them apart. Men cannot persuade other men to co-operate and to accept authority unless each believes the same, the same not about why they should co-operate in society, but about the nature of reality as a whole. In other words, man's juridical existence is conditional upon his religious beliefs. Without right religion, man cannot have rights and duties in relation to other men. The human personality as such, irrespective of acceptance of certain propositions about the destiny of the universe, does not endow a man with a moral or a

[1] What immediately follows does not apply to Ibn Khaldūn, for whom society and government were constituted naturally by the force of ʿasabiyya (group feeling). A community held together by ʿasabiyya may fall short of the best, which is governed by Divine Law in contemplation of the next world, but it is not inherently impossible.

[2] Santillana, *Istituzioni*, pp. 12–13.

juridical status *vis-à-vis* other men. Not his personality, not his psychology, not his policy but his piety renders man a social being. How then does he become committed and a being with social rights and duties? By making the affirmation (or, if a child, having it made by others for him), that there is no God but God and that Muhammad is His Prophet. This *shahādat* is an affirmation by the individual that he recognizes as binding for him the pact or *mīsāq* which God, of His uncovenanted Bounty, has offered the human race, the terms of which are to be found in the eternal uncreate *Qur'ān* which He has sent down to men through His Messenger, Muhammad the Prophet.[1] This *mīsāq* or pact is, of course, in no sense a social contract; it is not entered into between man and man but between man and God who has absolute power to vary the terms of the pact or to ignore them altogether.

Once entered into by pronouncing the *shahādat*, this *mīsāq* governs the individual's relations with all other men. He will find his status, social obligations and legal rights defined for him by Divine Revelation, by Divine Decree, the authority of which for himself he has now recognized. The *minutiae* of those rights and obligations he may find in the *Qur'ān*, the *Sunna* or model behaviour of the Prophet and in the *Sharī'a* or Holy Law founded upon the *Qur'ān* and the *Sunna*. They are positively commanded for him, in every detail, as much when they are deduced from the *Qur'ān* and *Sunna* as when they are patently prescribed in so many words in the *Qur'ān* and *Sunna*. Moreover, they are not deducible from other than the authoritative texts of Revelation. The *Sharī'a* is essentially 'that which would not be known had there not been a divine dispensation'.

The ideal community, or *umma*, is therefore the aggregate of those who have pronounced the Muslim affirmation; it is the only aggregate within which man can try to escape from his animal nature and fulfil his role in the universe. It is an open aggregate in the sense that anyone may join merely by pronouncing the *shahādat*. Within the *umma*, the source of authority belongs with God. All men are equal in the servanthood of God and no Muslim enjoys authority over another Muslim except by the positive command of God. Not only does all authority come from God, but there is no authority other than that of God. He has not conferred upon the community as such, some general discretionary authority to be exercised by it as the members may think fit according to some criteria of their own understanding or creation. All power comes from God, says classical

[1] Louis Gardet, *La Cité musulmane* (1954), pp. 197–9.

Islam, dwells in Him, and is entirely exercised by Him through human instruments.[1]

The *umma* is an aggregate created not by the rallying of human wills for co-operation, it is an aggregate created by individual acceptance of subjecthood of God. It is a compresence of individuals whose relations are defined and controlled by what God has decreed rather than by what they themselves have determined together. Within the *umma*, characterized though it may be by the brotherhood of all believers, joint activity is undertaken because it has been commanded by God; indeed, without God's Command, it is impossible that it should be undertaken. The *umma* is not made feasible by man's common humanity nor is it united by it. Without Islam, man would know only the war of all against all. For traditional Muslim thinkers, social life is not the completion of man's moral nature—indeed, for the dominant school of Muslim theology, man has no 'nature' as such. If man comes to fulfilment in the *umma*, it is because he has decided to accept God's Purposes as binding upon himself, not because he has realized that the recognition of obligations to others is a condition of moral existence. Indeed, it is not man who is to come to fulfilment in the *umma*, it is the purposes of God, in so far as He has deigned to reveal them, which are to be fulfilled. Moreover, for the *'ulamā'*, the Muslim community does not become a communion whose preservation as such is a claim upon the individual believer. On the Day of Judgement, 'no soul laden bears the load of another'.[2] On that day, no man could plead the service of the *umma*, the maintenance of its unity as such as a reason for disobeying a specific Divine Command in Revelation or in the Holy Law deduced therefrom. Life in the *umma* is an experience through which, by Divine Command, the Muslim must pass on his way to the Last Day, but the responsibility of the individual to God remains paramount; he may not place social ties before his personal duty of absolute obedience to God and His Holy Law. Traditional Muslim values cannot, in the last resort, be social or communal values. Social and political activity have value only in so far as God has specifically decreed in Revelation that it shall have value. If the end of politics be conceived merely as a species of diplomacy where everybody is 'kept in the picture' by ensuring that the picture never commits itself to any particular insight into reality, then traditional Muslim thinkers will regard such an end or such an activity as un-islamic.

The activity in which the Muslim community should engage is,

[1] Gardet, *op. cit.*, p. 36. [2] *Qur'ān*: liii, 39.

for traditional Muslim thinkers, essentially a normative activity. In the words of the *Qur'ān*, 'to command the good and to prohibit the evil'. Or again, 'Let there be one nation of you, calling others to the good, commanding the good and forbidding the evil'. Or again, 'You are the best community which has ever arisen among men; you bid the good and forbid the evil and believe in God'.[1] Few men would deny all normative purpose in social and political life. Even those who hold that the main function of politics is to secure peace and order rather than some ideal social condition are making the value judgement that peace is better than war, order better than anarchy. What however distinguishes the classical Muslim tradition is its conception of the good and of the means by which the good may be apprehended. Good is what God has ordained in Revelation, in His Holy Law, and evil is what He has forbidden by positive Divine Decree. Good is the *huqūq*, the rights of God, that which He has ordained as His due; evil that which He has expressly forbidden; evil acts are those to the commission of which He has attached a prescribed penalty. But more than that: good is wholly circumscribed by what He has commanded and evil by what He has forbidden. There is no intermediate area in which man is free to work out his own conceptions of what is best, his own conceptions of what is right or wrong. There is no aspect of life, individual or social which escapes the Divine Law. It is true that according to the fivefold classification of actions according to the orthodox *Sunnī* schools of jurisprudence, there is the category of actions regarded as *mubāh* or morally indifferent, but this category of actions does not embrace the fundamental purposes of the body politic or the fundamental constitution of the state. Moreover, within the area of *mubāh* actions, man is not being allowed to formulate his own moral code, he is merely being allowed to act without the prospect of either penalty or reward. Man enjoys no moral autonomy, he is allowed no scope for deciding himself, in the light of Divine Revelation, or of the nature of things, what is right or wrong. God has not written His Eternal Will for men on the face of nature and left mankind to decipher the meaning of the inscriptions for themselves. As Santillana writes, 'Se è vero che la comunità musulmana ha per capo Dio stesso, la legge altro non è se non la volontà di Dio ... chi la viola, infrange non solo l'ordine giuridico, ma commette, nell' ordine religioso, un peccato ("ma'siyah"—ribellione a Dio), poichè "non v'ha diritto in cui Dio non abbia la sua parte" '.[2]

It may help perhaps to bring this fundamental Muslim position

[1] *Qur'ān*, iii, 100 and 106.　　　　　　　　[2] *Istituzioni*, p. 5.

into even sharper relief, if a description of a quite contrasting position, held by St Thomas Aquinas, is quoted in extenso:[1] 'The eternal law is thus the plan of divine wisdom directing all things to the attainment of their ends. . . .But man, as a rational and free being, is capable of acting in ways which are incompatible with the eternal law. It is therefore essential that he should know the eternal law in so far as it concerns himself. Yet how can he know it? He cannot read, as it were, the mind of God. Is it then necessary that God should reveal to him the moral law? Aquinas answers that this is not necessary in the strict sense of the word. For although man cannot read off, as it were, the eternal law in God's mind, he can discern the fundamental tendencies and needs of his nature, and by reflecting on them he can come to a knowledge of the natural moral law. Every man possesses the natural inclinations to the development of his potentialities and the attainment of the good for man. Every man possesses also the light of reason whereby he can reflect on these fundamental inclinations of his nature and promulgate to himself the natural moral law, which is the totality of the universal precepts or dictates of right reason concerning the good which is to be pursued and the evil which is to be shunned. By the light of his own reason, therefore, man can arrive at some knowledge of the natural law. And, since this law is a participation in or reflection of the eternal law in so far as the latter concerns human beings and their free acts, man is not left in ignorance of the eternal law which is the ultimate rule of all conduct. "The natural law is nothing else but a participation of the eternal law in a rational creature."[2]

The implications of traditional Muslim attitudes for political life may now perhaps be easier to grasp. Politics cannot be a process whereby men attempt to secure for themselves the realization of a human vision of the good, even within limits set forth for them by their religious beliefs. Quite opposed to classical Muslim ideas are the large area left for human decision and the close limits set for the normative role of the law by, for example, the Archbishop of Canterbury in the debate on the Wolfenden Report in the House of Lords on December 4, 1957,[3] when he said, 'The right to decide one's own moral code and obey it—even to man's own hurt—is a fundamental right of man, given to him by God, and to be respected by society and the criminal

[1] F. C. Copleston, Aquinas (1955), pp. 215–16.
[2] See also Georges de Lagarde, Recherches sur l'esprit politique de la réforme (1926), pp. 29–32.
[3] 206 H. L. Deb. 5s., col. 753.

code'. In its actions the Muslim *umma* is always controlled and limited by the *hudūd* or determinations of the *Sharī'a*. The needs of the community do not shape the *Sharī'a*; it is the *Sharī'a* which shapes the needs of the community.[1] Politics should not be merely a means of attaining certain human and social satisfactions peaceably—a conversation between pressure groups intended to keep up the conversation by reducing the pressure. The beginning and end of the political life of the Muslim community is obedience to God in the ways which He has positively commanded.

The explanation of the refusal of traditional Muslim scholars to admit any moral autonomy for mankind outside Revelation, to allow the human reason and the human conscience to exist as a means of perceiving, however imperfectly, what is meet as well as expedient for life on earth, in society, is ultimately theological. Man as such has not been endowed with reason and conscience, with the faculty of glimpsing God's truth for himself. He is incapable, created as he is, of understanding what goodness and truth are, and of acting rightly and justly towards his fellows.[2] For, according to the Ash'arite school of theology, by AD 1100 accepted as orthodox by the consensus of the community, man has, in Louis Gardet's phrase, no ontological reality. 'Il n'y a pour la personne humaine aucun droit qui derive de sa nature telle que Dieu l'a façonnée. Le composé humain n'est qu'impermanence, et n'a d'autre stabilité que celle octroyée par Dieu de l'extérieur. Disons, si l'on veut, que, métaphysiquement parlant, l'invididu n'est rien, et que la personne n'existe que par l'intervention extrinsèque et discontinue de Dieu.'[3] Man is the slave ('*abd*) of God; he is the slave of God because he is nothing other than an aggregation of atoms held in juxtaposition from moment to moment. He has no nature as such nor is endowed with human faculties as such.[4] This doctrine, as we shall see later, was intended to preserve God's exclusive efficacy, His absolute sovereignty over His creation. Furthermore, to allow man any freedom, within however narrow a sphere, to decide questions of right and wrong, is to trespass upon Divine Omnipotence and to be guilty of *shirk* or of giving a partner to God. Justice and right would then be something other that what God was at the moment

[1] J. N. D. Anderson, 'Law as a Social Force in Islamic Culture and History', *BSOAS*, XX, 1957, p. 17.

[2] For a similar standpoint among early Protestant reformers see Lagarde, *op. cit.*, pp. 151–6.

[3] Gardet, *op. cit.*, p. 53.

[4] On the Ash'arite metaphysic of 'atomic occasionalism' see Majid Fakhry, *Islamic Occasionalism* (1958), pp. 26–43.

commanding. Orthodox Islam, in its Ash'arite formulation, has held fast to the position that what God commands is just and right, but that it is just and right because it has been so commanded, and not commanded because it is just and right. The orthodox doctrine of God's Unity and Omnipotence means that all determinations of right and wrong, truth and error are determinations of the Divine positive Law, the *Sharī'a*, which is itself not to be penetrated by the intelligence; it is *ta'abbudī* or to be accepted without criticism, as beyond human understanding.

But given that the Muslim community exists ideally to further the end of obedience to a Divine Law which embraces all aspects of man's individual and social existence, how far does traditional Muslim thought allow the understanding of the prescriptions of that Law and their enforcement to partake of a co-operative activity, to become an object of political association? How far is the *umma* an active association under Divine Law? The answer to this question may perhaps be found by glancing at the main features of the concept of *ijmā'*, or consensus of the community, and at the institution of *Khilāfat*, both of which at first sight may appear to offer scope for the joint activity of making decisions about the arrangements of Muslim society under Divine Law.

After the *Qur'ān*, the *Sunna* and *qiyās*, or analogical reasoning from the two first, *ijmā'* is recognized by all *Sunnī* schools of jurisprudence as a fourth source of the Holy Law. That which the Muslim community agrees upon it may be said has the force of Holy Law. Is this the element of popular decision, in Islam, of a rallying of wills in a lay and egalitarian theocracy? Does *ijmā'* contain the seed of the parliamentary principle in Islam? Some Muslims in modern times, for example Rashīd Rizā[1] and Sir Mohammad Iqbal[2] have argued so. But this view does not accord with the understanding of the traditional thinkers. And this is not merely because the ambit of *ijmā'* is circumscribed by a text, or *nass*, of the *Qur'ān* or *Sunna*, but also because not all Muslims may participate in *ijmā'* and because those that do are not acting politically when they do. For Ibn Taymiyya (661/1263–728/1328) and the Hanbalites, only the Companions of the Prophet and the generation of Muslims immediately following them, may join in *ijmā'*. For the *mazhab* of al-Shafi'ī, *ijmā'* is regarded as the consensus of the *'ulamā'*, that is of those who, in any given generation, are capable by reason of their character and scholarship of exercising

---

[1] Henri Laoust, *Le Califat dans la doctrine de Rašīd Ridā* (1938), pp. 98–104.
[2] Sir Mohammad Iqbal, *Six Lectures on the Reconstruction of Religious Thought in Islam* (1930), pp. 240–4.

ijtihād or personal effort at interpreting the *Qur'ān* and *Sunna* to meet contingencies not already provided for by existing determinations of the Holy Law. It is they alone who are entitled to be numbered among the *ahl al-hall wa al-'aqd*, those who unbind and bind the community. Thus, not every Muslim is considered fit to participate in *ijmā'*. Moreover, the *'ulamā'* are in no sense appointed, elected or selected by the community at large. They are a meritocracy founded on piety and scholarship. Again, *ijmā'* is not so much the description of an activity, but of a principle. It does not signify acts of discussion, deliberation, the process of voting or even of exchanging views until the sense of a meeting emerges. The *'ulamā* do' not form a synod, a parliament, a council or a cabinet; they are not members of an estate or of an order, but of an *élite* distinguished by the characteristic of learning in theology and law. *Ijmā'* is not reached by a process of conscious decision at all; it is something one detects by looking back after a certain interval of time. It is something one notices by silence not by animation. A single discordant opinion or voice on what constitutes the Holy Law and there is no *ijmā'*. *Ijmā'* is retrospective, not prospective; it is sanction of an opinion already acted upon; it does not so much take decisions as register them.

Perhaps the ideal ruling institution of the *umma*, the *Khilāfat*, is the subject of political activity as requiring the rallying of wills in the conferment of authority. For, although regarded by the *Sunnī* jurists as the integration or completion of the Holy Law, and as divinely ordained as necessary to the enforcement of the Holy Law, it is an elective office. Then, too, the ceremony of *bay'a* might be taken as signifying a reciprocal relation between the elected *Khalīfa* and the Muslim community, as recognition by the one of the duty to rule within the confines laid down by the *Sharī'a*, and as recognition by the other of a duty of obedience. By al-Bāqillānī (died 403/1013) for example, the *Khalīfa* is called the *wakīl* and *nā'ib* of the *umma*.[1] Perhaps the theory of a reciprocal relationship remained, but even in the earliest formulations of the *Sunnī* theory, the electors of the *Khalīfa* were to be drawn only from the notables or from the *'ulamā'* of the chief town of the Muslim empire and, by the fourth/eleventh century, the jurist al-Māwardī had legitimized appointment by only one elector.[2] Indeed, he states that the *Khalīfa* may be appointed by

[1] E. Tyan, *Institutions du droit musulman*, Tome II, *Sultanat et Califat* (1956), p. 319.
[2] H. A. R. Gibb, 'Al-Māwardī's Theory of the Khilāfah', *Islamic Culture*, XI, 3, July 1937, p. 295.

election *or* by nomination. In fact, the jurists were prepared to accept an hereditary monarchy so long as no one called it hereditary.

The jurists hold that a *Khalīfa* legally forfeits his office for wrong doing and evil living.[1] Can this be taken as sanctioning political activity among the members of the *umma* in order to depose a wicked ruler? The duty of commanding the good and of forbidding the evil, *al-amr bi'l-ma'rūf wa'l-nahy 'an al-munkar*, is one that is laid upon every believer individually and not merely on the community as a whole. But the jurists did not take their doctrines so far. The individual's duty of commanding the good and of forbidding the evil was whittled down to the obligation that if open resistance to over-whelming force was impossible, the believer should protest by words; if this also was too dangerous, then he should protest in secret, in his heart.[2] By the fifth/twelfth century, the emphasis was all on the duty of obedience to the ruler, repeatedly expressed in the *hadīs* that sixty years of tyranny are preferable to one hour of civil strife. As Sir Hamilton Gibb has pointed out, the upshot of the *Sunnī* theory is that a wicked ruler may legally be deposed, but that there is no legal way of deposing him.[3]

The explanation of this reduction of the political role of man in Muslim society, this apparent surrender of all initiative to the *Khalīfa*, wicked though he may be, must be sought, upon the plane of theory, in the religious beliefs of Muslims of the classical period. The *Khilāfat* is essentially an institution to implement the prescriptions of the Divine Law, the *Sharī'a*. It is necessary as an institution by Divine Revelation (the Mu'tazilite position that it was necessary only by reason was eventually rejected). The *Khalīfa* was to be chosen not for his sensitivity to human wants, or for his adroitness in satisfying them, but for his *'ilm* or knowledge of the Holy Law and for his *'adāla* or piety and excellence of morals as judged according to that Holy Law.[4] Providing that the *Khalīfa* is adjudged to possess these (and other related) qualities, the *Sunnī* jurists assume a complete identity of interest between the *Khalīfa* and the members of the *umma*. If the Holy Law is being properly understood and enforced, then man is getting his due, that is what God, by His Divine Law positive, has prescribed for him. In any event, if a believer should happen not to consider that

---

[1] H. A. R. Gibb, 'Al-Māwardī's Theory of the Khilāfah', *Islamic Culture* XI, 3, July 1937, p. 298.
[2] Gardet, *op. cit.*, pp. 184–7.
[3] Gibb, 'Al-Māwardī's Theory', p. 300.
[4] Santillana, *op. cit.*, p. 14.

he is getting his due from the ruler, the onus is nearly always on him to prove it. The presumption is in favour of the pious ruler as against the individual subject; later *Sunnī* jurists allowed the ruler considerable discretionary power to act in accordance with the spirit, if not the letter, of the *Sharī'a*;[1] individual interests take second place to the interest of the *umma*, which are that the principle of the supremacy of the *Sharī'a* be not challenged.

But why do not traditional conceptions provide some means of ensuring that the *Khalīfa* does in fact make the strict enforcement of the Holy Law his first, last and only concern? Ultimately, it is here considered, because of the Ash'arite theological formulations of the doctrine of God's Unity and Omnipotence. All power is from the One God whose Power too is One. Not only the *Khalīfa* but every other holder of executive office is, through the *Khalīfa*, a delegated wielder of this power. The channels may be many, but the stream of authority is the same. Let us assume, for the purposes of the argument, that there were to be a college of '*ulamā*' endowed with the authority to check the actions of a wicked or misguided *Khalīfa* and ultimately perhaps to depose him, all in the name of the Law of God. Since all power is by Divine Will this would in effect be one determination of the Divine Will curbing or reneging another determination of the Divine Will. This would be, in traditional Muslim thought, tantamount to imputing a duality to the Divine Will; this would be regarded as *shirk* or giving God a partner. Moreover, since God wills everything, in the Ash'arite view, everything must be taken to include present ill-advised or tyrannical rulers; to call a ruler to order in the name of justice and right, even if conceived on the basis of an earlier expression of the Divine Will, is to hold that justice and right are something other than that which God is currently willing—and this is a position rejected by the dominant Ash'arite school of dogmatic theology, which is concerned to preserve God's exclusive efficacy in creation.[2] A quotation from al-Ash'arī's *al-Ibāna 'an 'usūl al-diyāna*[3] (making clear the bases of religion) may help to clarify the point: 'We believe that God created everything by bidding it "Be" (*kun*) ... ; that nothing on earth, whether a fortune or a misfortune, comes to be, save through God's will; that things exist through God's fiat;

---

[1] N. J. Coulson, 'The State and the Individual in Islamic Law', *The International and Comparative Law Quarterly*, VI, 1957, pp. 50–3, 56–7.

[2] Louis Gardet et M.-M. Anawati, *Introduction à la théologie musulmane* (1948), pp. 62–4.

[3] *al-Ibāna* (1321/1903–4), p. 9.

that no one can perform an act prior to its performance, or be independent of God or elude His knowledge . . . ; that there is no creator save God; and that the deeds of the creatures are created by Him and predestined by Him, as it is written: "He created you and your deeds"; that the creatures can create nothing but are rather created themselves . . . ; We believe that good and evil are the outcome of God's decree and fore-ordination and we profess faith in God's decree and fore-ordination.'

To summarize the foregoing. In effect the traditional Muslim conception of the nature of politics is that political activity is a species of command and of enforcement of law. The *Khalīfa* alone is entitled to rally wills within the aggregate of the Muslim *umma* and this he does by drawing attention to the demands of the Holy Law and to the penalties for non-compliance with those demands. Upon him alone is conferred the right to exercise powers of initiative, to take what might be called, in other societies, political decisions, as for example, the decision to set on foot a Holy War. The members of the community, as such, do not possess the right to join in the taking of decisions. If in fact they do so, ideally it is as delegates, as appointees of the *Khalīfa*. The final responsibility remains his.

In the views we have been analysing, there is no recognition of politics as an activity whereby the divergent wills of different members of a community are adjusted peacefully. The classical jurists and *'ulamā'* would not recognize R. G. Collingwood's description of politics as a dialectical process whereby one condition of social life is converted, without violence, into another by agreement among those of the character, intelligence and will to share in the process of ruling.[1] The agenda of politics is not a matter for human wills to decide; it has already been drawn up by God.

The traditional Muslim theory of politics pre-supposes not only that Truth is One, but also that all who have made the Muslim affirmation, shall not differ about the nature of that One Truth. It therefore does not address itself to the problem of why a Muslim should obey, if indeed he should, a decision with which he disagrees as against the Will of God as he conceives it. The classical jurists—and one suspects—their modern descendants, are nonplussed by the question of what ought to happen when Muslims honestly and sincerely believe that they are believing and acting in good faith and in all humble piety and yet differ about which course of social action would be right, that is, truly Islamic. To admit majority decision

[1] *The New Leviathan* (1942), pp. 182–3, 212–13, 228, 259–60.

would be the thin end of the wedge of admitting fallible man as a judge of infallible truth and of beginning to regard social actions and social relationships as outside the purview of God's known Law, and to take such relationships out of the sphere of religion into the sphere of—politics—is against the whole bias of traditional Muslim views of the nature of politics'.

THE 'ULAMĀ' IN INDIAN POLITICS

WILFRED CANTWELL SMITH

Professor of Comparative Religion,
McGill University, Montreal

History is development, transition: not merely a sequence of events but a process of becoming. To understand history, is to see the evolution by which something is gradually transformed into something else; by which one situation 'becomes' (the word is so beguilingly simple!) another situation.

Moreover, we are increasingly finding that one of the most challenging aspects of historical studies is the need to see that the concepts in terms of which we analyse a development are themselves part of the flux.

I have been asked to address myself to the question of the '*ulamā*' in Indian politics. It is an excellent question; yet let us not be disarmed by it. In an earlier, more rationalistic day, we might perhaps have begun by defining our terms. Nowadays, more historically, we may see our task as rather that of gaining awareness of the gradual emergence over the years of a situation in India in which these terms come to have meaning, and then the gradual evolution of that meaning. Looking at India today, we note that there is politics in that country, and there is a class of people in Muslim society known as '*ulamā*'. We may well ask what has been the interplay of the two. Yet we must ask at the same time, what are the processes by which these two phenomena have gradually come into being—in their mutual impingement.

Political activity nowadays suggests a conscious participation in a complex procedure that pertains to government but is outside of it. It implies a rather rare and quite special type of rule that either explicitly and deliberately is open to be influenced and even determined by such procedure, or else implicitly is believed to be so. To govern, as either a bureaucrat or an emperor or a tribal chieftain does, is not to be involved in politics; but to influence government, and especially to try to do so, as either an electorate or a protest demonstration may do, is.

The kind of government that allows itself, or the kind of situation in which a government may be forced, to be much influenced by this extraneous activity is something of which the historian takes special note when he sees it. On the whole, he sees it rather seldom as he surveys the broad sweep of human development. That politics exists in India in 1960 in considerable intensity is a significant fact. It is one that has come into being over the course of several decades (with a striking leap in 1947). It has done so through a fascinating process in which the various factors have been many and diverse. The process is the result in part of situations and developments in other parts of the world; conspicuously in Britain, but also from America to Berchtesgarten and Moscow. It is the result in part of non-political matters, from economic and technological change to the writing of books. It is the result in part—and this inevitably is of salient interest though perhaps not of such salient importance—of previous politics in India, on a smaller scale. In the nineteenth century, a few people began to agitate, in what we may designate as an incipiently political fashion, in order that there should be more politics: in order that the government of the country should increasingly be that kind of government to which politics is relevant and where it is effective—ultimately, that there should be independence and democracy; that is, that a fully political situation should obtain. In this particular aspect—it is only one—politics is a dynamic and as it were narcissistic self-unfolding. The success of the movement was self-generating and expansive.

One other among the many factors that played a certain part in the emergence of an increasingly political process in India, one that we may single out for mention for obvious reasons but shall develop only later, is the activity in society of that class of persons known as Muslim '*ulamā*'. By this I mean, not only did these people play a role in politics as a process once politics had emerged, a role that we must investigate; they played a role also, I suggest, in that larger process by which politics in the modern sense came to be.

Before we turn to consider the '*ulamā*' as a phenomenon, however, I would ask to be allowed to make one further general point. The advent of what I have called a political situation—the emergence, that is, of a social complex in which a large number of people consciously participate in determining how they shall be governed—is a significant matter in the history of India, as indeed in the history of any other area. It is a political fact, but has plenty of extra-political consequences (as it had also extra-political causes). The attainment of democracy, whereby society in some degree self-consciously determines its own history and becomes collectively responsible for its own destiny; and also the preceding struggle to attain it, which was already the same thing in part, these are innovations of quite major profundity. Indian men and women have in these decades been entering that new phase of human life—recent for all mankind, though reaching different parts of our planet at somewhat different moments—wherein we are the masters rather than merely the victims of social development. The power to alter our situation that applied science gives us, is of course relevant here also. The fact that as creators of our own destiny we may be turning out to be no wiser than an erstwhile 'providence', and may indeed even use our freedom to commit race suicide, but makes the affair the more poignant.

The advent of political activity as a novel aspect in human life is a deeply significant matter not only in the history of India but—and we are coming now closer to the topic of our paper—in the history of Islām. For a society to become collectively responsible for its own development—for its own shape and stability and aspiration and achievement—is profoundly significant; not least, religiously.

For some centuries, at least, the Muslim's responsibility to God included many things but not, except in the case of sulṭāns, that of ordering society. To take one example, it is one thing to be a scholar responsible for telling what the books say Islamic law to be; it is another to be a voter responsible for deciding what law a Muslim society in the twentieth century shall choose to enforce on itself. Again, it is one thing to be a society of Muslims juxtaposed to a society of Hindus or Sikhs in an empire ruled from the top by a Muslim emperor, or a British government, or even a Hindu emperor. It is another thing to be a society of Muslims juxtaposed to a society of Hindus, in a political situation in which the course of events is determined by the complex of activities in which all these groups may and do, with varying vigour and success, conglomerately participate. And so on. One is not saying here that the new historical situation in which politics was evolving as a central activity was being intellectually grasped in all its immense impact by the *'ulamā'* or by any other class of Muslims. One is merely suggesting that not only is there a role of this group in politics which we may investigate, but also there is a role played by politics in inducing the new situation in which the *'ulamā'*, like everyone else, found themselves; and in which their constituency, the congregations to whom they would preach, have gradually found themselves.

So much, then, for politics, the sheer fact of whose emergence must give us pause. What about the *'ulamā'*? They, too, have emerged. There is a tendency, from which some of us at least have found ourselves suffering, to take this concept for granted; to suppose that there are *'ulamā'* in Islām and that this is somehow 'natural', that they have always been there. Not so. Like everything else on earth, they have come into existence historically; in certain situations, at certain periods, for certain reasons. They constitute a phenomenon the emergence of which is to be investigated, and the course of whose development is if possible to be understood. I am not satisfied that I have come to any adequate understanding here, and I therefore proceed with some caution, and ask you to take these observations as tentative. This much, at least, seems clear: that they emerge in Islamic history in consolidated form a good deal later than is usually supposed, and develop in the Muslim history of India, as a formal and constituted class, a very great deal later—and perhaps even, in certain significant senses, only in the modern period.

It would be startling, and would not even be true, to say that the emergence of the *'ulamā'* as a coherent and organized class, took place in the nineteenth century. This much rather is true, and is important even if tautologous: that the existence of a corps of *'ulamā'* in the modern sense is a modern phenomenon. In earlier times the class existed, but in a different form, and with somewhat different functions. The nineteenth-century meaning of the concept is not applicable to any previous century. Or again, the emergence of the corps of *'ulamā'* as a political force, and even as a politically significant force, is a phenomenon of the political, that is the recent, era.

In the general history of Islām beyond India, the emergence of the *'ulamā'* as a class[1] is a phenomenon of the Saljūq period, where the class was created by the state through the *madrasah* system that was set up to produce it. The formation and financing of this class was to provide an institutional basis for an ideological framework that could hold 'Abbāsī society together and counteract the wide opposition movement whose ideology was Shī'ah. Once the class was organized, however, it developed a momentum and function of its own, and the history of the *'ulamā'* under Muslim emperors is a see-saw of their functioning now as officials and spokesmen of the state, now as the conscious custodians of the conscience of the community and its normative tradition over against the ruler. Therefore

[1] Before this period, *'ulamā'* (and perhaps even 'the' *'ulamā'*?) are found as a species, but hardly yet as a class.

there are moments when the *'ulamā'* functioned as a political group, in our sense of deliberately influencing, or trying to influence, government without actually governing.

In the Ottoman empire, especially from Süleyman, that is from the sixteenth century, the group is formally and carefully organized within and by the state, as an official institution. Otherwise, after the collapse of the 'Abbāsī empire, over wide areas and periods of governmental instability the *'ulamā'* group developed a new function, which it is very important for us to understand. It is that of carrying Islām in the absence of state support and through the vicissitudes of social upheaval. As armies marched back and forth, and principalities abruptly rose and fell, the social order and especially the moral order existed in so far as they did exist for most of the population not, as in a happier or anyway more stable day, because of the ruler and the state structure but almost despite them—certainly despite the chaos that their warfare and plundering produced. In classical Islamic times it was the pious function of the individual Muslim to be personally obedient to God's specific commands, putting his particular share of Islām into practice; but it was the function of the ruler to see to it that the Islamic system as a whole went forward. Without an empire, on the other hand, the meaning of the Islāmic system as a whole' seriously shifted, but also the responsibility for its maintenance fell now on the *'ulamā'* class.

If this analysis is valid, the consequences, though subtle, are of the utmost importance. For this meant that Islām for them became the ideal not existentially of an operating social system, but, in essentialist fashion, of an abstracted entity, a pattern of intellectualized norms. In this pattern only a few of the norms could be actually implemented, but the whole disembodied pattern of them could be and was to be reverenced. In this situation one gets the emergence of an *'ulamā'* class whose function in society is that of custodian of a cherished, idealized tradition, enshrined as a static essence in their books.[1]

If I do not misread the situation, this may prove to have been the most important religious development in Islām for a thousand years.

This may be kept in mind as background; but in India, Islām had

[1] Some work that I am doing in another area of study suggests that perhaps their *'ilm* was at first of *aḥkām* rather than of a conceptualized *sharī'ah*. This matter is extremely complex, and more factors than are here noted went into the ossification (to use a modern Muslim's term) of the *sharī'ah*. Even before the political disintegration, the process of fighting against discontent ('heresies') contributed. We are here attempting to uncover one facet of a development, without claiming that it is the sole face.

to some degree its own history, or at least its own rhythm of development. The last of the *'ulamā"s* phases just mentioned crystallizes in India on a significant scale, so far as I have discerned, only after the disintegration of the Mughul empire and in full force only in the nineteenth century. Islām in India was structured somewhat differently from elsewhere. It arrived as a faith and idea whose institutionalization was first that of a state: conquest, dominion, power, social order, were the forms around which primarily it clustered. This continued, of course, and continued important—into the eighteenth century, and as an idea perhaps into the twentieth, as Jinnāh found. However, secondly, soon equally important, more intimate, and perhaps more lasting, came Ṣūfī forms. At a personal level the faith was spread in India chiefly by Ṣūfīs, and sustained chiefly by them. That their ideas and sensitivities, perhaps, provided the major content of Indian Islām at least to the seventeenth century is an hypothesis that I cannot altogether verify but that is anyway perhaps hardly extravagant. Certainly on the organizational level through all these centuries it is the Ṣūfī order (*ṭarīqah, silsilah*) that gives Islām its structure (apart from the state).

Many *'ālims* were also Ṣūfīs.

And even, curiously, it was in the end Ṣūfīs who called a halt to what eventually seemed the excessively Sufistic trend of Indian Islām.

Although my knowledge of pre-Mughul history is scanty, tentatively I see the evolution of Islām in India as falling, in the premodern period, into three main phases. They can be seen in the relations with Hindus. The first begins with the violent arrival with the armies of Maḥmūd of Ghaznah and his successors. It is a period of vehement iconoclasm and exclusivism: on the religion of the Hindus it was an overpowering onslaught such as India had never seen and has not yet quite forgotten or forgiven. The second, the Ṣūfīs' presentation of Islām, on the other hand, which presently gathered strength, won much of India's heart and indeed in later centuries formally converted to the new community many millions of its inhabitants, chiefly no doubt from the lowest castes. I must confess to not understanding, myself, how far Islām and particularly Islamic Sufism of extra-Indian origin influenced the rise and spread of the Hindu *bhaktii* movement (eleventh to sixteenth centuries) and vice versa; in any case the fact is that relations between the two communities not only improved vastly but even reached a stage where syncretism seemed a possibility. This culminated under the Mughuls, in the sixteenth and seventeenth centuries: at the level of government in the reign and policies of the Emperor Akbar; culturally in such creations as Fathpur Sīkrī, miniature painting, and music; ideologically in Dārā Shikūh. The Urdu language might also be instanced. Some Muslims viewed the process as threatening the utter absorption of Islām within Hinduism and its eventual death. A reaction set in; this is the third phase.

The governmental expression of the new development in the reign of Awrangzeb is well known; this is but one aspect of the widespread and multifaceted development that was going on as a deep religious and presumably social transition to an Islām that is *Sunnī*,—usually, though I think unjustifiedly, translated 'orthodox'.

This was a broad movement. In considering it, one may supersede any notion that Awrangzeb's policies reflect the whim of one man who chanced to be in power. For Awrangzeb came to the throne instead of Dārā Shikūh in considerable part because a larger portion of the *Manṣabdārs* chose to support him; that is, to support neo-classicism rather than liberalism. The movement religiously was led by Naqshbandī Ṣūfīs, of whom the most important is the major theoretician Shaykh Aḥmad Sirhindī (*c.* 1563–1624), who formulated a careful and eventually highly effective rejection of the pantheistic version of Sufism, insisting instead on an interpretation by which it could be, as it then increasingly was, subsumed under an Islām strictly within the bounds of the classical norms, especially the *Sharī'ah*. Sirhindī is, I think, the most historically consequential thinker of Indian Islām for these centuries, and so far as I am able at this moment to discern the evolving situation, this new movement, which involved eventually government, economics, art, communal structures and every facet of society, was fundamentally or primarily a religious movement, coming to formulation first in terms of ideas, of which Sirhindī is the chief representative; though my Marxist friends would doubtless argue that the ideas are subsequent or episodic to a primarily economic development. They may be right; one would delight to see their investigation of the case. It may be that my current tendency to see much of man's history as a history of religion is a trifle overdone. In any case, the more I delve into this particular movement in Indian affairs, the more persuaded I am of the depth and breadth of the transition that was taking place.

Another manifestation of the new development is the work of Sirhindī's influential contemporary 'Abdu-l-Ḥaqq Muḥaddith of Delhi (1551–1642), who as his name implies is remembered for his contribution of *ḥadīth* learning, that is for an emphasis on reintroducing classical formalism—though despite this he is remembered also as a Ṣūfī hagiographer.

Out of this movement can be seen emerging also systematic or institutionalistic expressions of the new orientation: in the field of law, in the major compilation the *Fatāwá-'i 'Ālamgīrī*; and in the eighteenth century, in certain systematizations in the field of education, to which we shall return.

It will perhaps be felt that I am being an unconscionably long while in getting around to the topic assigned to me, the role of the *'ulamā'* in Indian politics. I am ready to apologize for this, but also perhaps to defend it on the ground that historically Indian Islām was an unconscionably long while in getting around to producing an institutional *'ulamā'* class to play that role. What I am suggesting is that such a class is, as it were, an eventual product of the transitional movement of the seventeenth and eighteenth centuries that we have just been exploring. The trend back to a conservative Islām at the end of the Mughul period was not the work of an *'ulamā'* class (though individual *'ālims* who were also Ṣūfī were influential in it). Rather the emergence of such a class was the result, or social deposit, of that trend, a deposit that crystallized out only after the imperial power of Islām had been shattered; in fine, in the nineteenth century. Let us examine this more closely.

The most important thinker in Indian Islām in the eighteenth century was Shāh Walīyullāh of Delhi (1703–1762). If Sirhindī a century and a half earlier had elaborated the intellectual basis on which Awrangzeb's policy rested, Walīyullāh's ideas (which were more powerful than lucid; I must confess that I do not feel that I at all fully understand them) seem to have been those on which has rested any adjustment to the failure of Awrangzeb, or shall we say to the collapse of Mughul power. Walīyullāh was an *'ālim* Ṣūfī. His formal, institutional status was that of head of the Delhi branch of the Naqshbandī order (from 1719). He was a sensitive observer, not unaware that something quite serious had gone wrong, or was going wrong, with the Muslim position in India. His work was essentially purificationist and revivalist: aiming ideally at a restoration of a refurbished, more disciplined Sufism and a refurbished state power. In this last realm his immediate move was what most of us would call at least disastrous, to use no more pejorative a term: for he invited Aḥmad Shāh Abdālī to invade India, which proved hardly a contribution to the glory of Islām. This is *'ālim* participation in politics with a vengeance!

The disintegration of the Muslim order in India is virtually the theme of the late eighteenth century and early nineteenth. It is easy to observe in the sphere of government and power: the Marhaṭṭah domination of Delhi, 1782–1803, was flanked by the Sikhs' supersession of Muslim rule in the Panjāb on the one side and by the East India Company's on the other; and in 1799 Tīpū Sultān had spectacularly failed in the south to maintain or regain Muslim might. In the economic sphere the passing of the old order and, under the incipient impact of the results of the industrial revolution, its supersession by a new, have also been reasonably well studied, and the accompanying dislocation and misery are known. In Muslim education, one can trace in Bengal, at least, the crumbling of a school system economically feudal (that is, maintained by land endowments, specifically *muʿāfī* grants, which were gradually, or not so gradually, obliterated). What is not clear to me is what happened to the structure of the Ṣūfī orders. As I have argued all along, these, apart from the state, were the chief institutional form of Islām until this time. This presumably is the period during which they were giving way in this function to the gradual emergence of a structured *'ulamā'* institution; a transition of which one sees the result a little later but of which I do not yet see the process. Of the growth of the latter one gets one or two hints such as the expanding significance of the Farangī Maḥall, Lakhnaw, set up as a typical one-man school in 1698 but developing in the eighteenth century into perhaps India's first nationwide sunnī *madrasah* institution; and the spread of its curriculum as a standardized *Dars-i-Niẓāmī*, which came to prevail as dominant formulation for the formation of religious scholars.

However that may be, it was in 1803 again an *'ālim* Ṣūfī, the elderly son of Walīyullāh, namely Shāh 'Abdu-l-'Azīz (1746–1843) who formally, and in the name of Islām, inaugurated a movement to endeavour in overt action to reverse the worldly decline of Islām in India. For when in that year the Marhaṭṭah power in Delhi was overthrown and replaced not by restored Mughul might but by the British, he issued a famous *fatwá* declaring India to be *dāru-l-ḥarb*. This is the Islamic way of declaring war on behalf of the Islamic community; but the significant fact for our purposes is not only that it was proclaimed (with considerable consequences, as we shall presently see), but also that it was proclaimed not by a ruler but by a religious spokesman acting on his own. This was not yet 'the *'ulamā'* ' in Indian politics; but it was the first major step in modern Indian history towards such a situation, as it developed later and directly

47

from this. And in any case it was the closest thing to it of which the opening of the nineteenth century situation was perhaps capable.

Shāh 'Abdu-l-'Azīz was in the next few years paralleled in his pronouncement by other *'ālims* here and there (such as Sharī'atullāh), so that there was presently in effect an authorization by religious leaders to the members of the Muslim community to act.

If I understand the dynamics correctly, the declaration of *dāru-l-ḥarb* is not in itself an appeal for action, an eliciting of *jihād* (that comes twenty years later, as we shall see in a moment). It is rather simply a statement that—to use our modern terminology—analyses the situation in new and different terms. For eight hundred years Muslim India had been *dāru-l-Islām*, which means *inter alia* that the responsibility for its corporate as distinct from individual existence lay with the Muslim ruler. To assert (or shall we say, by 1803 to recognize) that this was no longer so, is to transfer that responsibility elsewhere. But it was not yet clear where else. With whom, with what groups or institutions, the new responsibility lay, was not yet, I think, thought out; nor just what it involved. In what did the responsibility consist? This latter was implied, in terms of the traditional concepts, by the word *ḥarb*, 'war'; and this is not unimportant, but was not yet explicated. As to the question of who would now take over the responsibility for Islām's corporate life, perhaps three sorts of answer were roughly possible: first, the community as a whole; secondly, a corps of *'ulamā'*; thirdly, the intervention of an outside Muslim ruler. In fact the history of the ensuing century shows the development in India perhaps of something of each of these, either in theory or in practice or both. However, before any of these considerations could be well worked out, the whole situation was, of course, immensely complicated by the altogether new and profound matter of the intrusion of the West, as a cultural and social as well as state phenomenon. But this is to anticipate.

The first great development was the Mujāhidīn movement, from the 1820's. Its enemies called it 'Wahhābī', and the term has stuck. I think one should take careful note of this name, particularly as stressing the impression that it made as fundamentally a movement of religious revival and purification. Yet we should drop it in favour of the internal name, which also stresses the Islamic character and includes, not unjustly, an emphasis on martial zeal. It was a mass movement, both funds and personnel being supplied from popular sources, not by rulers. It was inspired, organized, and led by religious dignitaries, *'ālims*. The chief of these was Sayyid Aḥmad Barelawī

(1786–1831), though he was himself commissioned and inspired by Shāh 'Abdu-l-'Azīz of the *fatwá*, and was accompanied and assisted by the latter's nephew, Ismā'īl (d. 1831).

Sayyid Aḥmad, as apparently Shāh 'Abdu-l-'Azīz's ablest disciple, had previously been sent by the latter to take part in an operation already on foot, namely a traditional type of resistance to British power by Indian feudal forces, with a Muslim apparently free-lance leader Amīr 'Alī Khān who was operating with a Marhaṭṭah noble Jaswant Rā'o Holkar. It is significant that in the anti-British orientation an alliance with Hindūs was acceptable; this persists right to 1947. This particular venture failed. Nothing came, either, of an approach to the Sindhiyā of Gwālior's administration, talking of joint anti-Britishness. Thereupon Sayyid Aḥmad, an able organizer, was turned into a popular agitator, to lead a mass movement. He toured North India, stirring up the Muslim populace to take on themselves the re-exalting of the purity and power of Islām, including a *jihād*, enlisting men and raising money. He seems to have organized a considerable army and met with considerable success. For reasons that are not entirely clear the action when it came was in the Panjāb and Frontier against the Sikhs. An independent *khilāfat* under Sayyid Aḥmad was set up in Peshawar for a time (1830–1), and there were other successes; but a decisive battle at Bālākot in the Panjāb (1831) brought 'martyrdom' to the leaders and a major setback to the venture. It did not altogether cease: with the major leaders gone, the minor ones divided, the armies dispersed and many lost heart. Nonetheless the movement continued, with headquarters at Sittana in the Sawat valley, and continued to harass the Sikh state and later the British.

Meanwhile in Bengal peasant uprisings protesting against the heartlessness and hardship of the new order also took the form of Islamic movements led by *'ālims* in the name of a purified Islām: the Farā'izīyah, from 1804, under a Bengali *mawlawī* called Sharī'atullāh, who had had his training mostly in Arabia; and the uprisings of 1834, 1841, 1844, and 1846 organized by his son Dūdū Miyāṇ, whose socio-religious activities were co-ordinated with those of the Mujāhidīyah in the North-west, and who seems to have given them more theoretical formulation than his father. On a more circumscribed sphere there was in Bengal and Bihar a more strictly religious reform led by Mawlawī Karāmat 'Alī of Janpur, as an outcropping of the Walīyullāhī impetus.

I personally am not quite clear as to how mighty these enterprises were; perhaps about as substantial as was in fact practicable in the then context, for non-state forces. This kind of operation culminated, of course, in 1857—the Mutiny, First War of Liberation, last attempt to restore the Mughuls, or whatever one opts for calling it. A lot of work has once again recently been put into studying this affair; I am not one of those who have gone much into it, but it is perhaps fair enough to generalize that it was complex, and that one of its strands was the Islamic *jihād*. Many *'ālims* were involved in this, their activities consisting at times, apparently, in actually fighting, 'sword in hand', but chiefly in organizing, inspiring, and Islamicizing Muslim participation in the struggle. They gave a considerable section of the movement, it would seem, an ideological content and emotional fervour; and, as well, direction.

The uprising, however, as we know, was crushed, with sufficiently decisive power to make it evident that this particular way need not be tried again.

What, then, to do next? What new phase of Islām's Indian evolution could be envisaged as possible or desirable? Some of the *'ālims* migrated to Makkah: Ḥājjī Imdādullāh, for instance, who had been one of the prominent leaders in 1857; also the father of the future Abū-l-Kalām Āzād; and others. This was presumably out of sheer discouragement; though I find myself speculating about this, and wondering whether conceivably there was as well some longer-range aspiration in view. Already in 1841 Mawlānā Muḥammad Isḥāq (1778–1846) had gone to Makkah. He was the grandson of Shāh 'Abdu-l-'Azīz and his successor at the Naqshbandī *madrasah* at Delhi, and is said to have been in some ways the brains and even the programmatic organizer of the Walīyullāhī tradition after the failure at Bālākot. He postulated two basic principles for a programme, namely strict observance of Islamic law and an alliance with the Ottoman empire. He died in Makkah five years later; but apparently his going was no escapism but a move aimed at exploring the possibility of Ottoman support for his cause.

The next move in India is altogether crucial for our purposes; namely, the setting up in 1867 of a Dāru-l-'Ulūm at Deoband. That it was founded by a group of *'ālims*, chiefly two who were prominent in the 1857 effort, is significant. Equally significant is that, once founded, it flourished: it attracted and sustained support, won the allegiance and services of first-class men, and developed a strong tradition of vitality and quality. In other words, its emergence represents something of fairly widespread significance happening in the Indo-Muslim community. We have already seen something similar happening, a little earlier, with the Farangī Maḥall of Lakhnaw. Deoband was distinctive in that it was considerably more dynamic and deliberate, with a richer and more revivalist tradition behind it (Walīyullāhī) and a clearer, more comprehensive ideal before it, namely, the active rehabilitation of the Indo-Muslim socio-religious situation. It was founded by men who had fought in the 1857 struggle, and who explicitly set out to develop an alternative means towards a similar goal: to produce a corps of 'ulamā' devoted to the cause of Islām and the freedom of India. The economic aspect is interesting. We remarked above that the traditional Muslim educational system had been tied to feudal patterns in that its financial support was in the form of endowments in land; and we saw that in Bengal the dissolution of those patterns meant the collapse of the educational system. Of the eight principles laid down by the Deoband founders as basic guides for the new Dāru-l-'Ulūm, the first is that its financial support must be in the form of contributions collected from the people; and it was affirmed that permanent sources of dependable income or governmental support would weaken and divert rather than strengthen the institution. In this fashion, at least, despite the traditional learning, this is an institution of the modern rather than the medieval age.

Deoband, then, from the latter part of the nineteenth century, became the chief of a group of institutions that produced that modern phenomenon of Indo-Muslim society, the politically active 'ulamā'. We need not trace further the role that these played, since this has been ably and informatively done in a recent thesis;[1] and the role of Indian politics in the development of these 'ulamā' and their corporate function may perhaps be inferred. The career of Abū-l-Kalām Azād should also be studied. If meanwhile here we have been at all successful in asking the right sort of question as to the appearance and significance of this class, it is enough.

[1] Ziyā'u-l-Ḥasan Fārūqī: *De'oband and the demand for Pakistan*. A thesis presented in partial fulfilment of the requirements for the degree of M.A. in Islamic Studies, McGill University. In the library of the Institute of Islamic Studies, McGill University, Montreal. This is currently being published in Delhi. The material of my two preceding paragraphs is also elaborated here.

CASTE AND POLITICS IN SOUTH ASIA

C. VON FÜRER-HAIMENDORF

*Professor of Asian Anthropology
in the University of London*

When India, Pakistan and Ceylon attained the status of sovereign states within the Commonwealth they found themselves with systems of government largely modelled on western lines. The foundations of these administrative and constitutional systems had been laid by Britain. In India a policy of introducing a measure of local and provincial self-government had been pursued ever since the First World War, and this policy had culminated in the constitution of 1935, which served as a point of departure for the constitutional arrangements in independent India. The development of western systems of government was made possible by the acceptance of the ideal of parliamentary democracy on the part of the politically conscious middle class, whose leading members had been educated in European schools and universities. These men associated the ideals of freedom and national independence *not* with a return to the indigenous forms of government, which colonial rule had superseded, but with the establishment of those institutions which they considered essential features of a modern democracy. Yet side by side with the intellectual preference for an essentially foreign system of political organization, appeared an emotional craving for the re-establishment of traditional cultural values, expressed, for instance, in the emphasis on indigenous forms of dress and on the use of the vernacular as the medium of education and cultural activities. In these conflicting attitudes there is perhaps an element of 'split personality'. Just as the Indian intellectual had become used to move in his professional life within the realms of western traditions and values, while conforming in his private and family life to values rooted in Hindu or Muslim tradition, so political leaders accepted wholeheartedly western ideals of democracy and parliamentary rule, without being fully conscious of their inevitable inconsistency with some of the basic principles of the traditional social system. Others, who were aware of this inconsistency, evinced a certain lack of realism in assuming that with the coming of freedom and democracy caste loyalties and discrimination based on caste would soon lose all importance as political forces. We shall see presently that this assumption was wildly erroneous.

The present position is that in India and Ceylon, as well as in other parts of Asia, there prevail systems of government conceived and developed in the West, and basically inconsistent with the traditional indigenous social order. The problem created by this position is briefly as follows: as it is against all historical experience that such an inconsistency can persist, we must assume that some kind of an adjustment is in the process of taking place. Theoretically there are three possibilities: the system of government may gradually adjust itself to the traditional social order, or the social order may change to such an extent that it will ultimately fit the prevailing type of government, or, lastly, both the social order and the system of government may change until they reach a tolerable degree of consistency.

If we consider the legislation passed since Independence by the Indian parliament, we must inevitably come to the conclusion that the Union government is making every effort to reform the social order in such a way as to bring it into line with the ideals of democracy as understood in the West. The introduction of universal franchise, abolition of untouchability, legalization of inter-caste marriages, and the removal of legal discrimination against women, are all measures inspired by ideals derived from western social thinking. It is well known, of course, that much of this legislation, such as the abolition of untouchability, is difficult to enforce and has had little practical effect on inter-caste relations, and from this we can conclude that government policy and popular social consciousness are still widely out of step. Yet, there can be no doubt that legislation has some effect on the direction in which Indian society is developing, however slow such development may be.

It is much more difficult to discern to what extent the values and principles inherent in the traditional social order are modifying the system of government. For the time being any influence they may be exerting is expressed in the manipulation of the prevailing system of government rather than in a demand for a change in the system. Before I deal with the extent and manner of this manipulation of parliamentary democracy, it may be useful to restate the problem in greater detail:

Parliamentary democracy and the system of political parties competing for the support of the electorate developed in a society where the individual was not born into a tightly organized group which demands his loyalty and affords him support in his dealing with the rest of the community. In India, on the other hand, such groups—the castes and sub-castes—dominate social life, and inevitably influence their members' attitude to other groupings of a social or political character. In other words, the very fact that a caste is capable of functioning as an effective pressure group, and that its members cannot leave it and join another group at will, places it into a position of a political power, which cannot be ignored by the political parties depending for their mandate on the goodwill of the voters.

This has been clearly recognized by M. N. Srinivas, who in 1955 wrote in the *Report of the Seminar on Casteism and Removal of Untouchability*:[1] 'One of the short-term effects of universal adult franchise is to strengthen caste. It is easily understandable that the villager, other things being equal, prefers to vote for his caste man. This is so widely accepted that during the recent elections in Andhra State, even the Communists were at pains to select candidates who had the proper "social base", which, when translated into simple English, meant that they belonged to the locally dominant caste.'

When discussing conditions in Mysore before the enlargement of the state, Srinivas was even more explicit:[2] 'The principle of caste is so firmly entrenched in our political and social life that everyone, including the leaders, has accepted tacitly the principle that, in the provincial cabinets at any rate, each major caste should have a minister. In the first popular cabinet in Mysore State, headed by Shri K. C. Reddy, not only were the ministers chosen on a caste basis, but each had a secretary from his own sub-sub-sub-caste. And today in Mysore State, this principle is followed not only in every appointment, but also in the allotment of seats in schools and colleges. Mysore is no longer ruled by the mythical demon Mahishasura, but by the very real demon Varnasura. One Okkaliga in Rampura told me: "Shri Hanumanthayya wants to rule strictly and impartially, but he must realize that the electors do not want it. They want him to confer favours on the people who have elected him. We want returns for what we have done" . . . the Okkaliga was right—voting is on a caste basis and voters do not understand that it is immoral to demand that the elected minister helps his caste-folk and village folk. . . . . Incidentally, no explanation of provincial politics in any part of India is possible without reference to caste.'

In the same report Srinivas pointed out that caste had gained in

[1] P. 137.   [2] *Op. cit.*, p. 133.

political importance already during the days of British rule. The earlier feudal political system had erected many barriers between one chiefdom and the other, and this political fragmentation had the effect of preventing the horizontal spread of caste-solidarity beyond the individual small state. With the establishment of *Pax Britannica* over the entire sub-continent, and the improvement in communications, caste solidarity could extend beyond narrow regional boundaries. Railways, an efficient postal service, printing presses, vernacular newspapers and books all enabled the representatives of a caste to spread out over different areas to meet and exchange views on their common problems and interests. The growth of caste institutions, hospitals, schools, hostels and publications is all a development of the last 100 years. One example must suffice: the Chitrapur Saraswat Brahmans, a wealthy caste of Bombay, issue their own caste census and directory, according to which there were in 1956 no less than 22 caste-operated educational institutions, 13 fraternal and social agencies and 12 housing co-operations all serving a community of just under 19,000 persons.

Caste consciousness and a sense of strength and importance among the members of the larger castes have been fostered also by the decennial returns of the Census of India. References to this phenomenon are found in many of the census reports. Thus we find as early as 1911 in the Madras volume the sentence '. . . the last few years, and especially the occasion of the present census, have witnessed an extraordinary revival of the caste spirit in certain aspects. For numerous castes *Sabhas* have sprung up, each keen to assert the dignity of the social group which it represents.'[1] And in the Bengal volume of the Census of 1921 we read '. . . the leaders of all but the highest castes frankly looked upon the Census as an opportunity for pressing and perhaps obtaining some recognition of social claims, which were denied by persons of castes higher than their own'.[2]

It was this exploitation of census statistics for purposes of caste aggrandizement, which decided the Government of India to omit the enumeration and tabulation of caste from the 1951 Census, a step which has since been deplored by many Indian sociologists and anthropologists. P. G. Shah[3] described it as an 'ostrich-like policy of neglecting the scientific study of Indian castes', which 'has created a great vacuum in the sociological information available to students of social progress and social welfare.'

[1] *Census of India*, 1911, vol. xii, Madras, pt. i, *Report*, p. 178.
[2] *Ibid.*, 1921, vol. v, Bengal, pt. i, *Report*, p. 346.
[3] *Report on the Seminar on Casteism* . . . , p. 79.

In a recent article in the *Economic Weekly* M. N. Srinivas[1] has reiterated and amplified the views expressed five years ago, and it is obvious that the General Elections of 1957 have confirmed Indian observers in their assessment of the political role of caste. It is particularly the so-called 'dominant' castes which have emerged as the focal points of political power, and Srinivas has analysed the shift of importance from the numerically small castes of highest ritual status and a tradition of literacy and learning, which enabled them to benefit most from western education, to numerically stronger castes of great economic power, which nowadays dominate village affairs and through the voting power of their members make their influence felt right up to the cabinets of states. Dominant castes in this sense are the Lingayats and Okkaligas of Mysore, the Reddis and Kammas of Andhra Pradesh, the Gounders, Padayachis and Muduliars of Tamilnad, the Nayars of Kerala, Marathas of Maharashthra, Patidars of Gujerat, Rajputs, Jats, Gujars and Ahirs of Rajasthan. The creation of linguistic states has enhanced the influence of some of these castes, and brought about a change of balance in areas where two dominant castes were rivals for political power. In Mysore, for instance, where the Okkaligas were the heirs to the power of the Brahmans of pre-Independence days, the inclusion of the Kannada-speaking districts of Hyderabad and Bombay altered the balance of power, for the numerical strength of the Lingayats now surpasses that of the Okkaligas. Srinivas quotes an ex-Chief Minister of Mysore as saying that no non-Lingayat could hope to become Chief Minister of the greater Mysore State.[2]

In South India the privileges and near-monopoly of government posts enjoyed by the Brahmans thanks to their intellectual and educational qualifications gave rise to an anti-Brahman movement, which as early as 1917 led to the creation of a separate political party known as Justice Party, supported by non-Brahmans of every caste and religion. The success of this movement, which soon gained a number of important concessions from the Government of India, can be gauged from a comparison of the share in government posts of the various communities in certain Andhra districts in 1922 with the position in 1959. In 1922 75 per cent of all district posts were held by Brahmans, 28 per cent by non-Brahman Hindus, 1 per cent by Muslims and 1 per cent by Christians. In 1959 Brahmans held only 29 per cent of the posts, the share of non-Brahman Hindus had risen

[1] 'The Indian Road to Equality', *Economic Weekly*, June 1960.
[2] *Ibid.*, p. 868.

to 44 per cent and those of Muslims and Christians to 10 per cent and 13 per cent respectively. The Christians in that case were mainly of Harijan stock though not classified among the scheduled castes.

But although the struggle against the predominance of Brahmans has largely been won, and the discrimination against this hereditary intellectual *élite* has inevitably led to a lowering of standards in the universities and liberal professions, opportunities are not distributed evenly throughout the non-Brahman population, but the chief beneficiaries of the new order are those high non-Brahman castes, which thanks to their large land-holdings and economic power became the new dominant castes. These castes are everywhere rather conservative, and it is in their interest to impede as far as possible the rise to economic and political power of the numerically strong, but economically still largely underprivileged Harijan castes. This tendency runs counter to the official policy of assisting the untouchables to overcome their disabilities, but paradoxically it is just the constitutional provisions guaranteeing to the Harijans a fair share of government posts, admittance to colleges and other benefits which has accentuated caste consciousness and even produced the previously unheard of competition for classification as 'backward'.

It is now being realized that the measures designed to bring about equality of opportunities and give the scheduled and other backward classes a chance of raising their social and economic status, tend to perpetuate the caste system, the ill effects of which they try to combat. Groups which have been classified as 'backward' and enjoy such privileges as reserved seats in the legislatures and an assured quota of places in educational institutions, are naturally reluctant to forgo these benefits and, holding on to their 'backwardness', are in the process of becoming a new privileged class. The Government of India has therefore tried to establish new and objective criteria of 'backwardness', but a commission appointed for this purpose did not produce any practical solution, and the list it compiled contains no less than 2,399 communities whose claim to backwardness has been admitted. Alone the 913 major communities on this list account for an estimated population of 116 millions and to this figure 70 millions of Scheduled Tribes and Castes have to be added.[1] The impracticability of providing special benefits for so large a percentage of the population is patent, but this does not deter many groups from clamouring for classification as 'backward'.

[1] M. N. Srinivas, 'Caste in Modern India', *Journal of Asian Studies*, vol. xvi, 1956–7, p. 547.

Thus there is at the one end of the scale a striving for higher caste status, exemplified by the claim of many economically dominant cultivating castes to Kshatriya status, and on the other end the unashamed espousal of 'backwardness' as a means of obtaining material benefits at the hands of government.

Both trends can operate only within a system of unequal castes and there is indeed no effective social movement, which does not, in the one or other way, utilize the concepts and rules of this system. M. N. Srinivas expressed this very clearly when in his presidential address to a section of the Indian Science Congress, 1957, he said explicitly: 'Caste is so tacitly and so completely accepted by all, including those most vocal in condemning it, that it is everywhere the unit of social action.'[1]

The way in which caste-feeling and caste-discipline affect political relations and specifically the conduct of the major political parties can best be demonstrated with the help of a concrete example. While general statements on the relevance of caste-solidarity for the conduct of election campaigns and the vote-catching power of more or less veiled appeals to caste-feeling abound in Indian journals and newspapers, there are not many detailed studies of the political situation in a specific area with reference to the local caste set-up.

The most illuminating example is probably the growth and development of the Communist party in Andhra Pradesh. In view of the Communists' avowed commitment to the ideal of a secular society free of all distinctions of caste and class, the importance of caste solidarity for the success of the Andhra Communists is particularly significant. Thanks to an excellent study by Selig S. Harrison[2] we are able to trace the fortunes of the Andhra Communist party in considerable detail. Ever since it was founded in 1934, the leadership was in the hands of the Kamma caste, which dominates the Krishna-Godavari delta. The Kammas are a caste of prosperous farmers, who are said to own about 80 per cent of fertile delta land. Their-caste status is that of 'clean' Sūdras, and approximately equals that of the other main Telugu cultivating castes of Kapu and Reddi. The Kammas, like the Reddis, pride themselves on the tradition of having been warriors in the armies of the Andhra kings, and they tend

[1] M. N. Srinivas, 'Caste in Modern India', *Journal of Asian Studies*, vol. xvi, 1956–7, p. 548.
[2] *Caste and the Andhra Communists* (1956); *India: the Most Dangerous Decades* (1960), pp. 204–45.

to claim Kshatriya status, though this claim is not admitted by the higher castes.

The number of Kammas in the delta districts, once known as Kamma Rashtra, was over 600,000 in 1921, the year of the last census which provided district caste-tables, while all other peasant proprietor castes taken together number only about half that figure. About as many Kammas are scattered over the other Andhra districts, in some of which the Reddis are the dominant caste.

The Kammas have always been a fundamentally rural caste, and though they were rich, and fourteen Kamma zamindars were the biggest estate owners in the delta regions, they showed little ambition to acquire western-type education. While in 1921 nearly 30 per cent of the literate Telugu Brahmans knew English, only just over 3 per cent of the literate Kammas were also literate in English.

Selig Harrison attributes the Kammas' political development largely to this educational difference. Whereas the Brahmans became the natural leaders of the Andhra Congress, the Kammas became active in the anti-Brahman movement, which before the Second World War spread over most of South India. Thus they were in opposition to Congress, and it was probably due to this caste-antagonism that they were ready to support another political party, and the natural opponent of Congress happened to be the Communist party. And just as the delta districts provided the Brahmans for the Congress leadership, so the Communists drew their leaders from the delta Kammas. The Reddis, concentrated in the politically less active districts of the Rayalaseema hinterland, showed less inclination to join the Communist party. Its leadership was already monopolized by Kammas from the delta, and as they were making their entry to party politics in any case belatedly, the Reddis found that there was little to choose between joining the Communist Kammas or the Congress Brahmans in the role of junior partners. It was by accident rather than owing to basic social causes that they assumed the role of non-Brahman supporters of Congress, a role which was to prove increasingly profitable when, with the introduction of universal adult suffrage, Congress had to adjust its leadership so as to appeal to the great masses of non-Brahman voters.

It may appear paradoxical that a caste of wealthy landowners should provide the leadership as well as a great part of the electoral support of a Communist party. But the issue before the young Kamma intellectuals, who in 1934 had founded that party, were not those of international Communism, but local issues such as anti-Brahman feeling or—in later years—intense Telugu patriotism agitating for an Andhra State in the face of Congress caution. True, the Andhra Communists wooed from the very beginning the landless labour, which consisted mainly of such untouchable castes as Malas and Madigas, but as late as the election of 1946 franchise limitations excluded most of the landless farm labourers from the effective electorate, and the party had no other choice than to rely mainly on Kamma voting strength. At the time of the elections in 1951, Kammas were so firmly entrenched in the Communist leadership, that there was no question of any change of party alignment in terms of caste. Of the successful Communist candidates fourteen were Kammas, two Reddis, three Brahmans and six members of other castes.

By that time the Kamma landlords had reaped some of the fruits of their support of the Communists. In the Communist rebellion of 1948–50, which extended over the Telingana districts of Hyderabad and large parts of the delta—an episode in the history of Andhra I cannot discuss here in detail—most wealthy Kammas remained unharmed, for party strategy had laid down that as long as such farmers remained aloof from the fight, they should be classified as 'neutralized' and left unmolested. In a report to the Indian Communist Politbureau, of 1948, the Andhra Communists had explicitly declared: 'Propaganda should be carried on to convince the *ryots* [landowners] about the just demands of the workers, and we should also effect compromises with such of those *ryots* who would follow with us. Assurance should be given that we should not touch the lands of rich *ryots*.'

This policy of class collaboration in rural areas, however, came ultimately under fire on the part of the Communist All-India high commnad, and there followed a long drawn out fight between the Party Secretary B. T. Ranadive and the Andhra Secretariat.

But at the time of the 1951 election the Communists still had the confidence of the Kamma landlords, many of whom supported Communist Kamma candidates with their funds and their local influence.

In the following years the rivalry between Congress and Communists took largely the form of a tussle between Kammas and Reddis. What agitated the popular imagination was not a conflict between Communism and Congress ideology, but the conflict between the interests of a Reddi-dominated Congress, favouring the selection of Kurnool in Rayalaseema as the state capital, and those of the

Kammas who championed the claims of the delta. A Communist leader described this situation as follows: 'The Congress raised the slogan of Reddi versus Kamma. It says: if you want to change from Kurnool to any centralized place, then Kamma domination will come and Reddi domination will go. These are the facts that cannot be controverted by anybody who knows anything about Andhra.'[1]

One of the many paradoxes of the situation was, moreover, that the Communists were not only the spokesmen of the local patriotism of the delta communities, but were representing also the interests of big business and real estate, both of which were vitally concerned with the location of the capital.

Space does not permit me to pursue further developments in Andhra in detail. But the Congress high command did not allow the Kamma–Reddi quarrel to play into the hands of the Communists in the 1955 election as it had done in 1951. A united anti-Communist front was created and the Congress set out to beat the Communists at their own game of manipulating caste-sentiments. It held back until the Communist list of candidates had been announced, and then matched every Communist candidate, selected with a view to local caste-support, with a candidate of the same caste or sub-caste. Thus every Communist Kamma candidate faced an anti-Communist Kamma rival, and the election could no longer be fought on issues of caste-loyalty. Many Kammas realized that they were in a strong bargaining position for Congress favours, and saw an alternative to the dangerous alliance with a party which outside Andhra attacked landlords and vested interests in no uncertain terms. Though the Kamma Communists still commanded the loyalty of a large section of their caste, and ran Kamma candidates in 29 delta constituencies, their percentage of the votes polled in those constituencies dropped by 6 per cent and this lost them the election. Kamma–Reddi rivalry, however, has remained an important factor in Andhra politics. Mr Hugh Gray, who is at present studying party politics in Andhra Pradesh, comments in a personal communication (dated December 2, 1961) on this problem as follows: 'In Andhra the evidence I have from two districts shows that there has been no change in traditional leadership. . . . In both these districts the struggle for office and power is overtly between the Kammas and the Reddis, and no attempt is made to disguise it. . . . At the state level alliances are fluid, the Reddi and Kamma networks are in opposition, but seek allies from each others' groups and from outside.'

[1] *For Victory in Andhra* (1955), p. 13.

The inclusion of the Telingana districts of the dismembered Hyderabad State in the greater Andhra Pradesh has definitely tilted the scales in favour of the Reddis, who in these districts are far stronger than the Kammas. Moreover Communism in Telingana was not specifically associated with Kammas, but gained the support of Hindus of various castes when it first sprang up in opposition to H.E.H. the Nizam's régime, and particularly the short-lived Ittehad-ul-Muslimin government immediately preceding the occupation of the state by the Indian Army. In the present government of Andhra Pradesh Reddis are firmly entrenched even though the post of Chief Minister recently went to a Harijan of Mala caste after the powerful Reddi leader Shri N. Sanjiva Reddi had resigned it on his election to the Congress presidency. The four remaining Reddi ministers are all rich landlords, and so are the other ministers with the exception of one Muslim lady and a Hyderabad Brahman lawyer, whose influence in Congress circles is said to be not unconnected with the fact that his brother-in-law is the Governor of Kerala.

References to 'Reddi rule' can be frequently heard in Andhra Pradesh, and when I recently visited a newly constructed Harijan colony in Medak District, the inhabitants told me that no doubt the possession of the vote had made some difference to their community, but that their masters were more than ever the Reddi landlords; 'now', they said (and I happen to have a tape-recording of this conversation) 'the Patwari is a Reddi, the Revenue Inspector is a Reddi, the Tahsildar is a Reddi, and the Revenue Minister is a Reddi'. The latter, Shri Ranga Reddi, a wealthy landlord of Hyderabad District, incidentally is also the Deputy Chief Minister.

I do not suggest that the picture is everywhere as simple, and F. G. Bailey has recently shown that in Orissa, the state adjoining Andhra Pradesh, to the north, political divisions do not run so much along caste-lines as along the line dividing the more advanced plains populations from the inhabitants of the hills where traditional rulers were able to reassert their influence through the mechanism of elections to the Legislative Assembly.[1] But the example of Andhra Pradesh illustrated the role which caste-interests may play in state politics, and I doubt whether Indian party politics can ever be understood without a very full knowledge of the caste—and family background—of the leading politicians. The influence of caste and regional interests on the thinking and conduct of politicians has been well described by the prominent Andhra Congress leader, B. Pattabhi

[1] 'Politics in Orissa', *Economic Weekly*, August–November 1959.

Sitaramayya, who wrote in a symposium on 'Group Prejudices in India':[1]

'All patriotism works in concentric circles. The man in power is apt in general to think of his family, relations and people of his sect or group, village, tahsil and province. . . . In the [state] legislatures . . . we think of our Districts, and on the Local Boards of Districts we think of our Tahsils, while on the Tahsil Boards we think of our Mandals or Firkas, our villages and in the Village Panchayats we think of our streets. So far the circles run on a territorial basis, but concurrently or intercurrently we have our biases running along religious, caste and sectarian channels. These centrifugal tendencies have struck deep roots in the administrative and, what is worse, in the educational world of India today. It is sufficiently bad that highly placed people should be accused of parochialism and provincialism, but when to this is added the charge of nepotism based upon consanguinity or sect bias, the position becomes intolerable.'

Writing in the same symposium on 'Group Prejudices and Political Parties' Asoka Mehta, the Socialist leader, puts the same ideas even more bluntly:

'As the franchise is widened, each social group and sub-group within the generally immobile Hindu society struggles for predominance or at least a share in the loaves and fishes of offices and jobs. Democracy in India has so far been a clever balancing of different caste interests.'[2]

Even the struggle between the Communist Party and the Congress and its allies in Kerala can be seen as a conflict of caste-interests, and such an interpretation finds expression in a recent letter to the Editor of the *Economic Weekly*, which draws attention to the 'deep conflict between the Nairs and Ezhavas':

'The Nairs and Namboodiris are by and large landowners while the Ezhavas and Harijans, like Pulayans and Cherumans, are landless labourers. The first group by and large support the Congress and P.S.P., while the second the Communists. A big bone of contention is the Backward Class reservation provisions which benefit Ezhavas, etc., but not Nairs. M. Padmanabham wants the reservation to go while the Ezhavas don't want it to go, naturally.

'If this kind of cleavage is superimposed on other cleavages (rural, urban, Christian, Muslim) what will happen? And above all, will Kerala Communism be identified with Ezhavas and a few other castes?

[1] Ed. Sir Manilal B. Nanavati and C. N. Vakil, Bombay, 1955, p. 160.
[2] *Ibid.*

In Andhra, people referred to Communism as Kammaism as the Kamma landlords were at the back of it and identification with them was one of the reasons for the downfall of Communism in Andhra.'[1]

This letter reflects some of the confusion in the minds of Indian political observers, who are faced by the fact that on the level of the region each political party is associated with certain caste-interests, whereas on the All-India level a party stands for a specific ideology. But whatever this ideology may be, in order to get its candidates elected, a party must put up candidates which belong to the caste dominant in their constituency. Similarly the castes want representation in the legislature in order to obtain for their members, as Ashoka Mehta puts it, the loaves and fishes of offices and jobs, and they have there- fore an incentive to ally themselves with a party capable of winning the elections. And as the electors think, of course, not only as mem- bers of their caste, but also as Indians, considerations unconnected with local issues may affect the poll. The Chinese threat to India's northern frontier, for instance, aroused considerable criticism of the Communist party's pro-Chinese policy, but such times of great national indignation are comparatively rare, and Frank Moraes, the editor of *Indian Express*, was probably correct when in a recent contribution to *The Guardian*,[2] he wrote, 'the average voter thinks on a dual plane—national and local—and is more concerned with regional grievances than with national issues'. It is this tendency which, in the words of the same author, 'enables parties such as the Communists to espouse regional chauvinism and gain local adherents, thereby endangering democracy'. Frank Moraes further pointed out that 'in India today the electorate by and large vote not so much on an individual as on a caste, communal or local basis, exposed to and influenced by its immediate rather than by the national environment'.

Indian observers are not agreed on the relative strength of regional and caste loyalties on the one hand, and national sentiments or ideological convictions formulated in All-India terms on the other. Thus K. M. Panikkar, writing in the same issue of *The Guardian*, took a view opposed to that of Frank Moraes, pointing out that 'the party system in India cuts through castes and sub-castes, and though there has been some tendency to exploit caste-loyalties the conflict of interests has generally tended to split the groups on economic and political lines rather than unite them'. He emphasized that national parties, such as the Congress and the Communists, could not afford to appeal publicly to caste-sentiment, but seemed to overlook that

[1] *Economic Weekly*, August 15, 1959.   [2] October 27, 1959.

there can be a great deal of off-stage manipulation of caste-interests and caste-loyalties, without any public pronouncement.

As Selig S. Harrison has pointed out,[1] caste-divisions make it impossible for Communists to follow traditional Marxist class pre-conceptions. Where there are two rival castes of approximately equal economic status the Communists or any other political party must choose between them as it may be impracticable to combine both in the same organization. Thus in Uttar Pradesh the Communist-led Kisan Sabha is supported by the Jats, and this means that the Chauhans had to be forfeited to the Congress, while the untouchables remain uncommitted in order to be able to sell their support to the highest bidder. Where the party had to make a choice between peasant proprietors or untouchable landless labour, expediency paradoxically compelled the Communists to depend on the landed peasant, whose support is of much greater value than that of the rural proletariat. Caste and outcaste have been kept apart even by Communists, for they could not attract to the Kisan Sabhas caste-peasants and untouchables at the same time.

There is, however, one state in which caste seems to play only a minor role in politics, and this is Western Bengal. Many of the urban intellectuals including Brahmans have largely broken away from the ties of caste, and some of the younger members of leftist groups have found within their political party new group loyalties and an exclusive new set of values. Such party workers, who consciously and often dramatically broke away from the ties of joint family and caste, must have been in the mind of Myron Weiner when he stated that 'Indians do not generally have multiple group memberships' and 'there are few outside loyalties to temper the intensity of party membership'.[2]

While this may be true of some of the leftist intellectuals, and explains perhaps the extreme bitterness of party strife, it is certainly not true for the greater part of India where caste-loyalty comes usually before party sentiment and ideological alignments.

In Ceylon we find the same conflict between western and traditional values as in India, but it would seem that there the influence of caste-loyalties on political conduct is on the whole less blatant. Though Buddhist Sinhalese society is organized on caste-lines, conformance with caste-rules is not subject to the same religious sanctions as in Hindu society, and caste-endogamy is not as rigidly enforced as in India. Bryce Ryan summarized his assessment of the influence of

[1] *India: The Most Dangerous Decades*, pp. 269 ff.
[2] Myron Weiner, *Party Politics in India* (1957), p. 8.

caste-sentiments on politics as follows: 'The modern urban world has brought the decay of the behavioural manifestations of caste-hierarchy, but caste-feeling and solidarity have not been shattered. . . ' For many years to come, caste-loyalties and antipathies, along with other functional irrelevancies, will serve to cloud real issues, and to retard the formulation of public opinion along lines of significance for national development.'[1]

Until recently political power lay mainly in the hands of the land-holding Goyigama *élite* of the low country, whereas leadership in commerce was held by Karavas, a caste of lower status, large sections of which had been converted to Christianity. Both among lowland Goyigamas and among urban Karavas there are many families which are so westernized that they are more proficient in English than in Sinhalese. These families furnished the political leadership throughout the years when the United National Party was in power, and the late S. W. R. D. Bandaranaike started his political career as a member of that party. The Shri Lanka Freedom Party, which he later built up, and which under the leadership of his widow has now gained a clear parliamentary majority appeals, however, mainly to those sections of the population which have not had the benefit of an education on western lines and wish for a return to traditional values. The replacement of English by Sinhalese as the official language and the take-over of Christian schools are symptomatic of this tendency. The division between these two parties does not run along obvious caste-lines, for the Shri Lanka Freedom Party could not have won the last election had it not had the support of large numbers of Goyigamas. But the fact that caste-sentiments are still of some account can be gathered from the recent change of leadership in the S.L.F.P. At the time of the inconclusive elections of March 1960 it was led by C. P. de Silva, a member of the Salaga caste. This caste of cinnamon-pickers ranks low in the caste-hierarchy, and though C. P. de Silva was an educated man, unconnected with the traditional caste-occupation, many Sinhalese felt uneasy about having a Salaga prime minister. In the March elections the party lost heavily to the U.N.P., though the latter did not obtain a working majority. At the new elections in July C. P. de Silva was dropped and Mrs Bandaranaike, herself a member of the Goyigama Kandyan aristocracy, officially led the party, even though she did not contest a seat. The result was an overwhelming victory for the S.L.F.P.

I do not think, however, that too much should be made of the

[1] *Caste in Modern Ceylon: The Sinhalese System in Transition* (1953), p. 334.

caste background of Sinhalese politicians, for in Ceylon the political scene is now dominated by two major conflicts: the conflict between the Sinhalese and the Tamils on the one hand, and the conflict between the western-educated and the traditionalists on the other. Time will show whether the recent victory of the Sinhalese traditionalists, which incidentally was so overwhelming that it deprived the Tamil parties of all bargaining power in parliament, will lead to changes in the operation of the democratic system in Ceylon.

Reference to the role played by caste in present-day politics, both in India and Ceylon, are so numerous that little purpose can be served in adding to the list of examples. Even the emphatic denunciation of what is described by the ugly term 'casteism' reflects the widespread belief that caste-loyalty is still a powerful force, and one inconsistent with the ideals for which all political parties claim to stand.

But beyond the fact of this persisting dichotomy of political trends and systems of social values, the literature tells us little about either an open clash or a gradual harmonization of traditional and modern attitudes. Are the electors or at least their chosen representatives conscious of the discrepancy between the manipulation of traditional influence groups determining the composition of the legislatures and the new democratic principles supposed to guide the work of these legislatures? How does a regional caste-group reach the decision to support the one or other political party, and what happens to caste-cohesion on the frequent occasions when two opposing political parties nominate candidates belonging to the same caste?

Are we, indeed, justified in seeing the contrast between the traditional political system and representative democracy as a pattern in black and white, or are both systems already far advanced in a process of change, though they continue to use on the one hand the terminology of the traditional caste-order and on the other hand the imported language of the western parliamentary system?

A study of current writings does not provide the answer to any of these questions, and what is needed are studies in the field, studies of the type known as 'grass-root' investigations. Only such studies can tell us how the members of the state legislative assemblies and the Indian parliament reconcile their responsibility to the nation with their special obligations vis-à-vis the caste- or regional-group to which they owe their election. One small indication is perhaps the fact that locally the position of M.L.A. carries much more prestige than that of Member of Parliament. For an M.P. can do little for his constituents, whereas a member of the state legislative assembly is expected to use his influence for the immediate benefit of his constituents, and in doing so may well intervene in matters of local administration.

To what extent does this activity on two levels and according to two apparently different value systems become part of the political pattern characteristic of India, or perhaps of any country moving rapidly from a feudal order to modern parliamentary democracy? In this essay I can do no more than pose this and other questions, but studies undertaken on the ground like those of F. G. Bailey are likely to provide at least some of the answers. Some recent books on Indian politics, on the other hand, such as Myron Weiner's *Party Politics in India* and John H. Kautsky's *Moscow and the Communist Party of India*, do not even begin to answer these questions and altogether throw very little light on the 'social base' and ultimate motivation of Indian politicians. Thus Kautsky in his analysis of the quarrel between the Andhra Communists and the Indian Politbureau under the party secretary Ranadive fails to explain that the Andhra committee showed little enthusiasm for Ranadive's 'proletarian' and anti-capitalist policies because they derived their strength from their landed Kamma supporters, and aimed at a common front of agricultural labourers, smallholders and middle peasants, and even at occasional collaboration with the rich peasants.

Other political scientists, writing on India, seem to base their attitude also on the unproven assumption that Asian politicians who talk in such western terms as 'democracy, capitalism, socialism or communism' must be motivated by sentiments comparable to those of western parliamentarians, and will therefore automatically move away from traditional attitudes. The few field studies which have so far been made do not bear out such an assumption, and the present position is succinctly expressed in the following quotation from an article by Maureen L. P. Patterson in the *Economic Weekly Annual* of January 1958:

'It must be emphasized that a high level of western education, considerable contact with westerners, and much travel abroad, do not automatically imply a permissive, liberal attitude towards marriage, diet, caste and social customs. . . . Among the highly educated persons of all castes whom I met in Maharashtra, many of those who were apparently thoroughly imbued with western ideas did not allow such intellectual westernization to change their personal mode of living. . . . Caste in Maharashtra has not been upset, undermined, or even much modified in its essentials, during the present period of socio-economic and political change in India as a whole.'

From my personal experience of other areas, I would say that this observation applies to the greater part of India with the possible exception of some sections of the urban communities of Bengal and some very small, cosmopolitan circles in Delhi and Bombay. The position described by Maureen Patterson is likely to persist as long as there is no radical change in the traditional social ideal. We have only to look at the Indian and in particular the Hindu family to realize how great is the emphasis on stability and submission to authority. Even grown-up married men, themselves the fathers of children, are expected to act in accordance with their father's advice and wishes. As members of a joint family they are not in control of property as long as their father is alive, and submissiveness and deference to elders are more highly valued virtues than initiative and independence of spirit. All this makes for conservatism and resistance to change; for with authority in the hands of the oldest members of the family, there is a curb on the activities of the age-groups most likely to favour innovations.

Arthur Koestler has recently suggested that the nation's unconditional deference to Gandhi, significantly referred to as Bapu, was modelled on the father–son relationship, and that Nehru, though temperamentally and by education a very different type, could not help stepping into the same role. 'India', Koestler says, 'is a democracy in name only; it would be more correct to call it Bapucracy.'[1] This is no doubt an oversimplification, but Koestler is probably right when he says that India 'could only become a working democracy in the Western sense after a revolution which strikes at the very roots of Hindu society and Hindu tradition'.[2]

One is inclined to ask with Koestler whether such a transformation, even if practicable, is really desirable, or whether India can work out a different solution in accordance with traditional Hindu ideals. An attempt on those lines is perhaps the policy of decentralization recently introduced in Andhra Pradesh which tries to revive the self-government of small units through the institutions of Zilla Parishad and Panchayat Samitis. The sense of responsibility to people's immediate social surroundings, which in the old days had made possible the working of village- and caste-*panchayats* can

[1] *The Lotus and the Robot* (1960), p. 156.
[2] *Ibid.*, p. 160.

perhaps be harnessed to the development of such a 'grass-root democracy', which—if successful—may combine some features of western democratic institutions with a recognition of such basically Indian concepts as caste-solidarity and a mutually beneficial give-and-take between traditionally distinct social groups.

THE POLITICS BEHIND THE
MONTAGU DECLARATION OF 1917[1]

S. R. MEHROTRA

Research Fellow,
School of Oriental and African Studies,
University of London

British policy in India, though liberal and progressive on the whole, lacked until 1917 a sense of direction. Conditions which had made the establishment and continuance of British rule possible in India were fast changing—mainly as a result of that rule itself. There was, however, little conscious effort to direct these changes to a definite and preconceived goal. Concessions were made to the demands of Indian nationalists, but no attempt was made to think out and work out a policy of continuous advance. The reforms of 1892 and 1909 did not shift the foundations of British rule; they merely adjusted the machinery of British government to the changed circumstances in India. They aimed at associating Indians more closely with the administration and allowing them better opportunities of influencing it, while retaining intact its foreign and autocratic character.

The purpose of this paper is to describe how the need for a well-defined and forward-looking British policy *vis-à-vis* the growing nationalist feeling in India came to be increasingly felt and how in August 1917 the British Government committed themselves explicitly to the policy of preparing India for responsible government within the Empire. As most of the official records of the period under review are not yet available, the account presented in the following pages can lay no claim to definitiveness. It is, so to speak, an interim report.

With the impressions of the Calcutta session of the Indian National

---

[1] On August 20, 1917, Edwin Samuel Montagu, the Secretary of State for India, declared in the House of Commons: 'The policy of His Majesty's Government, with which the Government of India are in complete accord, is that of the increasing association of Indians in every branch of the administration, and the gradual development of self-governing institutions, with a view to the progressive realisation of responsible government in India as an integral part of the British Empire.' 97 H.C. Deb. 5s., col. 1695.

Congress fresh in his mind, Samuel Smith[1] wrote to John Morley the Secretary of State for India, on December 26, 1906, about the' demand for Indian self-government put forward by Dadabhai Naoroji in his presidential address: 'I felt the force of the appeal. No one with a sense of humanity could but feel the great wave of emotion which is carrying India towards an unknown future. It was an epoch-making occasion . . . the demand was explicit, and momentous consequences will hang on the answer that we give.'[2] Morley had already given his answer to G. K. Gokhale in the summer of 1906. He had privately assured the leader of the moderate Indian nationalists that he and the Viceroy, Lord Minto, were eager to make an effective move in the direction of 'reasonable reforms'. But he was frankly sceptical about Gokhale's 'ultimate hope and design—India to be on the footing of a self-governing colony'. 'For many a long day to come', he had told Gokhale, '—long beyond the short span of time that may be left to us—this was a mere dream.'[3] It was Morley's considered belief that parliamentary democracy was not suited to Indian conditions. He repeatedly denounced in public the idea of introducing it in India as 'a fantastic and ludicrous dream'[4] and a 'gross and dangerous sophism'.[5] He spiritedly repudiated the suggestion that his reforms could in any way lead to a parliamentary system in India.[6]

India was too vast and too divided. She was educationally and economically backward. One can, therefore, understand why the disciple of John Stuart Mill did not 'think it desirable or possible, or even conceivable, to adapt English political institutions to the nations who inhabit India'.[7] But what one cannot understand or excuse is the fact that Morley did not suggest an alternative method of India's political evolution. This omission was all the more reprehensible on the part of a statesman who realized that the British *Raj* was 'intensely

---

[1] Business man, politician and philanthropist; Liberal M.P. for Flintshire, 1886–1905; a keen student of Indian affairs; went to India to attend the 1906 session of the Congress; died suddenly at Calcutta on December 28, 1906.

[2] Smith to Morley, December 26, 1906, Morley Papers, India Office Library, London.

[3] Morley to Minto, August 2, 1906, *ibid*.   [4] 161 H.L. Deb. 4s., col. 587.

[5] Morley, *Indian Speeches* (1909), p. 36.

[6] Morley's oft-quoted remark: 'If it could be said that this chapter of reforms led directly or necessarily up to the establishment of a parliamentary system in India, I, for one, would have nothing to do with it. . . . If my existence, either officially or corporally, were prolonged twenty times longer than either of them is likely to be, a parliamentary system in India is not the goal to which I for one moment would aspire.' 198 H.L. Deb. 4s., col. 1985.

[7] Morley to Minto, June 6, 1906, Morley Papers.

artificial and unnatural' and surely could not last.[1] The reforms which he, in collaboration with Minto, introduced into the government of India in 1909 were a typical product of that nineteenth-century English liberalism which believed that statesmanship was mainly a question of determining how far popular demands should be conceded, but which seldom bothered to think out the fundamentals of policy or relate it to a well-defined larger purpose. 'Lacking a clearly distinguishable and steadily developing British policy towards the growth of politics in India,' justly comments Professor C. H. Philips, 'Morley and Minto were driven to devising not so much a coherent plan as a series of expedients to meet the particular and admittedly difficult situation.'[2] A few Indians were admitted to the arcana imperii.[3] The numbers and powers of the existing legislative councils were increased.[4] The avowed purpose of these changes, however, was not to train Indians in self-government, but simply 'to enable Government the better to realize the wants, the sentiments, of the governed, and on the other hand, to give the governed a better chance of understanding as occasion arises, the case for the Government against the misrepresentations of ignorance and malice'.[5] In a sense, Morley and Minto refused to face the basic question posed by Indian nationalism: what is the goal of British rule in India? They really gave no serious thought to the future. Morley believed in leaving the day after tomorrow to Providence,[6] and Minto thought he could not afford 'to speculate on

[1] '... how intensely artificial and unnatural is our mighty *Raj*, and it sets one wondering whether it can possibly last. It surely cannot....' Morley to Minto, August 15, 1907, *ibid.*

[2] C. H. Philips, *India* (1949), p. 107.

[3] Two Indians were appointed to the council of the Secretary of State and one Indian each to the executive councils of the Governor-General and the Governors.

[4] The number of 'additional members' was increased to a maximum of 50 in the larger and 30 in the smaller provinces. In Bombay, for example, of the total membership of 47, 5 were ex-officio members, 21 were nominated (of which not more than 14 could be officials), and 21 were elected. All provincial legislative councils had now non-official (nominated + elected) majorities. Bengal even had a clear elected majority. The central legislative council also received an addition of Indian members, but there an official majority was retained. All the legislative councils were allowed more time to discuss the budget, to move resolutions, and to call for a division. The right of interpellation was extended and members could ask supplementary questions.

[5] *Proposals of the Government of India and Despatch of the Secretary of State*, Cd. 4426, 1908, p. 50.

[6] 'Do you know something said by Déak, the Hungarian statesman? "I can answer for today, I can pretty well for tomorrow, the day after tomorrow I leave to Providence." So do I.' Morley to Minto, July 15, 1909, Morley Papers.

the problems of coming generations'.[1] Nor is there anything to show that they ever considered what would be the next step to be taken from the point reached in 1909. 'But what will the next great change be, and when?' asked Minto, only to add 'Not in our time'.[2] For the tired and ageing Morley one step was enough. And he hoped that Indians, too, in so far as they were wise, would not concern themselves with the distant scene. Speaking on the second reading of the Indian Councils Bill in the House of Lords on February 23, 1909, Morley remarked that the effect of his reforms had been, was being and would be to persuade those who hoped for 'autonomy or self-government of the colonial species or pattern' in India to give up their dream and be content with admission to co-operation with the British administration.[3]

This was mere wishful thinking. Men do not give up their dreams so easily: and national dreams are, perhaps, the most tenacious. The eyes of most educated Indians were now fixed on the future and, despite the assertions of Morley and Minto to the contrary, they had welcomed the reforms of 1909 as an advance towards parliamentary self-government. As was to be expected, Indian nationalists, instead of relinquishing their dream, began persuading the British Government to accept it as their own. In July 1911 Gokhale wrote that the political evolution to which Indian reformers looked forward was 'representative government on a democratic basis'. In his view 'the first requisite of improved relations on an enduring basis between Englishmen and Indians' was 'an unequivocal declaration on England's part of her resolve to help forward the growth of representative institutions in India and a determination to stand by this policy, in spite of all temptations or difficulties'. 'I think the time has come', Gokhale added, 'when a definite pronouncement on this subject should be made by the highest authority entitled to speak in the name of England, and the British Government in India should keep such pronouncement in view in all its actions.'[4]

Nor did Indian nationalists stand alone in demanding a definition of British policy in India. Indian unrest and the controversial character of the Morley–Minto reforms had set reflecting Englishmen thinking about the future and purpose of the *Raj*. Men of religion were, perhaps, the first to respond to the challenge of Indian nationalism.

[1] Minto to Morley, June 17, 1909, Morley Papers.
[2] Minto to Morley, February 25, 1909, *ibid.*
[3] 1 H.L. Deb. 5s., coll. 118–19.
[4] G. K. Gokhale, 'East and West in India', *Hindustan Review*, July 1911, p. 9.

The Bishop of Southampton,[1] for example, enquired in January 1908 whether the English administrators in India ever cared to think where their work in India was leading to. 'Is India', he asked, 'always to remain a subject country? Is that our intention? Is that our desire and inward purpose? Is that our conception of our mission, or have we in our minds something better and nobler, something of more world-wide importance? Have we visions of an Indian nation as a far-off possibility, and are such visions the inspiration of our work? Do we feel that our duty to India and mankind can only be accomplished through the evolution of a united, free, intelligent, self-governing people, and that it cannot be accomplished through the indefinite continuance of foreign bureaucratic rule, however good and beneficent?' The Bishop argued that English-men and Indians were working at cross purposes because they did not have the same aim. He pleaded for a meeting of minds on the subject of the future goal and a definite acceptance by the British people of the Indian ideal of self-government.[2]

The enlightened English administrator in India also felt the need of a definite, far-sighted policy. Lovat Fraser[3] noted in 1909: 'Many of our difficulties are due to the fact that we have never made up our minds as to our purpose there. . . . Reflecting civil servants have said to me: "What are we here for? If I only knew that, I should know how to order my life and my duty." The civilian nowadays is perplexed and puzzled. He sees the conflict of rival ideas—the one that we are in India for the good of the people, and the other that we are there for our own good.'[4] In the same year William Marris[5] was telling Lionel Curtis[6] that 'self-government . . . , however far distant, was the only intelligible goal of British policy in India. It needed a guiding principle and no other was thinkable.'[7] In June 1912 another

[1] He had formerly been the Bishop of Bombay.

[2] The Bishop of Southampton, 'The Unrest in India and Some of Its Causes', *The East and the West*, January 1908, pp. 1–20.

[3] On the editorial staff of *The Times*, 1907–22; formerly editor of the *Times of India*.

[4] 'Britain's Future in India', *The Times*, June 28, 1909; *The History of The Times* (1952), vol. iv, pt. ii, p. 834.

[5] I.C.S., 1896; Governor of Assam, 1921–2; Governor of the United Provinces, 1922–7.

[6] 'The Prophet' of Milner's 'Kindergarten'; Fellow of All Souls College, Oxford; a leading exponent of federalism; one of the most influential 'backroom' figures of his day.

[7] Curtis, *Dyarchy* (1920), p. 41.

distinguished member of the Indian Civil Service, Sir James Meston,[1] was arguing with his friends of the Round Table group in England: 'Do we intend to give her [India] self-government or to hold her permanently in the status of a subject country? Many people would reply that our duty to India is fulfilled when we give her peace and ensure the maintenance of law and order. I do not agree with this narrow conception of our duty. It seems to me that we owe to India an endeavour to raise her by degrees as near to our own plane of civilization as we can. If this be true, self-government, being one of the characteristics of our civilization, must become one of the ideals at which our rule in India is to aim.'[2] Meston disclosed later that the far-reaching and constantly spreading spirit of nationalism in India made it impossible for the British officials in that country to carry on without a declared policy of what England meant to do in India and with India, and that it was largely in response to their appeals that the search for a policy was undertaken.[3]

The radicals in England demanded that the issue should be burked no longer. In July 1910 Josiah Wedgwood[4] asked bluntly in the Commons: 'Do we actually want India some time to be free and self-governing or do we not?' If not, the British Government should, he argued, drop cant and say so. If, on the other hand, they did want India to be ultimately self-governing—'whether it be in twenty or fifty or a hundred years'—they should tell that frankly to the Indian people and lay their plans accordingly.[5]

In 1911–12 there was an episode which, though it brought forth renewed and more emphatic official disclaimers of the ideal of dominion self-government for India, revealed that even the Government of India felt the need of looking ahead and at least one member of His Majesty's Government realized that a clear and authoritative enunciation of British policy in India was imperative. In a dispatch to the Secretary of State, dated August 25, 1911, the Government of

[1] I.C.S., 1883; Lieutenant-Governor of the United Provinces, 1912–18; Baron, 1919.

[2] Meston, 'Memo. on India and the Empire' (unpublished), p. 2, Curtis Papers. Quoted with the kind permission of Mr D. Morrah, the present editor of the *Round Table*.

[3] 37 H.L. Deb. 5s., col. 1034; C. Ilbert and J. Meston, *The New Constitution of India* (1923), pp. 94–5.

[4] Liberal, later Labour, M.P. for Newcastle-under-Lyme, 1906–42; joined the Labour Party in 1919; Chancellor of the Duchy of Lancaster in the Labour Government, 1924.

[5] 19 H.C. Deb. 5s., coll. 2043–4.

India had pointed out that 'in the course of time, the just demands of Indians for a larger share in the Government of the country will have to be satisfied, and the question will be how this devolution of power can be conceded without impairing the supreme authority of the Governor-General in Council'. To the Government of India 'the only possible solution of the difficulty' appeared to be 'gradually to give the Provinces a larger measure of self-government, until at last India would consist of a number of administrations, autonomous in all provincial affairs, with the Government of India above them all and possessing power to interfere in cases of misgovernment, but ordinarily restricting their functions to matters of Imperial concern'.[1] The dispatch was published on December 12, 1911, and was at once seized upon by Indian nationalists as indicating the aim and intention of the British Government in India. Speaking at Cambridge on February 28, 1912, Edwin Samuel Montagu, the Under-Secretary of State for India, confirmed the Indian interpretation of the dispatch. He dwelt at length on the Liberal ideal of the Empire, based on freedom and free association. He remarked that Curzon as Viceroy was a mere administrator who had no policy at all. He compared him to a chauffeur who spent his time polishing up the machinery, screwing every nut and bolt of his car ready to make it go, but never driving it or knowing where to drive it to. Referring to the celebrated passage in the Government of India dispatch, Montagu remarked: 'That statement shows the goal, the aim towards which we propose to work—not immediately, not in a hurry, but gradually.' He pointed out that the British Government could not 'drift on for ever without stating a policy'. A new generation had grown up in India which asked 'What are you going to do with us?'; the extremists had drawn up and published their own exposition of the exact form of *Swaraj* which they wanted; the moderates looked to the authorities to say what lines their future policy was to take. 'We have never answered that,' Montagu added, 'and we have put off answering them far too long. At last, and not too soon, a Viceroy has had the courage to state the trend of British policy in India and the lines upon which we propose to advance.'[2]

A storm of controversy raged for a few months in England over

---

[1] *Announcements by and on behalf of His Majesty the King-Emperor at the Coronation Durbar held at Delhi on December 12, 1911, with the Correspondence relating thereto*; Cd. 5979, p. 7. The dispatch was in connection with the proposed transfer of the capital of India from Calcutta to Delhi.

[2] *Speeches on Indian Questions* (1918), pp. 247–59.

the passage in the Government of India's dispatch. The Opposition in Parliament accused the Liberal Government of contemplating the introduction of some sort of federal home rule in India. The Secretary of State for India, Lord Crewe, repeatedly denied the charge. He explained away the controversial passage in the dispatch as a casual remark, indicating 'the inevitable trend and tendency of things in India' towards further decentralization in all matters of a provincial nature.[1] He referred to the political school in India which cherished the dream of self-government on the dominion model and remarked: 'I say quite frankly that I see no future for India on those lines. I do not believe that the experiment . . . of attempting to confer a measure of self-government, with practical freedom from Parliamentary control, upon a race which is not our own . . . is one which could be tried.'[2] Crewe affirmed that there were three objects of British policy in India: 'to devolve upon local and provincial governments as many of the functions of government as can be safely entrusted to them'; 'to employ as many Indians in the public service as can reasonably be employed'; and 'to continue the pursuit of the two first with the maintenance and permanence of British rule in India'.[3] But though Crewe tried, with all the weight of his great authority as Secretary of State, to dismiss the idea of a self-governing Indian dominion as 'a world as remote as any Atlantis or Erewhon that ever was thought of by the ingenious brain of an imaginative writer',[4] the last word in the debate lay with the Liberal peer, Lord Courtney. The latter deprecated the tendency 'to put the limit of impossibility on the development that may occur in India'. He recalled the extraordinary changes going on in the eastern world and the remark made to him by Sir Alfred Lyall[5] shortly before his death, 'It is not impossible that the twentieth century may see the complete withdrawal of Europe from Asia'; and observed: 'However comfortable it may be to ourselves to attempt to dismiss these speculations, we cannot get rid of them.'[6]

Crewe's invocation of what William Archer called 'the dogma of perpetuity',[7] failed to silence the heretics in India or in England. In December 1912 the Council of the All-India Muslim League adopted

[1] 11 H.L. Deb. 5s., coll. 243-4.   [2] 12 H.L. Deb. 5s., coll. 155-6
[3] *Ibid.*, coll. 742-3.   [4] *Ibid.*, col. 745.
[5] Alfred Comyn Lyall (1835-1911); famous Anglo-Indian administrator and author; I.C.S., 1853; Lieutenant-Governor of the North-west Provinces, 1882-7; member of the council of the Secretary of State for India, 1888-1902.
[6] 12 H.L. Deb. 5s., coll. 748-51.
[7] William Archer, *India and the Future* (1917), p. 295.

as one of its objectives 'the attainment of a system of self-government suitable to India'.[1] Returning from India after a short visit in 1912, Philip Kerr[2] wrote in the September *Round Table* that, whether the pace be fast or slow, the goal towards which events in India, propelled by Indian and British alike, were travelling was self-government like that of the dominions.[3] Under a very suggestive title 'India: Old Ways and New', another contributor wrote in the December 1912 issue of the same quarterly that conditions in India were changing with a rapidity unknown to previous generations, which made it impossible for the English in that country to go on doing their work empirically, avoiding a philosophy or a creed. And he added: 'It is time we defined our ideas; that we knew clearly what it is that India wants, and how far and by what stages we are going to assist her to get it.'[4]

With all their habitual disinclination to speculate about the future, with all their distaste for the conscious and the explicit, the British could not for long avoid defining their policy in India. The need for such a definition was being felt by many. It was, in a fundamental sense, made inevitable by the challenge of Indian nationalism. The impact of the First World War only brought the issue to a head and allowed it to be treated from a new angle of vision. The reforms of 1909, which Morley had hoped would suffice for a generation, had revealed their inadequacy even by 1912–13.[5] They had carried the representation of Indians on the legislative councils up to a point at which the question of responsible government in India was bound to arise. Their extension could not be undertaken—as was realized in 1916–17—without first answering the pregnant question 'Whither?'.

India's splendid rally to the cause of the Empire in the First World War both surprised and gratified the British people who had been hearing so much and so often of Indian unrest in the preceding years. And the more they were surprised and gratified, the more fulsome and

---

[1] *Indian Review*, January 1913, p. 54.

[2] The later Lord Lothian; editor of the *Round Table*, 1910–16; private secretary to Lloyd George, 1916–21.

[3] 'India and the Empire', *Round Table*, September 1912, pp. 623–5; J. R. M. Butler, *Lord Lothian* (1960), p. 175.

[4] *Round Table*, December 1912, p. 52.

[5] See, for example, the evidence of Sir Claude H. Hill, ex-member of the executive council of the Governor of Bombay and of the Governor-General of India, before the Joint Select Committee in 1919; *Report on the Joint Select Committee on the Government of India Bill*, H.C. 203, 1919, vol. i, p. 31.

vocal were their admiration and gratitude. It was recognized on all hands that India had qualified for closer partnership and a further instalment of reforms. The revelation that India had proved to be not a cause of anxiety but a source of immense strength in the Empire's hour of peril converted even the most conservative imperialist in Britain to view the problems of her internal development and place in the Empire from a changed angle. Even in the past it had been morally impossible for most Englishmen to reject outright the Indian claim for self-government. In view, however, of India's comradeship in the war and Britain's declared war aims, the Indian claim became irresistible. Wherever the question was debated—in the Round Table group, in the Viceroy's executive council, or in the War Cabinet— there seemed to be but one answer, consistent with logic, history and tradition: self-government was the only conceivable goal of British rule in India; and the Indian demand for it was a sign of grace and not an evidence of original sin.

Like most of his countrymen, Lord Willingdon, the Governor of Bombay, had been profoundly impressed by India's loyal and magnificent services in the war and felt that she should be rewarded handsomely. Early in 1915 he asked Gokhale privately to submit to him a scheme of minimum reforms which would satisfy India after the war. Gokhale submitted his suggestions on February 17, 1915.[1] Tragically two days later he died. Willingdon wrote to leaders at home to make a reassuring move, but 'either got no answer or no encouragement'.[2] Pherozeshah Mehta soon followed Gokhale to the grave, and the Congress was thus robbed of the moderating influence of two of its most prominent leaders. Under the influence of the excitement of the times, the uncertainty as to the intentions of the Government, and the apprehensions regarding India's position in a probable federation of the Empire, the political cauldron in India began to boil. Mrs Annie Besant acted as the peacemaker between the moderates and the extremists and began preparations for launching a home rule movement. The followers of Gokhale and Mehta were anxious that nothing should be done which might embarrass the authorities in any way during the period of the war, but neither did they wish to allow India's case to go by default. The loyalty of the moderates was as firm as their patriotism. They stood for a gradual and peaceful advance of India towards self-government, in co-operation with their British

[1] V. Srinivasa Sastri, *Life of Gopal Krishna Gokhale* (1937), pp. 112–13.
[2] Willingdon to Lloyd George, January 22, 1916, Lloyd George, *War Memoirs* (1933–6), vol. iv, p. 1739.

rulers. For themselves they believed 'with the fervour of a religious faith'[1] that India would some day achieve her self-government within the Empire and that British statesmen would prove true to their traditional genius and recognize India's aspirations as legitimate and worthy of encouragement. But how could they—without appearing ridiculous—avow their faith openly while the solemn disclaimers of Morley and Crewe were fresh in public memory? These disclaimers, the moderates knew, had made large classes of people in India distrustful of British good intentions and hostile to British rule. Clearly there was need that these unfortunate disclaimers themselves should first be disclaimed. And this, the moderates felt, could easily be done if the British Government made an authoritative and unequivocal declaration that it was their aim and intention to grant India self-government similar to that enjoyed by the dominions in the fullness of time. There was yet another reason why the moderates considered such a declaration of British policy in India necessary. They were wise and practical-minded enough to realize that the war had given rise to excessive hopes and demands in India which no reforms granted by the authorities at the end of the war would suffice to satisfy. Dissatisfaction with post-war reforms might even lead to a recrudescence of serious unrest in the country. But if the Government could be persuaded to avow an intention of leading India to self-government, the differences between the rulers and the ruled would be narrowed down to questions of method and pace of advance. In such a situation it would not be difficult for moderate and reasonable men to throw the weight of their influence and co-operation on the side of the authorities, thus ensuring the peaceful but steady political progress of India.

The desire of the moderates for a definite statement that ultimate self-government for India was the goal of British policy found earnest expression in the presidential address delivered by Sir Satyendra Sinha to the 1915 session of the Congress held at Bombay. Sinha remarked on the occasion that nothing but 'a rational and inspiring ideal' could 'still the throbbing pain in the soul of awakening India'. After reiterating that self-government within the Empire was the goal of Indian nationalism, he went on to appeal to the British people 'to declare their ungrudging approval of the goal' to which Indians aspired, 'to declare their inflexible resolution to equip India for her journey to that goal and furnish her escort on the long and weary road'. Such a declaration

[1] The phrase quoted is Sir S. P. Sinha's. See *Speeches and Writings of Lord Sinha* (1919), p. 86.

by Britain, Sinha said, would be the most distinguished way of marking her appreciation of India's loyalty and services; it would touch the heart and appeal to the imagination of Indians far more than any specific political reforms. These latter, he argued, might fall short of the high expectations raised by the utterances of English statesmen as to the future place of India in the Empire and cause general disappointment, but an authoritative declaration of Britain's resolve to lead India to self-government would, without causing such disappointment, convince the Indian people that the pace of reforms would be reasonably accelerated and that henceforth it would be only a question of patient preparation. Sinha referred to the 'unhappy statements and even actions of responsible [British] statesmen' in the recent past which had, he said, aroused widespread suspicion in India that Britain did not contemplate giving India freedom even in the most distant future. He demanded, therefore, 'an authentic and definite proclamation with regard to which there will be no evasion, no misunderstanding possible'—'a frank and full statement of the policy of the Government as regards the future of India'—'so that hope may come where despair holds sway and faith where doubt spreads its darkening shadow'. And he warned that unless the British Government 'steadily, consistently and unflinchingly' adhered to the policy of preparing India for ultimate self-government within the Empire 'the moderate party amongst us will soon be depleted of all that is fine and noble in human character'.[1]

That was how Sinha—the most loyal and moderate and sensible of Indians—tried to pin down the British nation and Government, and tempt them into making a declaration of policy. Lord Chelmsford revealed later that 'the ball was set rolling' by Sinha's remarkable address to the Congress in December 1915.[2] It apparently inspired him—the future Viceroy of India—and many others to think about the goal of British policy in India and to realize the need for its announcement.

The ruling Viceroy, Lord Hardinge, was a wise and imaginative statesman, fully alive and sympathetic to the new developments in India. Convinced that peace and tranquillity in India and the future good relations between India and the British Empire would depend to a large extent upon what concessions were made to legitimate Indian aspirations, he had already in August 1915 drawn up a memo-

[1] *Report of the Thirtieth Indian National Congress*, 1915, pp. 21–30.
[2] 69 H.L. Deb. 5s., coll. 266–7; C. H. Setalvad, *Recollections and Reflections* (1946), p. 284.

randum on the reforms which he thought should be introduced in India at the end of the war.[1] In October 1915 he had sent his memorandum to the Secretary of State, along with the overwhelmingly favourable comments on it of the heads of local governments and the members of his executive council. Hardinge openly avowed his friendliness to the Indian ideal of self-government. Speaking at the United Service Club at Simla on October 8, 1915, he remarked that it was 'not enough for [England] now to consider only the material outlook of India', she must cherish the aspirations for liberty of which she had herself sown the seed in the country. He asked the English officials in India to prepare themselves for the 'far more glorious task' of the future, that of 'encouraging and guiding the political self-development of the people', and he himself looked forward 'with confidence to a time when . . . India may be regarded as a true friend of the Empire and not merely as a trusty dependent'.[2] Although in his valedictory address to the Imperial Legislative Council on March 24, 1916, Hardinge discouraged 'extravagant hopes . . . and unrealisable demands' with regard to post-war reforms in India, he did not fail to add: 'I do not for a moment wish to discountenance self-government as a national ideal. It is a perfectly legitimate aspiration and has the warm sympathy of all moderate men.'[3] Hardinge's remarks encouraged Indian politicians to think that it would not be very difficult to persuade the authorities to make a formal and definite declaration that self-government for India was the ultimate goal of their policy.

A powerful combination of intellectuals and politicians in England known as the Round Table group,[4] was at this time busy exploring

[1] 'Memorandum by H.E. the Viceroy upon Questions Likely to Arise in India at the End of the War', Austen Chamberlain Papers, Birmingham University Library. The main recommendations of Hardinge were: (i) commissions for Indians in the army; (ii) modification of the Arms Act; (iii) abolition of the Indian excise duty on cotton goods; (iv) modification of the regulations of the central and provincial legislative councils (elected majority in the provinces, increase of elected members at the centre, wider electorates); (v) relaxation of control exercised by the centre over the provinces, and by the Secretary of State over the Government of India; (vi) India's representation at the Imperial Conference; (vii) abolition of indentured labour; (viii) state-aid for Indian industries; (ix) appointment of Indians to the Privy Council; and (x) increased employment of Indians in the public services.
[2] *Times of India*, October 11, 1915.
[3] *Proceedings of the Council of the Governor-General of India*, 1915–16, vol. liv, p. 559.
[4] The prominent members of the group were: L. S. Amery, Robert Brand,

the possibilities of Imperial federation. During the autumn of 1915, while the group was engaged in examining the position of India vis-à-vis a future federated Empire, it met regularly once a fortnight in London. Among those who attended these meetings were Lionel Curtis, Philip Kerr, Reginald Coupland,[1] Sir William Duke,[2] Sir Lionel Abrahams,[3] M. C. Seton,[4] C. H. Kisch,[5] and J. E. Shuckburgh.[6] The group began by agreeing that the attitude taken by the Indians in the war had proved that the country was riper than had been supposed for further reforms. Curtis, however, insisted that it was imperative to decide what was the goal of British policy in India before discussing any further steps in constitutional advance. The only conceivable goal, it was recognized, was self-government. A closer examination of the term 'self-government' revealed that it was ambiguous. 'The only meaning of self-government as a goal which bore the test of examination was responsible government for India within the Commonwealth which could not stop short of those by which the Dominions had reached their present position.'[7] It was obvious that India could not advance by one step to full responsible government and that her progress towards it must be by stages. It was also realized that any further progress on the lines of the Morley–Minto reforms would lead to disaster, for a further increase of the non-official element in the legislative councils would give the latter the power of paralysing government at every turn, but not the power and responsibility of conducting government for themselves. The essence of the problem was, therefore, to find a method of introducing true responsible government in a limited and manageable field of

Robert Cecil, Valentine Chirol, Reginald Coupland, G. L. Craik, Lionel Curtis, Geoffrey Dawson, John Dove, Patrick Duncan, Richard Feetham, Edward Grigg, Lionel Hichens, Philip Kerr, D. O. Malcolm, William Marris, James Meston, Lord Milner, F. S. Oliver, Lord Selborne, Arthur Steele-Maitland, and A. E. Zimmern.

The account of the activities of the Round Table group which follows is based on Curtis, *Dyarchy*, pp. xx ff. and the Curtis Papers. For permission to make use of the latter the author is indebted to Mr D. Morrah.

[1] Historian; Beit Lecturer in Colonial History, Oxford, 1913; editor of the *Round Table*, 1917–19; Beit Professor of Colonial History, Oxford, 1920–48.

[2] Member of the council of the Secretary of State for India; formerly Lieutenant-Governor of Bengal.

[3] Assistant Under-Secretary of State, India Office.

[4] Secretary, Judicial and Public, India Office.

[5] Senior Clerk, India Office.

[6] Assistant Secretary, Political and Secret, India Office.

[7] Curtis, *op. cit.*, p. xxii.

administration, which could be contracted or extended in accordance with the practical results attained, without imperilling the structure of government itself. The method by which this gradual and safe advance to responsible government could be made in India was suggested in a memorandum prepared for the group by Sir William Duke.[1] It was later nicknamed 'dyarchy' and became the basis of the Montagu-Chelmsford reforms. Chelmsford had shown interest in the inquiries of the group and at his request the final draft of the Duke memorandum was sent to him in May 1916. The part played by the Round Table group in determining the form of the announcement of August 20, 1917, in securing the representation of India at the Imperial Conference, and in the subsequent stages of the Montagu–Chelmsford reforms, though not always easy to trace with precision, was certainly significant, if not decisive.

Chelmsford came as Viceroy to India in April 1916 with his mind made up that a declaration of British policy was necessary.[2] At the very first meeting of his executive council, held in May 1916, he propounded two questions: '(1) What is the goal of British rule in India? and (2) What are the steps on the road to that goal?'[3] The deliberations of the council led to the conclusion that 'the endowment of British India as an integral part of the British Empire with self-government was the goal of British rule' and that an advance towards this goal should be made along three roads, viz. the development of local self-government; the more responsible employment of Indians in the administration; and the expansion of the provincial legislative councils.[4] On November 24, 1916, the Government of India sent a dispatch to the Secretary of State, containing their final proposals for reform, along with the comments of the local governments on them.[5] The two main features of the Government of India dispatch related to the reform of the provincial legislative councils and the declaration of the goal of British rule in India. As regards the provincial legislative councils, the dispatch had recommended that their electorates should be widened, that the number of Indian representatives in them should

---

[1] Originally issued under the title, *Suggestions for Constitutional Progress in Indian Polity*, it later became famous as 'the Duke Memorandum'.

[2] See the remark made by Crewe in the Lords on December 12, 1919. 37 H.L. Deb. 5s., col. 986.

[3] *Proceedings of the Indian Legislative Council*, 1917–18, vol. lvi, p. 17.

[4] *Ibid.*, pp. 17–18.

[5] Government of India, Home Department, Political, No. 17, Austen Chamberlain Papers.

be increased, and that they should have elected majorities.[1] In making these recommendations the Government of India had followed the lines laid down by the reforms of 1892 and 1909. They had rejected the method of advance—by way of dyarchy—suggested in the Round Table (Duke) memorandum.[2] Not only had they not recommended any immediate enlargement of the constitutional powers of the provincial legislative councils, they had expressly told the Secretary of State that they had 'no wish to develop the councils as quasi-parliaments'.[3]

As regards the declaration of the goal of British rule in India, the Government of India had proposed a long and verbose formula: 'The goal to which we look forward is the endowment of British India as an integral part of the Empire, with self-government, but the rate of progress towards that goal must depend upon the improvement and wide diffusion of education, the softening of racial and religious differences, and the acquisition of political experience.

'The form of self-government to which she may eventually attain must be regulated by the special circumstances of India. They differ so widely from those of any other part of the Empire that we cannot altogether look for a model in those forms of self-government which already obtain in the great Dominions. In all parts of the Empire which now enjoys self-government, it has been the result, not of any sudden inspiration of theoretical statesmanship, but of a steady process of practical evolution, substantially facilitated by the possession of a more or less common inheritance of political traditions, social customs and religious beliefs.

'British India has been built up on different lines, and under different conditions, and must work out by the same steady process of evolution a definite constitution of her own. In what form this may eventually be cast it is neither possible nor profitable for us to attempt now to determine, but we contemplate her gradual progress towards a larger and larger measure of control by her own people, the steady and conscious development of which will ultimately result in a form of self-government, differing perhaps in many ways from that enjoyed by the other parts of the Empire, but evolved on lines which have

[1] Government of India, Home Department, Political, No. 17, Austen Chamberlain Papers, pp. 19–24.
[2] See Chelmsford to Chamberlain, May 30, 1917 (telegram), Austen Chamberlain Papers. Also, 69 H.L. Deb. 5s., coll. 267–8.
[3] Government of India, Home Department, Political, No. 17, p. 20, Austen Chamberlain Papers.

taken into account India's past history, and the special circumstances and traditions of her component peoples, and her political and administrative entities.'[1]

Unfortunately the Government of India could not take the Indian public into their confidence. Indian politicians had expected some announcement of policy in Chelmsford's opening speech to the Imperial Legislative Council in September 1916, but were disappointed. It was already rumoured that the Government of India were busy considering a scheme of future reforms, but when Indian members enquired in the Council whether it was so, and would the Government publish their proposals before final decision was reached, the Home Member merely replied that the Government were 'unable to make any statement in the matter'.[2] Anxious lest their case go by default, nineteen non-official members of the Imperial Legislative Council hurriedly put their heads together and produced a memorandum, containing what they called their 'humble suggestions' regarding post-war reforms in India, and submitted it to the Viceroy in September 1916.

Aided by the unnecessary reticence of the authorities, Indian nationalists closed their ranks. The extremists re-entered the Congress and before the year 1916 was out the Muslim League had signed a concordat with its old antagonist. Besides putting forward joint proposals for an early and far-reaching reform in the government of India, the Congress and the League, meeting together at Lucknow in the last week of December 1916, demanded that 'the King-Emperor should be pleased to issue a proclamation that it is the aim and intention of British policy to confer self-government on India at an early date'.[3]

---

[1] Government of India, Home Department, Political, No. 17, p. 16, Austen Chamberlain Papers.

[2] *Proceedings of the Indian Legislative Council,* 1916–17, vol. lv, pp. 45–6, 51.

[3] *Times of India,* December 30, 1916; January 1–2, 1917. The other main demands of the Congress and the League were: (i) provincial autonomy; (ii) four-fifths of the central and provincial legislative councils to be elected; (iii) not less than half the members of the central and provincial governments to be elected by their respective legislative councils; (iv) the executives to be bound to act in accordance with the resolutions passed by their legislative councils unless they were vetoed by the Governor-General or Governors, in that event, if the resolution were passed again after an interval of not less than one year, it should in any case be put into effect; (v) the relations of the Secretary of State with the Government of India to be similar to those of the Colonial Secretary, and India to have an equal status with the dominions in any body concerned with imperial affairs.

It was a definite and direct demand to which some answer would have to be given by the British Government. As a matter of mere courtesy the Congress and the League would have to be told whether their request for a statement of policy was to be granted or not. In February 1917 the Maharaja of Bikaner publicly expressed the deep sympathy of the princes for 'the legitimate aspirations of our brother Indians'.[1] Never before had such a unanimity of opinion been witnessed in India on any political issue. Hindus and Muslims; moderates and extremists; politicians and princes—all seemed to be united in their desire for self-government for India. This unique phenomenon could not fail to impress the British Government. It was not long before liberal non-official Anglo-Indian opinion reinforced the Indian demand for a declaration of British policy. 'We have never met an intelligent man', wrote the *Times of India* on May 15, 1917, 'who doubted the goal of British policy in India; it is clearly and irrevocably, the attainment of full self-government within the Empire.' The paper could 'discern no possible ill, and many positive advantages', in a 'clear and emphatic announcement' of this goal. 'Unless the end is clearly in view', it added, 'there can be no logical or definite purpose behind such constitutional changes as are made or contemplated.'[2] On June 21, 1917, the paper again urged 'the Government of India to place itself at the head of the best national forces in India, to avow boldly and uncompromisingly that the attainment of self-government within the Empire is the goal of its policy in India'.[3] Similar appeals were made by the Bishops of Calcutta[4] and Madras.[5]

An India Office committee, headed by Sir William Duke, examined the Government of India dispatch of November 24, 1916, and submitted its report to the Secretary of State on March 16, 1917.[6] The committee did not think that the proposals of the Government of India with regard to the provincial legislative councils constituted a coherent and well-thought-out plan of reform, or that they embodied sound and constitutional lines of political advance.[7] It pointed out that

[1] K. M. Panikkar, *His Highness the Maharaja of Bikaner: A Biography* (1937), p. 174.

[2] *Times of India*, May 15, 1917.

[3] *Ibid.*, June 21, 1917. Also August 2, 1917.

[4] *Indian Review*, August 1917, p. 542.

[5] *Nineteenth Century and After*, August 1916, pp. 265–83; *Indian Review*, July 1917, pp. 449–54.

[6] 'Report on Government of India Despatch, Home Department, No. 17, Political, dated November 24, 1916', Austen Chamberlain Papers.

[7] *Ibid.*, pp. 1–2.

a mere increase in the number of elected Indian representatives in th councils would effect 'no progress towards self-government', but simply 'perpetuate and aggravate a vicious system which makes it the main function of the Legislative Councils to oppose and criticise the Government while remaining completely free from responsibility for the results of their action'.[1] The committee considered it 'hazardous to increase their numbers while withholding responsibility' and suggested that 'training in functions ought to precede any considerable increase of numbers'.[2] Nor did the committee give its support to the enunciation of an ultimate goal for Indian constitutional development, such as formulated by the Government of India. 'We doubt the wisdom', said its report, 'of dangling before the Indian politicians a formula of political progress, hedged with restrictions that nullify its meaning, and calculated to embarrass, by the vagueness of its promises, our successors in Indian government. We feel that the situation demands not the visionary prospect of a development beyond the realisation of generations, but a frank and clear statement embodying practical progressive reforms capable of achievement within a definite future that can be foreseen.'[3]

The Secretary of State for India, Austen Chamberlain, agreed with the committee's criticism of the Government of India scheme and wrote to the Viceroy accordingly.[4] As regards a declaration of British

[1] 'Report on Government of India Despatch, Home Department, No. 17, Political, dated November 24, 1916', Austen Chamberlain Papers, p. 7.
[2] Ibid.   [3] Ibid., p. 8.
[4] 'After all, we want to train Indians in self-government. A mere increase in the number of their representatives does not really advance this object, unless we can at the same time fix these men with some definite powers and with real responsibility for their actions.' Chamberlain to Chelmsford, May 2, 1917, 'Extracts from Mr Chamberlain's Private Letters to the Viceroy', Austen Chamberlain Papers. Again, on May 15, 1917, Chamberlain wrote to Chelmsford: 'My difficulty in regard to this scheme is, first, that it makes no real progress towards self-government; and, secondly, that it will perpetuate and aggravate a vicious system which makes it the main function of the Legislative Councils to oppose and criticise the Government while remaining completely free from responsibility for the results of their action. . . . The vital difficulty of this scheme, as it seems to me, is that, while increasing the number of representatives, it does nothing to secure any increase in their sense of responsibility; it gives them no real training in affairs and will merely multiply the number of irresponsible critics who, dissatisfied with their own impotence and deprived of all sense of responsibility for their actions, may become a grave embarrassment to Government. I can see no use in multiplying elected representatives until we are prepared to entrust them with some degree of responsibility in financial or administrative matters.' Ibid.

policy in India, however, Chamberlain had begun to realize its necessity,[1] though he considered the formula proposed by the Viceroy to be unnecessarily elaborate and formal. 'I do not dispute your goal,' he wrote to Chelmsford, 'though I dislike the elaboration and the formality of your definition. I should prefer to say in the least formal manner possible and in the shortest words, that our object is to develop free institutions with a view to ultimate Self-Government within the Empire, and I should not attempt to define, at a time so distant from any point at which we could expect this aspiration to be realised, the form which such Self-Government must take or the extent to which our aspiration can ultimately be realised.'[2] Chamberlain was also anxious that any such statement of the goal of British policy in India should be 'accompanied by a very clear declaration that this is a distant goal' and that 'the rate of progress and the times and stages by which it is to be reached must be controlled and decided by His Majesty's Government'.[3]

In the spring of 1917 the Maharaja of Bikaner, Sir James Meston and Sir Satyendra Sinha came to England, as delegates from India, to attend the meetings of the Imperial War Conference. They ardently pleaded India's case for ultimate self-government within the Empire from various platforms in the country and created a very favourable impression. Commenting on their speeches—particularly those of Bikaner—*The Times* wrote on May 2, 1917: 'The question is whether the time is not now upon us for something more than pious aspirations about the future of India. . . . The broad lines of British policy in India are perfectly clear. It looks steadily forward to a gradual increase of the self-governing function, and is only concerned to regulate that increase as good order within and security against aggression from without require. But this policy is too seldom expressed in terms, and we believe that the moment to declare it with authority is now, while the war is still in progress, and not as a reply to agitation when the war is over.'[4] In private Bikaner, Meston and Sinha pressed the need for an announcement of British policy upon the Secretary of State for India and apparently succeeded in converting him to their view.[5]

[1] 'I am coming round to your view that a statement of our object is necessary.' Chamberlain to Chelmsford, May 2, 1917, Austen Chamberlain Papers.
[2] Chamberlain to Chelmsford, May 15, 1917, *ibid.*
[3] Chelmsford to Chamberlain, May 2, 1917, *ibid.*
[4] *The Times*, May 2, 1917.
[5] See the remark of Bikaner to this effect, reproduced in *Speeches and Writings of Lord Sinha*, appendix, pp. xix–xx. Also K. M. Panikkar, *op. cit.*, pp. 185–9; 'Memorandum by H.H. the Maharaja of Bikaner', dated April 17, 1917, Austen

An additional and a very potent argument, if not for making the announcement, at least for launching India as speedily as possible on the road to responsible self-government, was furnished by the decision of the Imperial War Conference in April 1917 to admit India to the full membership of the regular Imperial Conference. Self-government was the prerequisite for membership of the Imperial Conference and if an exception had been made in India's case, a payment in advance, so to speak, made to her, it was only on the understanding that self-government was her destiny.[1]

Willingdon had, as noted above,[2] since long favoured a bold and liberal gesture in India by the British Government. He was in close touch with the leaders of moderate Indian opinion and sympathetic to their aspirations. Moreover, his province—Bombay—was particularly affected by the home rule agitation of Besant and Tilak. In the autumn of 1916 he had strongly advised the Government of India and the Secretary of State to make an early declaration of their policy in order to strengthen the hands of the moderates, but was told that it would be useless to make a general declaration until the authorities were prepared to state specifically the reforms which they intended to carry out at the earliest.[3] In May 1917 Willingdon renewed his pressure upon the Viceroy[4] and with better effect. On May 18, 1917, the latter telegraphed to the Secretary of State requesting an immediate announcement of British policy in India. The Viceroy pointed out that the political situation in India had materially altered during the past few months as a result of the revolution in Russia, the publication of statements as to the right of the peoples to govern themselves, the reception accorded to the representatives of India at the War Conference in England, and India's admission to the Imperial Conference. The absence of any definite announcement of policy was, he wrote, causing embarrassment to the local governments, alienating the moderates, and leaving the field free to the extremist propaganda. The Viceroy realized the difficulties of making a declaration of policy

Chamberlain Papers; 'Note on Constitutional Reforms in India', May 1917, by Meston, *ibid.*; Chamberlain to Chelmsford, May 8, 1917 (reporting a talk with Sinha), 'Extracts from Mr. Chamberlain's Private Letters to the Viceroy', *ibid.*

[1] On this point see Lloyd George, *op. cit.*, vol. iv, pp. 1763–4 and 231 H.C. Deb. 5s., coll. 1314–16.

[2] See p. 80, above.

[3] See Chamberlain to Chelmsford, November 27, 1916, and Chelmsford to Chamberlain, December 1, 1916 (telegrams), Austen Chamberlain Papers.

[4] Chelmsford to Chamberlain, May 18, 1917 (telegram), *ibid.*

while not yet being in a position to state specifically what their proposals for reform were, but he considered the declaration necessary 'in order to arrest the further defection of moderate opinion'.[1]

On May 22, 1917, Chamberlain invited the attention of the Cabinet to the very serious problems with which the Government of India were faced and asked for an early decision on the action to be taken. He circulated to his colleagues the reform proposals submitted by the Government of India, along with his comments, and his suggestions for making known the policy of the British Government.[2] Lloyd George's small War Cabinet was, however, overburdened with work and could not find time early to deal with the Indian issue.[3] And when at last it did take up the question on June 29th, and again on July 5th, valuable time was wasted in a fruitless discussion over the meaning of the term 'self-government'. Lord Balfour, in particular, objected to the use of the term 'self-government' in any declaration for the reason that in the mouths of Englishmen it had acquired a definite meaning, namely, a parliamentary form of government, and in his view it was unwise to graft parliamentary democracy on India.[4] The result was that when Austen Chamberlain suddenly resigned on July 14, 1917, over the Mesopotamian affair,[5] the Cabinet, even after having discussed the question twice, had failed to reach any decision on the form of the announcement or whether it should be made at all.

In India the political situation had meanwhile further deteriorated. The internment of Mrs Besant in June 1917 had led to a countrywide agitation. The publication of the Report of the Mesopotamian Commission at the end of June, containing severe strictures on the

[1] Telegram from the Viceroy to the Secretary of State, Home Department, May 18, 1917, 'Indian Political Reforms, Collection of Telegrams (unparaphrased) between Viceroy and Secretary of State', pp. 1–3, Austen Chamberlain Papers.

[2] 'Memorandum by the Secretary of State for India on Indian Reforms', *ibid.*

[3] Austen Chamberlain, *Down the Years* (1935), p. 132.

[4] Lord Ronaldshay, *The Life of Lord Curzon* (1928), vol. iii, p. 164. Ronaldshay did not disclose the name of Balfour, but simply referred to him as 'one prominent member of the Cabinet'. It is significant that Curzon considered Balfour's note to be 'very stubborn and rather reactionary'. See Curzon to Chamberlain, August 25, 1917, Austen Chamberlain Papers.

[5] A royal commission which inquired into the mismanagement of the campaign in Mesopotamia revealed a very disquieting state of affairs, particularly where the medical services were concerned, and accused the Government of India of administrative inefficiency. There was never any suggestion that blame attached to Austen Chamberlain, but he was Secretary of State for India, and as it was his department which was involved he felt it to be his duty to resign.

Government of India for their lack of judgement and administrative efficiency, had dealt another blow to their prestige. The debate in the Commons on the Report turned out to be a censure motion on the Government of India. Montagu, in a bitter and impassioned speech, described the Government of India as 'too wooden, too iron, too inelastic, too antediluvian', 'illogical and indefensible', and pleaded for a more responsible and democratic administration. He outlined his vision of future India as 'a series of self-governing provinces and principalities, federated by one central government', and remarked: 'But whatever be the object of your rule in India, the universal demand of those Indians whom I have met and correspond with is that you should state it.' 'The history of this war shows', Montagu went on, 'that you can rely upon the loyalty of the Indian people to the British Empire—if you ever doubted it! If you want to use that loyalty you must take advantage of that love of country which is a religion in India, and you must give them that bigger opportunity of controlling their destinies, not merely by councils which cannot act, but by control, by growing control, of the executive itself.'[1]

Montagu's speech gladdened the hearts of Indian nationalists. He had ever since his days as the Under-Secretary of State for India (1910–14) been known for his deep sympathy with Indian national aspirations. And when on July 18, 1917—within a week of his performance in the Mesopotamia debate—Montagu was appointed as Chamberlain's successor at the India Office, the event was widely acclaimed in India and gave rise to excessive expectations. Many believed that he had been selected to carry into effect the views expressed in his Mesopotamia speech. Indian politicians now became more active than ever before. The Committee of the Indian National Congress and the Council of the Muslim League met together at Bombay in the last week of July and reiterated their demand that the Imperial Government be pledged to the policy of making India a self-governing member of the Empire. They also urged the authorities to adopt the Congress-League scheme of post-war reforms, to publish the official proposals for discussion, and to reverse 'the policy of repression'. In order to secure these objectives they decided to send a deputation to England and even threatened to launch a campaign of passive resistance in India.[2]

Recognizing 'the gravity and urgency of the situation' in India, the Viceroy repeatedly impressed upon the home government the view that, whatever be the decision regarding the nature and extent of

[1] 95 H.C. Deb. 5s., coll. 2202–10.   [2] *Times of India*, July 30, 1917.

future reforms, 'it would be fatal to put off any longer an unmistakable declaration in India of our future policy'.[1] Montagu energetically took up the threads where Chamberlain had left them. On July 30, 1917, he circulated a memorandum to the Cabinet, drawing their attention to the rapidly deteriorating situation in India and to the increasing insistence of the Viceroy and the heads of provincial governments for an immediate announcement of policy.[2] But he could not get the Cabinet to find the time to discuss the question soon.[3] On August 7 he was still pleading with the Prime Minister: 'You can save India. You can set your foot, and force England to set its foot, firmly on a path of progress on democratic lines....'[4]

Montagu was anxious that any declaration of British policy must include the word 'self-government', not only because it was so current in Indian discussion, but also because he feared that its avoidance might cause dissatisfaction in India and thus defeat the very purpose of making the declaration.[5] The formula which he had suggested to the Cabinet in his memorandum of July 30th was substantially the same as that proposed earlier by Chamberlain. It read: 'His Majesty's Government and the Government of India have in view the gradual development of free institutions in India with a view to ultimate self-government within the Empire.'[6]

This, however, did not satisfy Lord Curzon, who like most members of the Cabinet disliked the phrase 'self-government'.[7] He devoted a good deal of time and thought to the phraseology of the proposed declaration. In order to make it 'rather safer and certainly nearer to [his] own point of view',[8] he redrafted it as follows on the eve of its publication: 'The policy of His Majesty's Government, with which the Government of India are in complete accord, is that of the

---

[1] 26 H.L. Deb. 5s., col. 768; 31 H.L. Deb. 5s., col. 597.

[2] 'Indian Reforms', encl. Montagu to Chamberlain, August 7, 1917, Austen Chamberlain Papers.

[3] See Montagu to Chamberlain, August 7, 1917, *ibid.* On August 15, 1917, Montagu wrote to Chamberlain: 'The number of times that I have sat trembling for a Cabinet summons, the number of times that I have hoped to see the Prime Minister, the number of messages that I have got from the Viceroy,—all this would make a story which would bring tears to your eyes....' *Ibid.*

[4] F. Owen, *Tempestuous Journey: Lloyd George, His Life and Times* (1955), p. 416.

[5] See Montagu to Chamberlain, August 7, 1917, and encl. *op. cit.*, p. 2, Austen Chamberlain Papers.

[6] 'Indian Reforms', *op. cit.*, p. 3; Ronaldshay, *op. cit.*, vol. iii, p. 167.

[7] Montagu to Chamberlain, August 7, 1917, Austen Chamberlain Papers.

[8] Ronaldshay, *op. cit.*, vol. iii, p. 168.

increasing association of Indians in every branch of the administration, and the gradual development of self-governing institutions, with a view to the progressive realisation of responsible government in India as an integral part of the British Empire.'[1]

It was this formula which the Cabinet sanctioned on August 14, 1917, and Montagu repeated in the Commons six days later—on August 20th—in reply to a question from Charles Roberts. Montagu also declared that substantial steps in pursuance of this policy would be taken as soon as possible and that he would be proceeding to India shortly to discuss matters with the Government of India and receive representations from Indians. 'I would add', he went on, 'that progress in this policy can only be achieved by successive stages. The British Government and the Government of India on whom the responsibility lies for the welfare and advancement of the Indian peoples, must be the judges of the time and measure of each advance, and they must be guided by the co-operation received from those upon whom new opportunities of service will thus be conferred, and by the extent to which it is found that confidence can be reposed in their sense of responsibility.'[2]

The announcement laid down clearly and definitely the ultimate aim of British rule in India. It recognized India to be potentially a dominion. It committed the British Government to the policy of

[1] Ronaldshay, *op. cit.* vol. iii, p. 167. It is not possible, in the present stage of our knowledge, to account for the choice of the phrase 'responsible government' in preference to 'self-government' by Curzon and the Cabinet. The following comments by Montagu on the point are interesting, but not very enlightening: 'For some reason which I am absolutely unable to understand people prefer "responsible Government" to "Self-government". I do not know the difference. If there is a difference, "Self-government" might mean that India was to be placed under a Hindu or Parsee dictator, but "responsible Government", I should have thought, meant that that Hindu or Parsee dictator would be responsible to some form of Parliamentary institutions. So I think they [the Cabinet] have given more than your formula would have necessitated.' Montagu to Chamberlain, August 15, 1917, Austen Chamberlain Papers. 'It was a strange discussion. I had hoped that the word "Self-government" would be used, because it appeared in everyone of your communications and because I thought it was a pity to boggle at a word so current in Indian discussion. The Cabinet in its wisdom preferred "responsible Government" to "Self-government". It requires a better educated man than myself to know the difference, but if it lies anywhere, "responsible Government", I should have thought, pledges one to more than "Self-government".' Montagu to Chelmsford, August 21, 1917, Sir David Waley, 'Life of the Hon. Edwin Samuel Montagu (Unpublished), p. 174. Quoted with the kind permission of the author.

[2] 97 H.C. Deb. 5s., coll. 1695–6.

introducing parliamentary self-government in India on the English
model. It was not only 'the most momentous utterance ever made in
India's chequered history',[1] it was also a landmark in British Imperial
history, for it marked a definite repudiation of the concept of 'the two
empires'[2]—the concept that there could be, under the British flag,
one form of constitutional evolution for the West and another for the
East, or one for the white races and another for the non-white. The
declaration of August 20, 1917, signified the passing away of the
second British Empire and the beginning of what Zimmern called 'the
third British Empire',[3] the transformation, in principle, of the Empire
into a Commonwealth of Nations.

[1] *Report on Indian Constitutional Reforms*, Cd. 9109, 1918, p. 5.
[2] The phrase is Lord Milner's. See his *The Nation and the Empire* (1913),
p. 289.
[3] A. E. Zimmern, *The Third British Empire* (1926).

POLITICS AND SOCIETY
IN CONTEMPORARY ORISSA[1]

F. G. BAILEY

*Reader in Asian Anthropology
in the University of London*

The newly independent territories in Asia and Africa equipped themselves at the beginning of their freedom with the institutions of representative democracy, including free elections. In Asia, within ten years, these institutions have in some countries been discarded, in others they are modified, and in others they appear to have produced crippling conflict. There has arisen an idea that representative institutions based upon free elections cannot survive in Asia with the possible exception (among the larger nations) of India.

The new nations are faced with problems of economic development and of maintaining national unity now that their people are no longer held together by the struggle for independence. Both these tasks, so the argument runs, can better be done by political institutions which are more forceful and less given to compromise and delay than parliaments and legislative councils: in fact, by totalitarian régimes. China and Soviet Russia are there to prove it.

Those in India whom I have heard advance these arguments do not believe that parliamentary institutions are inherently incompetent or vicious: quite the contrary. Apart from Communists, they consider these institutions desirable but, in their circumstances, impractical. They are impractical because they evolved in western countries, and have been imposed in India upon quite a different social and cultural base. In brief, this argument holds that representative institutions and free elections based on total adult suffrage are not suited to the indigenous social structure of India.

This simple opposition of the indigenous social structure and representative institutions in fact contains a series of complex questions. The problem can first be simplified by removing the evaluative element from the discussion and asking not 'Are representative institutions

[1] This essay is based upon research done in 1959 and takes no account of events since that date.

suited to traditional Indian society?' but 'What are the connections between the new democracy and the old society?' What are the points of contact between the new institutions and the traditional society? Concretely: How do the politicians keep in touch with their electorate? This question guides the analysis, but it is to be remembered that it is only one in a battery of questions which have to be answered before one can begin to understand and evaluate the relationship between democratic institutions and traditional Indian society.

Our operative questions are even narrower, and of a deceptive simplicity: How does a candidate win an election? What use does he make of existing social allegiances and cultural characteristics? What new patterns of allegiance does he create in order to win an election, and to what extent are these allegiances changing the existing structure?

Orissa at the present day has an area of 60,000 square miles and a population almost at the 15 million mark. It has a Legislative Assembly of 140 members, no upper house, and a cabinet which has varied in size from three to fourteen members.

The original Orissa consisted of three coastal districts, which were a division of Bengal, and later part of the combined state of Bihar and Orissa. There had been from the end of the nineteenth century a determined effort to unite all Oriya speakers into a single administrative unit, and by 1936 a separate province comprising seven districts had been created. All but two of these districts lay in the coastal plain. Up to 1948 the remainder of the present Orissa consisted of Tributary States in the hills of western Orissa, governed as kingdoms by their own rulers under the guidance of a British official. These Tributary States were merged with Orissa in 1948, and the Orissa State now contains thirteen districts. This historico-geographical division between the coastal plains, which were British administered, and in the west the hill states under their own rulers, has had an important effect upon Orissa's politics in the decade since Independence. The population is approximately equally divided between the two areas, and there are crucial social and cultural differences between them.

The history of democracy in Orissa can be synoptically seen through the four elections, 1936, 1947, 1952 and 1956, and through an important event—the formation of a Coalition Government—in 1959. The first two elections were conducted on a restricted property franchise: the latter two on a total adult franchise. The first two were conducted in British Orissa only, that is by and large in the coastal areas: the latter two in the whole of present-day Orissa, taking in the former Tributary States.

The first election was won by the Congress and it held 36 seats in a House of 60 representatives. The Opposition in this Assembly, which supported and—I think it is fair to say—was supported by the British, spoke for a rentier class of zemindars and big landlords, who had been victims in a Congress campaign to recruit peasants by ventilating peasant grievances against their landlords. The elections since Independence have shown that at least some of these traditional leaders (zemindar and landlord), still have influence over, even when they do not hold the affections of, their peasants.

The 1947 election, on the eve of Independence, gave a triumphant Congress 45 seats in a House of 60 members, 37 of them returned uncontested. But the 1952 election—now to a House of 140 members —upset Congress expectations by returning them to only 67 seats, and admitting a new opposition party, the Ganatantra Parishad, to 31 seats. In the 1956 House Congress had 56 seats against the G.P.'s 51. Government with a majority that never reached double figures, and rested upon the uncertain allegiance of a few individuals, led to many difficulties and in 1959 a new Coalition was formed out of the two major parties, the Congress and the G.P.

I recount these events for three reasons. First, they are required as a background. Secondly, they will be of use in demonstrating certain points about our main inquiry into the relationship between a member and his voters. Thirdly, they reveal a connection between representative democracy and the larger social structure in the following way.

Up to 1947 the division between Government and Opposition in the Assembly reflected not only alignments in the struggle for Independence, but also a major social cleavage in British Orissa: between the rentier class on the one side and on the other side the peasants led and represented by Congress politicians. But the 1952 election showed that at least some of the traditional leaders could win seats as Independents against Congress candidates. By 1956, with the danger of an outright G.P. victory, Congress leaders healed the breach between themselves and the rentier class (this in spite of the very strong socialist element in Congress policy statements) and important individuals in the rentier class were given Congress tickets, duly won their seats, and in some cases were given office. There are two ways of looking at this: perhaps the rentier interest has captured the Congress (this is how the Socialists and Communists see it): alternatively the Congress has converted the reactionaries. Only time will say which is the right view. But whichever view is correct, a

POLITICS AND SOCIETY IN INDIA

cleavage in the traditional society has been contained and controlled by the typically democratic method of compromise. This is one instance where democratic institutions have proved able to deal with a potentially destructive cleavage in the traditional society. Or, from a different point of view, democratic institutions have removed the threat of an earlier political system, by giving its leaders a place in the new system.

The same interpretation can be put upon the Coalition of 1959. The threat of disintegration arising from traditional cleavages and the ambitions of dispossessed rulers, has been met and countered by the new institutions. All but one of the G.P. members fill seats representing the western hill area of Orissa: the great majority of the Congress seats are on the plains. The Coalition represents the first political group to cut across this plains–hill cleavage, and is one step towards that network of cross cutting relationships which integrate a nation, and foster the spirit of compromise upon which the successful practice of representative democracy depends. My own opinion is that this Coalition will speak for the middle classes, and by its creation the territorial cleavage of East and West has been replaced by a class division, which may eventually become a class conflict when the peasants are better able to present their case in the democratic forum. Whether this is good or bad is beside the point: the point is that in this instance democratic institutions have succeeded in doing more or less what they are expected to do.[1] Our main inquiry is into the way in which a successful candidate wins an election, but before asking this, it is first necessary to describe the electoral framework within which the candidates work.

Election is by a simple plurality on a total adult franchise. One hundred and forty members are returned from 101 constituencies, 39 constituencies being double seats. Fifty-four of the 140 seats are reserved for candidates of Scheduled Tribe or Scheduled Caste. Everyone votes to fill these seats, but only members of the privileged communities may stand for them. They may also stand for the general seats.

The two elections have been sufficiently well managed to deserve the adjective 'free'. Although there have been many charges of corruption and intimidation practised both on the voters and on the officials, and charges of inefficiency particularly in the registration of voters, I think it is fair to say that the Election Commission com-

---

[1] This argument is set out at length in the *Economic Weekly*, November 7, 1959.

mands the confidence both of the voters and the candidates. In other words, so far as the actual mechanics of voting are concerned, it has not proved impossible to make an electoral machine work in Indian society, and there is no evidence that dishonest candidates could gain any advantage by manipulating the electoral machine. Instances may occur: but they are exceptional and do not affect the question at issue.

Within the framework provided by this organization, the candidate has three aims: firstly to influence public opinion in his favour; secondly to mobilize active support for himself; and thirdly, to split the opposition, or in other ways prevent it from influencing public opinion or enrolling active workers. These last two sets of activities so much complement one another that I will analyse them together.

I have given an arbitrary meaning in this context to 'public opinion'. I take it to be that part of a candidate's activities which are aimed at making a 'mass contact', the purpose of which is not to gain active agents and workers who will influence voters, but to speak directly to the voters themselves.

Mass contacts are most easily made through highly developed media for mass communication, the most striking example being the use now made (or which could be made with more skill) of television. An appeal to the voters implies that, at least to some extent, they have open minds and are ready to be persuaded by argument to vote one way or the other. Yet in those countries where mass communication is most highly developed, voting is for most people not so much a rational act, with the arguments re-examined at each election, but rather a habit. This does not mean that reasoning is entirely absent: spectacular failures can change people's minds: and there is a small but important floating vote, to which probably these general appeals are addressed. But it seems that the majority in the advanced countries let the propaganda pass over their head and vote the way they have always done.

In underdeveloped countries like India, the vote by habit is much rarer than in, for example, this country. Perhaps there has not been time for voting one way or the other to become a habit. Potentially a large section of the voters are floating and could be steered one way or the other by convincing propaganda. But, paradoxically, the media for mass communication are poorly developed and the floating voters cannot be influenced by this type of propaganda because they cannot be reached.

Communications are poorly developed. Some double-member constituencies are a thousand square miles in area, and many parts of the constituency can be reached only on foot. The literacy rate in Orissa varies from 5 per cent in one district to 23 per cent in the most advanced district, and there is no reason to suppose that literate people are evenly distributed throughout the district. Therefore printed appeals, in newspapers, pamphlets and manifestoes, cannot reach a wide audience. The candidates do their best: public meetings are held n towns and in market villages; pamphlets are circulated; bards are hired to travel about extemporizing satirical songs about rival candidates; and the candidates spend a lot of time and energy touring their constituencies making speeches.

There are also difficulties in finding issues which are particular enough to seem important to the ordinary man and general enough to appeal even to the width of one constituency. Except on a few issues (leaving aside the politicians' generalities about prosperity and low taxes and so forth) there is no such thing as public opinion for the whole of Orissa or even for one district, except among the middle classes. The outlook of the peasant voter is entirely parochial.

This is evident in the voter's expectations of what his representative should do for him. The representative is not seen as a legislator and a part of the government. He is regarded as a representative, not even in the sense that he will look after the interests of his constituents in the forming of policies, but in the narrower sense that he is an influential intermediary who can intervene with the Government (which means with the Administration) to secure a favour or prevent an injustice. M.L.A.s (Members of the Legislative Assembly) spend much of their time finding places in hospitals for their constituents, getting jobs for them, finding them grants or loans to build a well or repair a school, and so forth. Many M.L.A.s resent the time which they spend in this way, when they would rather be thinking constructively about Orissa's future: but if they neglect constituency work then the wrong kind of stories are spread about them and they pay the price by losing the next election.

To be acceptable to his voters a candidate needs a reputation for two things, first, for being wholeheartedly interested in his constituency and ready to put its welfare before that of the larger community; secondly, for being a forceful and influential person (what is in Orissa called 'a good fighter').

The demand for a person with evident parochial loyalties means that in all but a very few cases, the candidates are natives at least of the district and usually of the constituency for which they stand. This is not, of course, only a question of the voters' judgement about his loyalty. A local man is known, and he is already connected by ties of caste, locality, kinship, friendship, possibly business, and so forth, with his voters. He can use these ties to gain himself votes: and his constituents can use the same avenues to approach and influence him after he has been elected.

The criterion of 'a good fighter' or an influential man is measured partly by qualifications, and partly by past performance. Apart from candidates for reserved seats (for which it is often difficult to find suitable persons), the voters, other things being equal, prefer an educated man, one who 'can stand up to officials and make them respect him'. It is this type of advantage which candidates from the Princely families enjoy and which, in all but a few cases, has ensured them sweeping victories, whether they stood for Ganatantra or Congress, over some experienced and able opponents. The heroes of the Independence Movement enjoy the same advantage. They have proved themselves big men, were 'good fighters', and have, most of them, considerable records of self-sacrifice and public service. Such reputations can also be made today, for the frictions which arise from the acts of the Government and Administration give ample scope for a young and energetic politician to raise an agitation and ventilate a popular grievance, and such agitations are a royal road to political success.

These are the ideas which the candidates would like public opinion in their constituencies to hold about them. I do not think that the voters are much concerned with their candidates' attitude towards China and the border question, or where he stands in the conflict between socialism and private enterprise. It is enough that he is a local man, and an energetic man.

A suitable reputation can be got either from traditional status, as is the case with those Rajas or landlords who have been successful candidates, or it can come from achievements within the framework of democratic activity—the agitators, the 'freedom fighters', and so forth. But whatever the source of this reputation, the candidate's personal qualifications count for much more than they do in Britain. The parties cannot parachute into alien constituencies people whom they would like to have in the Assembly: only a very exceptional candidate can win a constituency where he is a stranger.

For a few persons—ex-Ministers, the Rajas, a few exceptional individuals—their own reputation is enough to win them the seat and they need do no active campaigning beyond a few tours of the constituency and a few speeches. One ex-Raja told me 'I promised them nothing. I had no arguments. I just asked them to vote for me. I suppose there were a few party workers, but I had nothing to do with them.' But not every candidate is in this happy position, and most of them ran an active campaign. In the following sections I examine the methods used in such a campaign, the extent to which it can rely upon traditional social allegiances, and the extent to which it is creating new social groups and categories. For the majority, birth in the constituency and the right reputation is no more than the qualification which enables them to enter the race. All serious candidates have such qualifications, and the election is not decided on these criteria alone.

A candidate has 'ascribed' support through his local affiliations and through his caste membership. I will discuss these first, and then go on to consider party organization, both in its formal aspect and in the 'behind-the-scenes' organizations which in fact get most of the work done. It will be noticed that the former ties between candidate and voter belong immediately to the traditional social structure, while the latter, *prima facie* at least, are groups and networks of relationship created, so to speak, by the representative democracy for its own purpose, although they too may owe a good deal to traditional allegiances.

Whatever his party, and whatever the programme he stands for, a candidate hopes to get the support of his fellow villagers and the villagers from his own locality, because they know him and they can reasonably expect him to do favours for them, and they can get in touch with him through his family and friends, and, finally, the good name of their village is involved in his victory or defeat. But this alone will not bring him victory since his rivals enjoy similar support in their own villages and a village vote can only be a small part of the total. Secondly, to judge from my own experience and from various accounts of village elections and the working of village panchayats, there is hardly a village which is not divided into at least two factions. These factional loyalties may pervade every field of activity, and a candidate who becomes too closely identified with one faction, may for this reason alone lose the support of the other faction. Considering the voters' expectations of their candidate, this attitude is quite sensible, for they look upon him as a potential source of patronage and favour, and therefore will not support a man whom they consider is already committed to their rivals.

I have no figures to show systematically that a candidate is always supported by the people of his own and neighbouring villages. But the politicians themselves believe this, and in some cases have given covert support and encouragement to an Independent candidate, who has no chance of being elected, only because he comes from the same area as, or belongs to the same caste as, their most dangerous rival.

There is also a general expectation that voters will support a candidate of their own caste. I think this is a matter of simple unthinking loyalty, and possibly of caste prestige, and they do not expect immediate material gains for themselves *as a caste* (although as individuals they do, of course, presume that in dispensing patronage their member will give them preference over individuals of other castes).

It is against the law to make overt and systematic use of caste loyalties and prejudices either to win support or to undermine a rival. Whether it would also be illegal to campaign on issues of policy about caste I do not know: but it would be sailing near the wind. Congress candidates appeal to Harijan and Tribal voters on the grounds that Congress has shown practical evidence of its favour for these classes. I collected several instances of non-Congress candidates making use of the resentment which these policies had aroused among members of clean castes: but this was never done openly and in print. There are also said to be candidates who make systematic use of their own caste fellows. But this is probably done mostly in the recruitment of men for the 'network', which I will describe later. It is not done openly, and all those whom I interviewed denied that they made use of caste loyalties.

Leaving aside legal considerations, there are structural facts which make it difficult and dangerous for a candidate to rely too greatly or too openly on caste loyalties to get his votes for him. In all except the tribal constituencies, no one caste comes anywhere near constituting a majority of the electorate, so that their support alone cannot win an election. Secondly, as with the village, too close an identification with one caste will automatically line up other castes against a candidate. Thirdly, castes, like villages, are commonly split into factions, and to gain one faction is to lose the other. Fourthly, in Orissa, up to the present there is little evidence of widespread caste organizations. The point of getting hold of a caste—or indeed of any other kind of congregation—is that by capturing the support of the leaders, one draws automatically on the non-political loyalties of their followers. Caste leaders, in other words, might be potential vote-banks, and this would constitute one short cut through the difficulties of mass-contact. But in fact the great majority of caste organizations in Orissa are of the narrow traditional type, concerned with ritual and marriage, and covering small populations in restricted areas. Where All-Orissa caste organizations have developed, as in the case of the Oilmen, these have proved not to be a vote-bank for the politician who can capture them, but yet another arena in which the fight with his rivals is carried on. I was told, for example, that within the Oilman caste there is a bitter conflict between Congress supporters and Communist supporters, although I did not have the opportunity to investigate at first hand.

Undoubtedly candidates do make use of caste loyalties where they can. No politician lightly offends anyone (except another politician), and if he is approached by a caste organization and asked for a donation or a favour, he will give it. But caste is only one of the many kinds of loyalties upon which the politician can draw, and which he must balance one against the other.

But in a different way caste is essential to an understanding of the relation between the politician and the voters. Orissa has its dominant castes, the Karan and the Brahman. Together they cannot be more than about 8 per cent of the population, but they hold a very high proportion of responsible positions both in politics and in the services. The two castes are rivals, and some of the old manœuvres of the pre-Independence Congress are to be attributed to this rivalry. But this is not the case today in politics: members of both castes take a leading part in all political parties except the Jharkhand, and lines of cleavage both between parties and within parties are not illuminated by looking at caste membership. The position is that the members of these two castes, together with an increasing number of lower castes nowadays, and with the few members of the Princely families, constitute Orissa's very small middle-class élite, and it might be more correct to regard their dominance in politics and the Administration as a class phenomenon, rather than a caste phenomenon.

I have now discussed the part which caste and village loyalties play in the relation of the politician to his electorate. They do play some part, but there is no simple equation to be drawn between the politician's support and these traditional groupings, neither at party level nor at lower levels. Their significance is rather that politicians are constrained to attempt to make use of them, because any congregation is of use when the state of communications (in the wide sense of that word) make mass contacts very difficult.

The main function of a party at election times is to provide a team of workers, who will persuade the undecided voter or the apathetic sympathizer to come to the polling booth and put his vote in the right box. In the absence of mass media their role in making a mass contact and, indeed, in political education, should be of peculiar importance.

In their form, and in their intention, the five parties in Orissa are a diluted version of our own political parties and I can describe them briefly. At the bottom are ordinary members and active members: the latter pay a higher subscription and they alone are eligible for office. Ideally there are committees elected for each polling booth, each constituency, each district, and for the state as a whole. The reality is far less than this: sometimes there are only *ad hoc* constituency committees at election times and the booth committee is still rare: some of the parties have no organization whatsoever in some districts. The number of people active in politics is very small, and even the Congress in 1959 had only 120,000 members and only 1,381 active members in a population of almost 15 million.[1] Besides these committees, which consist mostly of voluntary workers, there is a cadre of salaried party workers organized by a central secretariat.

There are some small variations, but, roughly speaking, this description would apply to all the parties. Basically this is a model of party organization, taken like the Assembly itself, from the British example. But there are differences in the way these organizations actually work in the different parties. I will describe each of them briefly.

The Jharkhand Party held six seats in the 1956 House, all from the northern tribal areas of Orissa, close to the Bihar border. Jharkhand is powerful in Bihar and represents the main opposition in the Bihar House. The party declares its aim to be the founding of a tribal state in Chota Nagpur and adjoining areas. In so far as party support can be reduced to simple factors, I think the Jharkhand support rests on two things: the charismatic qualities of the leader Jaipal Singh; and the communal loyalties of Adibasis, which springs from their dislike of non-Adibasis and their bitter experience of exploitation by outsiders. The Orissa Jharkhand leaders whom I interviewed denied the communal basis of their support, but the broad facts are all against this denial. But it is fair to add that I did not have the opportunity to visit a Jharkhand constituency.

The nature of the two left-wing parties, the Praja Socialist Party (P.S.P.) and the Communists (C.P.I.), is substantially the same in both cases, quite different from the Jharkhand, and nearest to the British model of party organization. Both parties have their main

[1] *Amrita Bazar Patrika*, November 4, 1959.

following in the coastal districts. Almost all their active members formerly belonged to the Congress and their leaders are experienced politicians. My impression is that both these parties, as compared with the other three, least rely upon traditional loyalties and cleavages to get them the twenty seats which they had in the 1956 election (P.S.P.–11: C.P.I.–9). I have worked briefly in the offices of the four larger parties in Cuttack, and it became quite clear that the organization and administration of the two smaller left-wing parties was infinitely tidier than that of the Congress or the Ganatantra. This, of course, is partly because they are smaller in size. But I think it also reflects the fact that the two left-wing parties have no traditional loyalties upon which they can draw automatically: they are not identified with one caste or community; they have not the glamour of being led by the great figures of the Independence Movement or by former Princes; they are relatively poor in resources. Therefore their main effort has to be directed into building up a ground organization of voluntary workers. By British standards they are not very successful: but the other parties are even less efficient.

Support for the Ganatantra Parishad is confined, up to the present, almost entirely to the hill areas and the former princely states. Like the other parties they have an organization of committees at various levels, but their effective support lies elsewhere. Firstly, it lies in the continuing loyalty of the former subjects of the Princes. Secondly, many votes for the G.P. are protest votes against the alleged favouring by Congress Governments of the coastal districts from which most Congress politicians originate. Thirdly, the transition in 1948 from princely rule to bureaucratic Administration was accompanied by considerable friction, so much so that some of the halo of 'freedom fighting' now rests upon G.P. leaders, for the 1948 Congress Government used repressive methods against G.P. leaders, similar to those employed by the British against Congress leaders. It is also to be noted that the influence and authority which attached to traditional (mostly hereditary) village officers in the princely states is still with them, although their office is in the process of being abolished: and these men, supporters of the G.P., form the nucleus of a ground organization although they might not be formally incorporated as active party members.

Congress has the most extensive party organization. Yet, as a vote-getting machine, it has proved effective only in the former British-administered districts, and, although it is the largest party, it has only 1,381 active members. This would suggest that its voting strength is not gained mainly through the party organization in the country. It has, of course, inherited a great advantage in being the party that is associated with Independence. Within its ranks are many of the heroes of that movement, and, leaving aside the Orissa leaders, the names alone of Gandhi and Nehru are important electoral assets. It has also been—and this is perhaps the crucial factor—the party in power, at least up to the Coalition in 1959. But this concerns a different kind of organization through which the politicians influence their voters—the 'brokerage network'.

The main characteristic that emerges from this brief outline of party organizations in Orissa is that this ground organization is very meagre indeed. In terms of numbers it is thin: in terms of activities it would not be entirely wrong to say that the greater part of a worker's energy and time is spent not in propagating among the electorate, except for a very short period before the election, but in internal rivalries and contests for power. The fact that the parties have very few active workers should not be surprising, when the cultural and economic condition of the voters is taken into account. In the last resort a widespread party organization (except under totalitarian conditions) can only exist when sufficient volunteers come forward. These men have to be able to work without payment, and to be sophisticated enough (or naïve enough) to believe that the party's aims are intrinsically worth while. Neither of these conditions are to be found in Orissa: firstly, the great majority of the people are too poor, and in any case otherwise occupied in their leisure time: secondly, in the eyes of the common man, to be a politician (since 1947) is to be a self-seeker, and only a very few political and social workers escape this taint and are credited with sincerity. To some degree this applies everywhere: but in Orissa it is almost the whole story. Successful party organization rests on a general confidence in the integrity and efficiency of the party.

But while the general public may be indifferent to, or sceptical about, the activities and record of the party, and the values for which it stands, there is a core of active people who see in the parties a chance of personal reward. This is a wide category, stretching from careerist politicians down to the voter who accepts a bribe. Since Congress has been the party in power, and therefore best able to dispense favours, most of these people attach themselves to Congress. But it would be wrong to assume that therefore other parties consist only of idealists: they also contain people who have failed to climb on, or have fallen off, the Congress bandwagon, and also those ingenious people who make a profession of being against the Government and the Administration in ways that I have not room here to describe.

A brief enumeration of some of the favours which members of a network expect will indicate the main social characteristics which underlie the existence of networks. Many are seeking an appointment for themselves or their relatives—usually a minor appointment—in Government service, for example as a schoolmaster or a peon. Others want loans or grants for the development of their village school or to excavate a well. Others, less altruistic, want the contract to carry out the work. Some want a licence for trading in controlled commodities. Others have lost their job and want to be reinstated. These are a few examples selected from the reports of Election Tribunals inquiring into complaints of corrupt practice and intimidation.

The Government controls an enormous amount of patronage. The last word in the selection of an applicant for a job or for a contract rests with a politician or an official, and there is a firm conviction that merit alone does not count in these appointments; it is more important to have the backing of an important person. Nepotism and corruption are deplored in public, but in practice—so it is believed—they pervade all fields of activity. Economic conditions favour the creation of networks. There are the forms of a controlled economy and several lucrative economic activities can only be undertaken with a licence: to run a liquor shop, to exploit forest produce, to sell controlled commodities like cloth or, at times, foodgrains, or to procure foodgrains under the State Trading schemes. Relatively large sums of money are available for development work: there is competition to secure the benefits of the work and to get the contracts where construction is involved. All these things are favours at the disposal of the politician to reward those who will work in his interest.

Some of these favours are large, and are got by big entrepreneurs. These are in some cases a direct transaction between the entrepreneur and the politician: the entrepreneur gets his contract or his licence and in return he makes a contribution directly or indirectly to political expenses. But the network which I am here discussing is smaller than this and covers, typically, a part of a constituency. The boss of this network will be a shopkeeper or contractor. Under him is an army of agents who are obliged to him in various ways: they might be his relatives; they might be his employees; they might owe him money; they might want his help to get out of trouble; they might want him to intercede with the Administration to get some kind of favour for them.

Some of these agents are, so to speak, professionals, living on their wits, and known opprobriously in Orissa as 'touters'. But anyone who wants to get on in the world, or who has got into trouble and wants to avoid going under, is a potential recruit for the network.

What does the boss and his network do for the politician? The humbler members act as ordinary election workers, alongside or in place of volunteers, carrying messages, sticking up posters, starting whispering campaigns, and so forth. The network as a whole functions as an intelligence service, reporting on the activities of rivals, and seeking out their weaknesses. Its more responsible members can be employed on the delicate work unsuited to the agenda of a committee: for example, suborning the agents, or even the candidates, of a rival party, or persuading an inconvenient Independent to withdraw from the campaign.

This is a difficult field for the sociologist to investigate, and I am not clear about the relation of the boss and his network to the formal party committees. Many of them are not overt politicians, not even ordinary members of the party for which they work. But others, as they go up in the world, turn their energies to formal politics and become members of local committees, and hope eventually to become candidates.

The strength of the network does not lie only in its active self-seeking members. Viewed through the amoral glass of functionalism, the network does a job and a necessary job. It is a channel of communication between the common man and the administrators and politicians. At the bottom of the network—and this is where both its strength and its significance really lie—there is a huge army of simple honest people who have done no wrong and who want only something which they consider their right. But they are simple and ignorant people, they are frightened of the clerks through whom they must work, they do not know the proper approach, they can neither read nor write, and, above all, they believe that the only way to get their due is to employ some knowing intermediary: and he is likely to be the local boss. Once again our analysis comes down to the fundamental fact of an enormous social cleavage between the middle classes and the common people. The politician cannot reach his electorate: the voters cannot communicate with their politicians and administrators: the gap is bridged by the political brokers and their network.

But to recognize that the brokers fulfil a necessary function is not to claim that they do no harm. They are mercenaries, without political principles or conviction: they back the winning side: and in adversity they will change sides. For the common man they do nothing to educate him politically in the way that is expected of an orthodox political ground organization: they merely reinforce the present disastrous conviction that the only worth-while political principle is self-interest. On development work the brokers are a hidden cost, supplying communication at exorbitant rates. The common people undoubtedly respect these brokers, but they do not have confidence in their motives, and so long as Community Development is channelled through such people, the real leaders of village society do not participate: and from this comes both the frictions, which are so characteristic of Community Development, and the totally irresponsible attitude of everyone, from the top to the bottom, towards public money. The brokers undoubtedly provide education in the political techniques which are characteristic of some representative democracies: but they are a check upon the growth of civic responsibility among the common people.

*   *   *

Every line in the latter part of this inquiry has led back to the point that between the people and the politicians who represent and govern them there is a wide cleavage: there is an even greater cleavage between the people and their administrators. There is a cultural cleavage, in the sense that the middle class is educated and sophisticated, while the people are not. There is a cleavage in social relations, in the sense that quite literally neither side can get in touch with the other, neither the politician to win votes nor the ordinary man to make known his needs.

The result of this cleavage is that two things which are sometimes considered a normal element of representative government are either absent, or, at least, imperfectly exemplified. To cast a vote is not to pass a verdict on the past government or on the programmes and policies put forward by competing parties. This is a myth: there are too many other weights in the balance for an election to be a test of a party's popularity. Secondly, the Orissan voter has little sense of participating in government: the electoral mechanism does not appear to him to be a mechanism of consultation. The Government remains as remote and exterior as it has always been: there is no sense of self-government. It should be added that India and Orissa are not peculiar in this, and it could be argued that this is a defect not peculiar to

Orissa and the Indian scene, but the normal state of affairs in representative democracy.

The cleavage in outlook between the Government and their people is also perhaps a normal and inevitable feature in politics. The people have narrow horizons: the Government must look to general interests. There is an inevitable conflict between the interests of the local group and the interests of the whole to which it belongs. This conflict is found everywhere, but in Orissa it is the dominant characteristic, governing the type of man who stands for election, and his behaviour after election. The Government and ruling party is not judged by what it has done for Orissa as a whole, but by what every member has done for his own constituency. In turn this means that too much time and energy are spent in seeking compromise, and too little in getting things done. This too, perhaps, is the normal state of affairs in a representative democracy: but the fragmentation of Orissa society exaggerates conflict and compromise to the point of inertia. What the institutions of representative democracy require are a greater diversification of loyalties. They presuppose that loyalties should cut across one another, that the society, in other words, should be more homogeneous.

This change could come about—perhaps is coming about—in several ways. Education alone will not work the change. Greater spatial and social mobility, which may be the result of industrialization, are a step in this direction. The growth of pressure groups with a wider base than the village and its locality will help to bring about the change: and this is true whether the groups concerned are desirable ones, such as party organizations based upon voluntary membership, or ones that are normally considered undesirable, like regionwide caste associations. Even the brokerage networks, in spite of their evident defects, could eventually contribute to the wider diversification of loyalties and interests.

The question which has guided this analysis—the relation between the politician and his voter—provides no answer to the ultimate question of whether or not representative institutions are suited to, and therefore can survive in, India. The ultimate test is a pragmatic one: whether the present institutions can raise the standard of living in India and maintain national unity. Electoral systems which have been far more corrupt and inefficient than those in India have nevertheless put great men in power: what matters is not how these men got into power, but the use which they make of the power given to them. It is interesting that the political successes of the democratic system in Orissa—the successful compromise of deep-seated traditional cleavages in the wider structure—were in no sense the work of the voters or the response to public opinion. One is tempted to conclude that an election is a test of skills and abilities of persons, and the efficiency of organizations, at tasks which have little to do with framing policy and governing.

MUNICIPAL ELECTIONS:
A CENTRAL INDIAN CASE STUDY[1]

A. C. MAYER

*Reader in Indian Anthropology,
in the University of London*

Analyses of elections in India have mainly been made at the levels of the village and the State and Central Legislatures. But there is a third level, that of the Municipality, at which emerge certain features of Indian political behaviour, which tend to be obscured elsewhere. For example, alignments at the village level are mainly expressed in local and personal rivalry, in contrast to the party organization in Municipalities, where electorates, though of moderate size, are yet large enough to demand intensive and co-ordinated campaigns. Again, General Elections are so extended that, though detailed consideration of local and personal interests can be made in single constituencies or towns,[2] the analysis of the election as a whole must be done in mainly statistical and party terms. Municipal elections can, however, be studied intensively as complete examples of political parties in action at the 'grass roots' level.[3]

Elections of this kind were held recently in the Central Indian town of Dewas. The purpose of this article is to describe them briefly and generally. It is hoped to deal with special aspects in greater detail elsewhere. These would include the personal qualifications of candidates and their relations to the town's social configuration, the specific influences exerted by politicians on individual voters, and the influence of the elections on the internal structure of the parties. The material might also be compared with similar accounts of elections elsewhere. What follows is intended to be a basis for further analysis.

Dewas is a town of 35,000 people, situated 22 miles from Indore

[1] Research was done on study leave from the School of Oriental and African Studies, University of London, to whose Governing Body I express my thanks.

[2] For example, the analysis by Raghuraj Gupta of the 1957 General Election in a single town (*Janata*, vol. xii, nos 13–16).

[3] A general account of Municipal government is contained in H. R. Tinker, *The Foundations of Local Self-Government in India, Pakistan and Burma* (1954).

and 95 miles from Bhopal, the commercial and political capitals respectively, of Madhya Pradesh State. Until the merger of the Princely States in 1948, the town was the capital both of the State of Dewas Senior and Dewas Junior, being divided into two parts. After merger, the Municipalities of the two States were combined, and continued to operate with a large Congress majority. The first elections after Independence were in 1954, and resulted in a landslide victory for the Praja Socialist Party (P.S.P.) which won eleven seats to Congress's three. The main reason for the victory was a *lathi* charge a few months before, at a demonstration organized by the P.S.P. against the shortage of grain. Congress was held responsible for the use of force, traumatic to a town which had hardly known the struggle for Independence.

In 1957 both parties won the same number of seats, and an uneasy régime followed. The chairman, who held a casting vote, was chosen by lot for the first three years. In the fourth chairman's election, however, Congress managed to detach a P.S.P. member, and elected its chairman by a majority vote. At the time of the 1961 election, then, Congress controlled the Municipality.

Candidates were nominated for the elections of 1961 by Congress, the P.S.P., the Jan Sangh and the Lohia Socialists, and a solitary Independent also stood. The latter two parties were contesting Dewas elections for the first time; a further two parties—Communists and Swatantra—had Dewas branches, but did not feel themselves strong enough to enter the lists. Elections took place in twelve single-member and two double-member wards (the second member being a Harijan). They gave a sweeping victory to Congress, which avenged its 1954 defeat by winning fourteen seats to two for the P.S.P. None of the other parties won a seat. Besides this, Congress candidates were elected on an absolute majority of the votes, though in some three-cornered contests they won a minority of votes cast.[1] In short, it was complete victory, beyond the hopes of the most fervent Congressmen,

[1] The statistics of the election are:

Party	Candidates	Votes Polled	Seats Won	Deposits Forfeited
Congress	16	6,273	14	1
P.S.P.	13	3,669	2	2
Jan Sangh	11	1,899	—	4
Lohia Socialist	4	331	—	4
Independent	1	214	—	—

In addition, two P.S.P. and three Jan Sangh candidates had their nomination orms rejected by the Election Officer.

who were not prepared to think of victory in more than ten or eleven seats.

What were the factors behind this victory? What issues divided the parties and how were these presented? What kind of organization enabled parties to fight in more than a dozen wards? What was the attitude of the voter to demands for his support; and how did politicians use the voter's ties of caste, kinship, religion and occupation to obtain his support?

The first problem in the election concerned the selection of candidates. For several months before nomination day there had been discussion, sometimes intense, over the distribution of party tickets. Lists of both P.S.P. and Jan Sangh candidates had actually been published in the Indore press; these lists had been disowned, but were held by opponents to be a device for gauging popular reaction to more controversial names. But the final selection was made by each party in complete secrecy. Only when people were actually assembled at the Election Office to file their nomination forms did the lists become public. At that time, candidates moved about the office in great excitement, finding out their opponents.

Why was there this secrecy? Why did not the parties nominate their candidates in good time, and thereby give them a chance to cultivate the electorate and nurse the ward? In Dewas the reason was a pragmatic one; the method of open discussion and of selection by party or public had been tried and found to be impracticable.

The experience of Congress in previous elections will show this. In 1954, selection was to have been made by a committee of Dewas Congressmen, and then confirmed by a Civic Board formed by the District Congress Committee and containing the local members of the Legislative Assembly and other important leaders. But the list put up from Dewas was changed under pressure from various interested individuals and groups in a way which caused dissatisfaction amongst the Dewas rank and file. A third committee was then constituted, which made several further changes. Only eight of the fifteen names proposed remained unchanged; in six wards there was one, and in one ward two, substitutions. These produced discussions and bad feeling. The effect on party discipline can be imagined and this was said to have been a reason for the Congress defeat.

Because the selection by party committee had failed, it was resolved in 1957 to let the populace of the ward choose the candidate.[1] Accord-

[1] Formally, this included only Congress members in the ward; but it is probable that anyone was allowed to speak at the meeting.

ingly, ward meetings were held, and names were proposed. But where several names were sent forward because the ward was unwilling to decide, a choice had to be made, and this in practice meant control by the Congress leadership. The result was the same as in 1954, with the additional disadvantage that the names of those rejected had been made public.

There was much discussion in 1961 about the method of selection. Some people maintained that there should be no canvassing of prospective names at all. A single selector should be chosen, who would make a list and announce it on nomination day. Other Congressmen criticized the system of secret nomination by individuals or committee because it gave undue power to groups in the party. Whilst admitting that the 1957 experiment of public participation had failed, they insisted that any Congressman had the right to put his own name forward for consideration by the party's general membership.

In the event, a five-man selection committee from Dewas town forwarded a panel of names for each ward to the District Congress Committee's Civic Board, which chose a candidate from each. The selection committee used considerable discretion in sounding out prospective candidates and, it was said, managed to keep its selection and the Civic Board's decision private until shortly before nomination day. Then, in two wards there was some confusion, when men who had thought they had received final confirmation were replaced at the last minute by different candidates. In one other ward, the selection committee called for the choice by a public meeting of the large Muslim minority, instead of selecting the candidate itself. A dispute broke out over the chosen person, and the final selection (also by the public) of another candidate ended in feelings of the kind which had disfigured the 1957 election.

The problem of selection existed because party discipline was not always strong enough to overcome rivalry for office and the shame of being proposed and then passed over. Many names considered by the committee were of men who had only tentative and often selfish connections with the party, or who were not members at all. Such people felt no compulsion to be loyal to the party if not chosen. On previous occasions disappointed would-be candidates had defected to opposition parties. In 1961 there were no such departures, for selection had been tactfully made, and the few men with reasons for dissatisfaction happened to be staunch party members. The P.S.P. fared worse, for disappointed members resigned and took a large part in founding the branch of the Lohia Socialist Party two days before nominations closed.

Both parties, in fact, had similar problems because they were similar in structure. Each had a core of permanently active members, and a supporting number of men who rallied to the party mainly at election times; the more committed of the latter, together with those few active members with no party post, could be called the rank and file. Congress contained some thirty active members, and the P.S.P. about half that number. These quantities were clearly too small to produce the requisite number of candidates, so in each case men had to be chosen from the rank and file, or from purely nominal members or even non-party men. Records of both parties show that the P.S.P. had had to take in outsiders more often, since it was the smaller party—especially in the 1954 election when it was fairly new—whereas Congress could rely on its own members rather more.

The public is certainly attracted by fresh blood in the candidate list. But it is dangerous to provide this by enrolling people who may not respond to party discipline if elected. For example, no fewer than five of the eleven P.S.P. Councillors elected in 1954 had left the party by the 1957 election; all of them had been enrolled in this way. A fresh supply of new faces who *are* party members is more likely to come from the Congress, because the total Congress membership, however nominal, is much larger than that of the P.S.P. There were 853 primary Congress members, to approximately 300 P.S.P. members in the Dewas branches. Further, men are more likely to want to stand for the Government's party, from which they may derive added status and advantage. Hence, Congress has provided more new candidates over the years than the P.S.P. In 1961, for example, the P.S.P. retained six of the ten men available from the last election list, whereas Congress retained only four out of sixteen men.

These problems were not so serious for the Jan Sangh. Since the party was fighting its first election,[1] there were no sitting members pressing their claims. Nor was there any great pressure to stand as candidate for a new and weak party. Though membership in Dewas was estimated at between 200 and 800 (probably around 300), there were few active older members, and it was possible to leave selection to the chairman of the Dewas town branch, who consulted others informally. Candidates were chosen from sympathizers enrolled for the election and from old members in equal numbers.

[1] In 1957, five men said to be Jan Sangh members stood under Independent tickets. All but one lost their deposits, and only two stood again in 1961.

The problems of candidate selection vary with the size and organization of the parties. This is also true in the next phase of the election, that of canvassing the electorate.

Nominations closed one month before polling day, and during this period canvassing was carried out with a steadily increasing tempo. For the first fortnight, candidates were mainly making sure of their major supporters. Some of these were with them from the beginning; others, with records of work at elections only, had to be awoken from their political hibernation, and their loyalties dusted off. Then, for the last fortnight, the public at large was canvassed.

The more methodical candidates would go to each house in turn, armed with a voter's list, asking for support and trying to assess the allegiance of each voter. Others would make a round of a locality (*mohalla*) talking to those they met. Candidates never went alone. Sometimes they were accompanied by party leaders making a quick check of the situation; sometimes by their chief workers; and sometimes by other residents whom they had persuaded to support them, or simply to come with them. As I shall indicate, a candidate depended greatly on his helpers; but in this case their presence was not so much actively to gather votes, as to indicate that support existed for the candidate. It was said that the larger a canvassing party, the more impressed would voters be and the more inclined to join what was so clearly a bandwagon.

By far the commonest reaction from a voter was a promise of support for the candidate. Probably over 90 per cent of voters answered in this way. But it was well known that almost all these people answered all candidates alike. A few people would also complain about local problems—mainly about the lack of public taps and lights. The number of people who openly told a candidate that they would not support him, or who asked him questions about his party's municipal or national politics, could be counted on the candidate's fingers. Experienced politicians maintained that they could tell a voter's true allegiance from his expression, but even they admitted a margin of error.

Candidates, for the most part, did not attempt elaborate persuasion. Most simply asked for support if the voter thought they were the best qualified of those standing. Sitting Councillors would bring forward their record of work in the ward—or would try to excuse their lapses by saying that it was impossible to meet everyone's demands. Canvassing mainly took place in morning and evening, when menfolk were at home. At other times, the women were approached by male and occasionally female helpers brought for the purpose. The candidate would stand on the doorstep, listening to his virtues being extolled inside the house. It was considered to be a great advantage for candidates to have an informal enough relationship with womenfolk to be able to canvass them personally. For women were said to be impressed by such attention to their votes, and to be less fickle if their promises were given to the candidate in person.

These tours were for general publicity more than for exerting pressure on the voter. They were nevertheless essential, since voters were said to feel offended if not paid a visit, however casual. This canvassing was superficial because the arguments behind any pressure exerted could not be given publicly—and because the person who could press these arguments was often not the candidate himself, but another person with influence over the particular voter.

These arguments were of two kinds. One, roughly, was the obligation to the candidate, or his workers, which could be 'cashed' for a vote. Such obligations included jobs provided (or promised), court cases fought without charge, provision of Municipal facilities etc.: they did not necessarily include the obligation of a tenant or a debtor, for it was considered to be risky for a creditor to exert financial pressure lest he lose the vote.

The second kind of argument involved less the cashing of obligations than the manipulation of favourable relationships. By these are meant the ties of caste, kinship, common residence, or simply friendship.

In each ward there were localities in which particular castes[1] predominated. But in no ward was election said to be possible on the vote of a single caste. The average poll in Dewas is 65 per cent, which means that such a caste would have to comprise 33 per cent or 22 per cent of the roll in a straight fight and a three-cornered contest respectively. The former figure was said to be never, and the latter rarely, reached.[2] Even if it were, it was said to be impossible to get every single member to the poll, and to ensure that such a vote was one of absolutely solid support.

[1] There has been no Census of castes since 1941. At that time, the main castes in Dewas were the Brahman, Maratha, Rajput, Hindu Bania, Mali and Balai in that order—and this position has not changed materially. Subcastes exist in most castes, and are the units of internal operation; but outsiders generally view the caste as a single unit of action. What I say below about castes can be applied, *mutatis mutandis*, to subcastes.

[2] This is confirmed for half the wards by a 20 per cent sample of the voters' rolls.

It is significant, however, that in four wards the Muslim com-munity[1] provided over 33 per cent of voters, the highest proportion reaching 47 per cent, and could therefore in theory elect a man single-handed. There is no record of this having occurred in 1961 or any other year, but the point is important in view of the communal issues raised during the election campaign.

Why should members of a caste or community vote for a particular candidate? Many Muslims in 1961 voted for the party which promised to protect them best against communal prejudice. A party could also try to recruit Harijan voters by promising to work for their welfare; and a feeling of common Harijan interests could overcome inter-caste antipathies, and present a significant, though not necessarily total, 'Harijan vote'. Again, many people voted for caste mates from senti-ment or hopes of patronage. A solid vote was said to have occurred in some of the rare cases where members did not have prior obligations to different parties or candidates (or their workers), and where the caste's own internal cleavages did not affect its vote. Sometimes, prejudice or rivalry against the caste of a candidate gave his opponent an advantage. Some people, for instance, regarded Banias with sus-picion; others felt the same way about Maharashtrian Brahmans. There was no sweeping anti-Brahman or anti-Bania vote, but these and other castes could always be denigrated by their opponents, to some effect when the character and standing of the candidate could not counteract it. But it is by no means certain that to choose a candidate of a certain caste will result in the solid support of that or any other caste.

Economic interests (which cut across caste lines) were said to influence the vote. For instance, some middle-class people were expected to be anti-Congress in protest against a cost of living rising more swiftly than their salaries.[2] Congress hoped to benefit, on the other hand, from full employment of labour in Dewas, due in part to numerous Government building projects, and from the work of the Congress-led mill workers' union in improving working con-ditions and wages of the 550 or so cotton mill workers living in Dewas.

But local issues constantly intruded on such economic interests, and make it impossible to present such a tidy analysis of interest groups.

[1] Muslims as a whole form a 'community'. Amongst them, certain can be said to belong to castes, stemming from conversion (e.g. Mewati, Naita, Mirasi) Others (e.g. Pathan, Sheikh) provide no such record of caste division.

[2] At the start of 1961, for example, mainly economic discontent in the civil service became so acute that lower grade clerical staff went on strike.

For example, one ward contained a sizeable number of mill workers, on whom Congress had pinned its hopes. But when some eminent visitors addressed a union meeting on the day before the election, the workers were invited to hear the speeches, but not to drink tea with the guests afterwards. Anti-Congress propaganda on the strength of this lost the Congress some union votes, and contributed to the loss of the ward.

The vote of a kin-group is easier to obtain than that of a caste or a class—when the caste population is small, and contains but a single subcaste, the two coincide, of course. But this is numerically of little importance. Common residence, again, covers no more than a street, and cannot alone deliver a majority. In short, I suggest that a candidate cannot win through the manipulation of any single relationship; he must fight on several fronts and through workers having qualifications all of which he cannot himself possess. A candidate cannot win by himself, unless he be a charismatic leader of a kind not yet seen in Dewas.

Who are the political workers, and how much influence do they wield? I have already said that some are permanent party stalwarts, and others (the majority) are people who make their contribution at elections only. Men whom I never saw at any party meeting during 1960 suddenly blossomed with party badges and caps. This is not surprising, for the main party effort is precisely at elections. It is not possible to say, however, that all party members help in the election, for many are traders who join two or three parties, and therefore remain neutral.

One can distinguish between full-time election 'workers' (the English word is used) and those who aid the party in the course of their daily routine—they could be called primary and secondary workers. The number of primary workers in the election is hard to calculate, because no lists were kept and the distinction from secondary workers is sometimes slight. In some wards there were over a dozen Congress primary workers, and the total cannot have been short of 150; the largest source was the mill union, some of whose younger members were party enthusiasts. The Jan Sangh had around sixty to seventy primary workers, mostly young and often college students. Through the Dewas branch of the Rashtriya Swayamsevak Sangh, the Jan Sangh was able to recruit a small but energetic body of workers whose sincerity and enthusiasm was remarked on. The P.S.P. had no such pool of recruitment, and could not have had more than forty to fifty active workers.

All these primary workers were busy at such tasks as sticking up posters, arranging the microphone for meetings and advertising these, and in the routine work of canvassing and recruiting of secondary workers. The latter were people who would join a canvassing party and lend prestige to it, who would contradict other parties' propaganda when it was made before them in conversation, and who might, on election day, undertake to bring out the vote from their neighbours' houses.

It is even more difficult to calculate the number of secondary workers in a ward. There were around twenty or thirty for a strong party, less for others. Together with primary workers, they presented a core of votes which was strategically essential. In one ward, forty-six men were said to be workers; the candidate reckoned that if each brought his wife and one other voter, they could place him more than halfway to the 250 votes he needed to win.

Because the vast majority of voters pledged support to every candidate who sought it, it was necessary to get an independent assessment of one's position. Primary and secondary workers could not do this, since they were openly connected with the party. Candidates therefore tried to have secret workers who could find out the voters' true feelings. The number of such workers is clearly impossible to ascertain. Some were said to be spies in the other party's organization; others were independent. I happened to hear a report made by one such man to his candidate. It occurred on the edge of a public meeting, where it would be little remarked, in an area distant from the ward concerned. All parties were aware of these undergrounds, which added an extra dimension to the campaign. For the existence of secret workers could be used to disrupt the other party through the suspicion of its primary workers. In one case, it was said, the opposition had been demoralized to the point at which several primary workers were 'rested' lest they defect, and other primary workers were used to shadow these men. The moral is that one must have confidence in primary workers (until proved wrong) lest the party's energies be dissipated in counter-espionage.

I have used the neutral word 'worker' to describe the men who act as links between candidate and electorate, rather than the term 'broker'. This is because by no means all of these men gain from their work, many doing it from friendship or prior loyalties. To have gone to school together or to the same wrestling gymnasium, to be friendly as neighbours, to be friends of a friend (who may himself benefit materially)—all these are reasons enough to be a worker.

One might, of course, say that by his support, the worker is starting a credit balance of obligation, and that this is his gain; but such a balance would accrue through his support of any candidate. One must not forget that many workers are at the same time brokers, of course, and also that the broker and the worker are in the same structural position as middlemen, needed because they have adequate relations with both persons in the election transaction.

It is dangerous to accept everyone's assertions about how many votes he controls. If all were true, the election would be easy to win with the help of two or three ambitious workers with '100 votes in my pocket'. Candidates must appear to take such men seriously, for they control *some* votes, but it is unwise to count on promises often made to secure standing with party leaders. This is borne out in wards where subcaste votes were divided in spite of the statements of such people that they would bring their entire subcaste population with them. Formerly, it is said, subcastes or localities *did* vote *en masse*. As one candidate said:

In 1954, people would vote for the man they promised to support. Sometimes they decided this through a council of the subcaste, sometimes they were brought in through workers, or through the tempo [English word used] at public meetings. Now people only vote after they have each been reached and persuaded, and they vote because of their own benefit, or because of the person who talks to them; so they can be changed up to the last minute. Maybe in a few years they will vote because of Municipal policies. You see, we are progressing all the time, and our people are learning about elections.

In general, this analysis was confirmed by others, though in 1961 there may have been more weight given to Municipal policies than the informant suggested. Pleas to vote as a caste or a kin bloc were made mostly to women, who are supposed to feel the moral worth of such solidarity more than the men, being more conservative and family-centred. For the men, an important factor was the ability of a party or candidate to do better work for Dewas, or more specifically, to fulfil the needs of the ward in such matters as water supply and guttering. As will be noted, the fact that Congress could promise more Municipal work was a major asset in its campaign.

It is possible to distinguish two alternative strategies for candidates. One could call these the 'hard' and the 'soft' approaches. Each depended on the recognition, implicit or otherwise, of four categories of voters. First were the voters who made public their allegiance.

Second were voters who agreed to support all candidates but who had privately decided how they would vote. Third were those who supported everyone publicly but who had *not* decided and in fact cared little about the election. Last, were those who wanted to sell their support and so remained uncommitted though flirting with all parties.

These categories were suggested by a candidate (and confirmed by others) who maintained that each of the first two did not number more than 10 per cent of the electorate. (I myself would say that the second category grew larger than this in the two days before the election day, since people appeared to make up their minds at that time.) The last two numbered around 40 per cent each, it was said.

The 'hard' campaign consisted in trying to persuade the third category, and to buy the fourth category, after which the candidate had to repel counter-attacks by his opponents. This he did by following rival workers on their tours of the wards, afterwards sending his own men to repair any damage they might have done. The 'soft' campaign, on the other hand, was run on two assumptions; that the uninterested people were impossible to persuade and would vote for whoever persuaded them to go to the poll, and accompanied them there; and that the fourth category of waverers should be brought in at the last moment, since to attract them sooner would leave them open to counter-offers and so raise the bidding.

No ward followed completely either of these types of campaign. Candidates did not have enough workers to operate a completely hard system, which would involve shadowing every opponent all the time; nor did they have enough nerve to let their fortunes rest entirely on the efforts of the last day or two. Of the two, the hard campaign was more prevalent. A major reason was that workers had to be recruited at the start of the campaign, even if only to apply the final pressure of a soft campaign. But such people, if interested, would inevitably start to counter opposition tactics earlier than this, and so a hard campaign was started, even if the candidate himself did not take the initiative. Nevertheless, variations in activity and tensions could be ascertained in different wards.

Strategy in the ward does not appear to have been the result of co-ordinative decision by the party leadership. Such co-ordination existed mainly in the distribution of campaign material (badges and posters), the organization of meetings and to some extent of the speeches delivered therein, and the 'plugging of gaps' in the wards— i.e. the despatch of particular people to doubtful voters over whom they had influence. These activities were supervised by the top leaders of each party, either through casual encounters throughout the day, or from the party office. The ward campaigns were not closely co-ordinated or controlled from above, but there *were* leaders who saw to it that canvassing and other activities went ahead in a business-like manner, and who had some control over their content.

I have so far mentioned the influence of specific social relationships and benefits. How did general issues, expressed by party leaders at public meetings and afterwards used by ward canvassers, affect the voters?

The campaign of intensive canvassing started after the first public meeting held by Congress, and in the two following weeks each party held a public meeting almost every night. These were at places allocated by the District Magistrate, who saw to it that each party got its share of more distant places as well as the town's central square. Attendances varied widely, the largest crowds being drawn by Jan Sangh and Congress on the last two evenings and numbering perhaps 1,500 people. Most meetings had outside speakers as well as local leaders since the election was not part of a State-wide Municipal poll; Congress drew on Ministers, and all parties brought their state office-bearers. The average meeting lasted three hours; there was no heckling, but matters raised were usually answered by the other parties in their own meetings.

Major campaign issues were raised by the Jan Sangh and the Congress. One was the communal issue. A month before the election, riots between Hindus and Muslims had broken out in the State, first at Jabalpur and then at Saugor. These had shocked Dewas people and had brought to the surface latent communal tensions. At first, Jan Sangh speakers referred to these riots only to deplore them and to tell Muslims that they were welcome in India as long as they remained patriotic Indians. But little by little the tone of the meetings changed, until shortly before the election some speeches were frankly inflammatory, describing outrages said to have occurred in Jabalpur, and raking over past history in Punjab and Kashmir. In addition, Jan Sangh canvassers widened their attack on Congress from the mis-management of Government to its refusal to ban cow slaughter all over India, and its sponsorship of 'anti-social' legislation under the Hindu Code.

Reaction was immediate, especially from Congress speakers whose party was more severely attacked than the P.S.P. These ridiculed the Jan Sangh's supposed concern for Mother Cow (*gau mata*), saying, for instance, that if one's mother were in mortal peril one would go to rescue her, rather than make speeches about her plight; and they countered the communal statements by saying that India should try to rise above religious difference rather than make election capital from it.

Nevertheless, the Jan Sangh propaganda made an impression, together with the party's plea to be given a chance to prove itself in the town's administration. Other politicians were concerned at the rise in the communal 'tempo', and some were prepared for a surprise landslide to the Jan Sangh. But two things prevented this. One was an unsuccessful speech at the critical Jan Sangh meeting on the penultimate day. The election's largest crowd had come, to be either emotionally excited or rationally convinced, but in the end they were bored. The other was the youth and inexperience of the Jan Sangh candidates.[1] No last minute communal swing occurred, and though Jan Sangh leaders professed satisfaction that only four candidates lost their deposits in the first election fought by the party, the general public appeared surprised (if not relieved) that the party did not poll a heavier vote.

The election issue raised by the Congress concerned its favoured place *vis-à-vis* the State Government (controlled by a large Congress majority). Congress leaders suggested that they would best be able to make Bhopal disgorge large sums of money for Municipal development. Indeed, Congress was the only party to put forward a concrete programme, including a costly scheme for underground drainage.

The party to react most strongly to this point was the P.S.P., which, as the major opposition party, could hardly afford to let the matter go unanswered. P.S.P. speakers maintained that no State Government could starve a Municipality, whatever its political complexion, and that they would fight by every means for Dewas rights. But this argument did not impress the average voter, who reasoned that even if the P.S.P. could get the money, it would be easier to let Congress get it without the delays of a struggle with Bhopal.

Through this issue, the Congress tapped a general and deeply held feeling that it was best to 'vote for the Government'. Partly this stemmed from traditional attitudes towards an autocratic Government; many people appeared to regard the Congress Government in much the same way as they had done the Maharaja's Government a

---

[1] The average age of Jan Sangh candidates was 33 years, as contrasted to the 38 years of the P.S.P. and the 43 years of the Congress candidates.

bare thirteen years previously. Partly it was a feeling of self-interest—
that the Government's forces were so great, and that the local Congress
as its agent had so much larger resources in terms of members and
influence, that it would be foolish to vote against it, and perhaps forgo
personal advantage. The issue of Bhopal's relations with Dewas
high-lighted this feeling and gave it direction.

The issues raised by Congress and Jan Sangh went to the roots of
democratic life in India, and were also recognized as vital for the life
of the town. By contrast, the P.S.P. ran a less effective campaign.
Amongst major issues raised by both P.S.P. and Jan Sangh were the
corruption of the Congress Government, the rise in the cost of living,
and India's dispute with China. Unlike the Jan Sangh, P.S.P. speakers
also argued with Congress over the Municipal records of both parties.
Since the P.S.P. had controlled the Municipality from 1954 until 1959,
there was an adequate quota of alleged misdeeds over which Congress
leaders could expatiate. P.S.P. leaders therefore had to defend their
actions as well as attack Congress for its administration in 1960 and
before 1954. Both parties had their weaknesses, and a *tu quoque* was
often easy to deliver. For instance, accusations of P.S.P. extravagance
in buying a Municipal Landrover could be countered by the fact that
present Congress leaders were driving, rather than selling, the vehicle.
Claims for credit in Municipal works could be answered by saying
that the initial planning had been done by a previous administration.
The P.S.P. was more vulnerable because of its longer Municipal
control; but the controversy carried little weight with a cynical
public, which thought impartially that *all* politicians took advantage
of their positions once elected.[1]

The P.S.P.'s campaign tended to lack clearcut identification in the
public eye. There was no single word which could sum up the party's
impact, as could the word 'authority' (*hukumat*) for the Congress, or
'religious duty' (*dharma*) for the Jan Sangh. In addition, the split of
the Lohia Socialists on the election eve enabled other parties to
picture the P.S.P. as a dying party, kept together by self-interest and
gimcrack political devices.

Though few people went to meetings, and most audiences were

[1] The records of individual Councillors were more important than the overall
Municipal performances of the parties. One of the election's largest majorities
was gained by a P.S.P. man, against the run of voting, mainly through his work
for the ward. Conversely, it was safer to replace an ineffective Councillor rather
than allow him to try to justify himself, for the new candidate could disclaim
neglect. Personal attacks were made by some speakers, but to a lesser extent than
in previous elections; in general, personal controversies were not key issues.

composed of a few hundred *habitués*, the news of what had been said went round the town and created what the politicians called the 'tempo' of the election. But these election issues were not paramount in influencing the vote; first, because many of them were common to several parties (e.g. anti-communalism or the cost of living); and second, because other interests often cut across those which were exclusive (e.g. not all Hindus supported the Jan Sangh on the communal issue, because some disagreed with it, others disliked Jan Sangh leaders, and yet others had loyalties to other parties). Though the large issues might decide a vote, they were probably more often important as a means of acceptably rationalizing self-interest or obligation.

The absence of one factor must be noted; there was scarcely any reliance on the printed word. No full reports, and few controversial statements were carried by the Indore or Ujjain newspapers. A few 'bulletins' and biographies were issued, but party manifestoes appeared only on the last day, and few people had read them before they voted. In fact, internal party quarrels in 1960 had received fuller coverage than the entire Municipal election. Leaders said they had no time to write press reports; evidently they calculated that the Dewas public, with a literacy rate of about 40 per cent, would be little influenced. Meetings were therefore held for the spoken word to reach the public and not to achieve publicity through newspaper reports.

*   *   *

Congress won the election by a convincing margin. Factors behind this victory include: the swing of a considerable number of Muslim voters to Congress as the best guarantee of communal harmony, and a similar swing by many Hindus frightened of communal trouble in the event of a Jan Sangh victory; the generally good economic conditions for labourers which nullified much of the P.S.P. propaganda; the tradition of not going against the (Congress) Government; the large number of new candidates chosen by Congress who could disassociate themselves from previous dissatisfactions; the belief that Congress could get better terms for the Municipality from the Government; and the presence of a much larger number of Congress workers in the wards, who were able to recruit votes on various individual bases, some of them stemming from the control by Congress of the Municipality, which gave it added forms of patronage to attract uncommitted voters. In addition, Congress election expenses, on posters, badges and meetings, were greater than those of other parties.

It was calculated that the party spent close to Rs. 1,000, whereas the other parties did not rise above Rs. 600 or Rs. 700. In addition, individual candidates contracted expenses for hospitality and so forth. The inevitable post-election accusation of bribery and vote-buying should be generally discounted.

Several points emerge from this account. One is the way in which elections form key contexts for power struggles in the parties. In the P.S.P., for example, the 1961 election precipitated the split of the Lohia Socialist branch. On the other hand, the same election saw the consolidation of power by the then Congress leadership; and it also witnessed the first intervention of leaders of the rural system of local government into Municipal affairs.[1] In so far as party rivalries centre around the selection of candidates, we approach a universal dilemma of the democratic process—whether to select candidates by means of primary elections within the party, or by the decisions of the party leaders alone. The former method was tried unsuccessfully by Congress in 1957, and the latter in 1961. A reason for this variation is the relative newness of the elective process; there are no traditions to be respected. Another reason is the fluctuating influence of the rank and file members. I have suggested that there are few men constantly active in the party who do not at the same time hold some party position. Hence, the rank and file normally has little voice. But at election time, party leaders must consider the effects of their actions on rank and file members who may become important in the campaign. However, the loose definition of the rank and file in Dewas parties, and the degree to which such people influence party policy and the party leadership are topics beyond the scope of this paper.

A second point is that there is none of the traditional Indian dislike of open elections and a corresponding desire for unanimous choice. This is in marked contrast to elections in, say, the rural system (for Village Committees or the District Cooperative Bank), where great efforts are made to have a unanimous choice. There are, in fact, two ways of by-passing the elective principle. One is to choose a single list through a meeting of political leaders or the ward populace. This list would comprise the most capable man in each ward, whether of any party or not. The other alternative does no more than to minimize elections, by allowing the eminent party leaders unopposed election, whilst having contests in marginal seats; this is a party, not a public, decision.

[1] A key Congress candidate was elected largely due to the efforts of the Congress head of the District-wide system of rural committees.

The first method has been canvassed from time to time in Dewas, though with no great popular support. It is said that Congress leaders once informally agreed to a unanimous list, on condition that it was then given a Congress label! The second alternative appears to be impracticable, because there are strong reasons for giving party tickets in *all* wards.

One reason is that to leave a ward uncontested because the opposing candidate is strong gives the other party a chance to deploy its strongest leaders elsewhere—and political strategy clearly demands that the opposition machine be stretched to its limits. Another reason is that these wards are precisely those in which one's party has everything to win and little to lose. A defeated candidate can say that he hardly expected to win against such an eminent opponent, but can cherish the hope of an upset victory which will make him famous. It is therefore worth the risk of defeat, and—to the party—of the loss of his Rs. 75 deposit if necessary. Further, a party machine can only be built up by running candidates who, although they lose, will slowly attract a nucleus of followers. Hence, seats have been contested in Dewas which appear hopeless to the observer.

A third point: it seems that general campaign issues are not more important than personal loyalties and interests, and that these latter must be tapped by approaches to each voter. This implies that the candidate with most social strings to his bow has an advantage. The man who has caste fellows, employees, debtors and of course neighbours in his ward and who has taken the trouble to cement these ties with personal interest and involvement—if necessary going to marriages and funerals, and helping with domestic problems—will be a strong candidate. In other words, Dewas is a place where a political 'boss' with a paternal attitude is a popular and powerful figure. It may well be that as the town grows, so such bosses will lose their position and 'managerial' politicians whose basis of power is control of the party rather than electoral contacts will take their place. But the political leader in Dewas is still expected to be all things to all men; and it is hoped that even this brief survey shows the degree to which small-town Indian politics represent an amalgam of party-bounded and socially-orientated activities.

INDIA'S POLITICAL IDIOMS[1]

W. H. MORRIS-JONES

*Professor of Political Theory and Institutions
in the University of Durham*

Not long ago, someone outspokenly remarked: 'There hasn't yet been an honest book written on Indian politics.' This may have been intended to be arresting and wild, but it was not silly. It did not mean that authors had been lying, only that the whole truth had not yet come out.

I had a student from Asia whom I asked to write an account of his country's local government system. When I commented that his essay seemed very thorough but at the same time so formal that the reader could get no impression about the way things actually worked, he looked at first hurt and genuinely puzzled. Then he beamed suddenly and said: 'You wish to know how it works? Ah, then I shall write a different essay!' And so he did.

Every state's political life has an 'inside story' and every 'honest' book on politics has to try to bring it out. But is there some special difficulty in being 'honest' about Indian politics? Is its inside story very concealed and very different from outward appearances?

*   *   *

The study of the politics of a society undergoing transformation is indeed as difficult as it is important and exciting. All these qualities are enhanced when the transformation is being effected not by an outside power (as in India under British rule or in Tibet today) nor by a single coherent political force (as in China), but by a variety of internal pressures and pulls. One of the best entrances into an

[1] This is an extended and revised version of the paper read at the S.O.A.S. seminar in November 1960. The original paper is published as part of the proceedings of a seminar held at the Australian National University, Canberra, in August 1960, in *Constitutionalism in Asia* edited by Professor R. N. Spann. I should like to acknowledge my very considerable debt to the published and unpublished contributions of several fellow students but especially to those of Dr F. G. Bailey and Professor M. N. Srinivas.

understanding of Indian politics may be through a discussion of the difficulty of its study.

One very general way of putting the problem is to point out that the student of Indian political institutions soon forms the impression that the main thing he has to learn is that nothing is ever quite what it seems or what it presents itself as being. At first he may put this down to his own faulty vision, to his unavoidable tendency to try to fit new things into categories which he has brought with him. But later he realizes that the matter is not so simple; there are different categories operative within the Indian context itself. Perhaps this should not surprise us. Indeed, it would be odd if it were otherwise. Everyone knows that in India's economic life whole European centuries coexist within the present moment, and in her social life too. The bus-ride from the airport to city centre announces this enormous fact even to the passing traveller. Why then should we expect her politics to belong to any single simple style?

Yet while the complexity of styles should not surprise us, it is nevertheless worth emphasizing that for most students of politics this phenomenon is unusual and for that reason at first baffling to the understanding. Of course the idiom in which political activity is conducted certainly varies from country to country. The Britisher who seeks to understand American politics knows that he must master a new idiom—one which is dictated by the size of the country, the peculiar character of the nation-building process which has taken place there, the separation of powers, and so on. But at least it is, by and large, just one idiom. The regional variations are related to the main theme. The conversation of American politics may be 'tapped' at any level and any place and the language will remain the same. And I should say that this is true of most countries whose study has figured prominently in the development of political science.

It may be argued that the matter is one of degree only—but then the range is very wide. We may concede at one end that even in the socially tight little island of the United Kingdom politics looks rather different according as to whether it is seen in Whitehall or in a miners' lodge. But the differences are, as it were, of tone and volume, not of basic language. For all participants have shares in a common culture. In some other countries of Western Europe, such as Belgium and France perhaps, the variety of political styles may be more marked: it may be a long way from Clochemerle to Paris. Further along this scale would come a country like Italy where culture contrasts between the South and the North are pronounced. But even there—with the exception of Sicily's Mafia—politics could be said to be in one language with several dialects. The case of Communist régimes seems different in an emphatic way; if we are to speak of differences only of degree, then at least we must say that here is a sizeable jump along the scale. For in Communist countries it seems that an idiom of politics derived from Marxism is found along with a primarily national idiom; the two may not mix in such a thorough way as to form a coherent new language. The observer of the political life of such a state may easily get the impression that things are not what they seem. The confusion or incoherence is in the situation itself and can express itself in different ways. Men may act in one political fashion but give an account of their acts in another set of terms. Or some men may act more or less fully in one political manner while others of their countrymen, within the same political institutions, act more or less thoroughly in another manner. Or it could be that the same men act in different styles according to occasion and context.

This way of putting things may or may not be helpful in understanding Communist political life, but it certainly proves an aid to probing the nature of Indian politics. Tentatively I would distinguish three main languages in which political life in India is conducted. The least inappropriate of a poor set of labels for them would be 'modern', 'traditional' and 'saintly'.

It will have been already noticed that I speak of these as 'languages' and 'idioms' while also referring to 'manners', 'styles', 'fashions'. Perhaps all these terms indicate a particular view of politics. Perhaps they all seem ambiguous and unclear. Some of the ambiguity attaching in particular to the word 'language' is, however, quite fitting. As already suggested, I wish to talk both about behaviour and accounts of behaviour and I intend to use the same term to extend over both. I am content to do this partly because there is a similarity between learning or acquiring a language and adopting a way of behaviour, partly because it may be useful to emphasize the close interacting relation between practical behaviour and descriptions of behaviour.

It can be argued—and indeed the point has been put to me in discussion—that this talk of languages of politics is unnecessarily confusing and that the contrast between modern and traditional in particular is rather a contrast between the political institutions of a nation state and the structure of an ancient society. There is some force in this view. Certainly I am only too pleased to emphasize that the key to Indian politics today is the meeting of these two as strangers. Political system and social structure, so far from having grown up together, have only just been introduced to each other. Before Independence, limited franchise and alien rule kept them apart. Even the great national movement for all its long history and wide appeal seems in retrospect to have skated quite lightly over the surface of Indian social relations, cutting it up as it were only in one or two patches such as Gandhi's untouchability campaigns. With the disappearance of the white outcastes and the introduction of adult suffrage, 'politics' and 'society' come to meet. However, to speak of languages of politics still seems valuable. First, it serves to stress that no social relations—however ancient and no matter how far bound up with religious ritual—are devoid of political content. Traditional India is not non-political, only it contains a different kind of politics from that of the 'modern' state. Second, this way of putting the matter makes it easier to bring out the peculiar third language of saintly politics.

The language of modern politics is undoubtedly important in India —more so than perhaps in most other parts of Asia. This is less on account of the long period of British rule than because of the existence for nearly one hundred years of an Indian *élite* steeped in its grammar and masters of its accents. Members of this *élite* were not only the agents of much of the administrative and economic development of the country; they also provided the leadership of some of the more important movements of social reform and of the nationalist movement itself. It is true that an important change came over the nationalist movement with the impact of Gandhi's leadership after 1917, but it would be a mistake to imagine that Gandhi did not employ the modern idiom; he combined it with another, but by no means abandoned it or prevented its continuous development.

This language is so widespread in India that it has seemed possible to give a well-nigh comprehensive account of Indian political life without moving outside its terms. That indeed is what we political scientists have been doing. We have found so much modern behaviour and so much modern talk about the behaviour that we hardly found our own language of description deficient. This modern language of politics is the language of the Indian Constitution and the Courts; of parliamentary debate; of the higher administration; of the upper levels of all the main political parties; of the entire English press and much of the Indian languages press. It is a language which speaks of policies and interests, programmes and plans. It expresses itself in arguments and representations, discussions and demonstrations, deliberations and decisions.

Within this idiom are conducted several momentous conflicts of principle and tussles of interests. These are so wide-ranging that observers could be forgiven for greeting this Indian politics as a well-recognized familiar friend and assuming that this is the whole of Indian politics, the complete story. For what more could one ask? One kind of 'debate', for instance, is that which is carried on—partly within the Congress Party, partly between it and the Swatantra Party on the 'right' and the Socialist and Communist Parties on the 'left'—about the size of the public sector of the economy, the degree and forms of governmental controls and the direction and pace of land reform. This looks very like some of our doctrine-and-interest conflicts. Another 'argument'—still conducted within the modern idiom—relates to the 'federal' theme, and will also sound familiar to western ears. Here men will discuss the relative roles of centre and state governments, the impact of the Planning Commission on the federal structure, the Supreme Court's influence on the federal balance through its interpretation of the Constitution, and so on. (The whole range of disputes between India's linguistic units concerning the division and boundaries of territories—the splitting of Madras and Bombay, the demands of the Sikhs, the violent hostility between Bengalis and Assamese—can up to a point be regarded as falling within this category; but, as we shall see, only up to a point; to get the full meaning we have to move into a different language for the reason that those involved are operating in a different language. The same is the case with the strictly linguistic tussles between Hindi and the regional languages and between both and English.) A third example of 'debate' within the modern idiom would be mostly discussion about forms of political organization and relations between organizations. Here one would place conflicts between party organs and party groups in legislatures; relations between Ministers and back-benchers and between Ministers and civil servants; the composition and powers of the Planning Commission; relations between governments and opposition parties.

Most evidently, then, this is an important language of politics, covering most of what is to be expected as politics. A good index to a book written in these terms on Indian political life would bear comparison with a standard work on Britain or the United States. This is not to say that there would be no items peculiar to India; nor that many of the apparently familiar items would on closer examination prove so readily recognizable. It is only to say that if this modern language comprehended the whole of Indian politics, then as a subject it would for all its distinctiveness be susceptible to analysis by the same methods as French or Dutch politics.

But this is not the case. The observer of Indian politics will not look at his subject for long before he gets the feeling that he is missing something. This feeling can perhaps be described only by metaphors. The actors on a stage do not know why the audience should laugh just then, because they have not seen the cat which is playing with the stage curtains. Or, again, the audience may detect an awkward pause, but they do not know that the actors are pre-occupied because the hero's make-up is coming apart. Such a feeling with regard to Indian politics is perfectly justified; what the observer has so far not taken into account is a play within the play.

Indian politics is in part conducted in a very different language. The traditional idiom is that which social anthropologists and sociologists in India are busy discovering or rediscovering for us at the present time. In its purest forms it is spoken in rural India. It knows little or nothing of the problems of anything as big as India and its vocabulary scarcely includes policies and Plans. One way of indicating how different it is would be to use the term 'feudal', for this word, although in some ways misleading and inexact, would at least put us at an appropriate distance from the first idiom. 'Tribal' might also do the trick and would not be without some justification.

This language of politics is that of a particular kind of highly developed status society. It is far more important as a manner of behaviour than as a language of description; it is acted upon more than it is spoken about. It is the chief source of the contrast between the inside and outside stories of Indian politics, even of the gap between practice and profession which is a striking feature of Indian life.

Caste (or subcaste or 'community') is the core of traditional politics. To it belongs a complete social ethos. It embraces all and is all-embracing. Every man is born into a particular communal or caste group and with it inherits a place and a station in society from which his whole behaviour and outlook may be said, in idea at least, to be derived: his occupation, the range from which his parents will choose to negotiate for his bride, his fairly precise standing in terms of privileges and obligations to members of his own and other caste groups, his attitude towards them. For this reason, caste cannot easily be assimilated within the world of modern politics. It is seldom *merely* a group operating as a unit within a modern whole—as perhaps the Roman Catholics in Australian politics or the Irish in parts of earlier U.S. politics. When it comes into politics it comes not with a list of demands but with a way of life.

But that is already an over-simplification. For that way of life is itself undergoing change. Indeed, the presence of organized caste pressures within Indian political life is itself a sign of the changing of traditional India; this is behaviour unbecoming to units of a status society. It is easy for the modern eye to see caste as a recalcitrant and limited focus of loyalty in stubborn competition with 'the state'. But this tends to overlook the rather different role of caste in the proper setting of its own society. There it contributes to social cohesion, it organizes the parts into the maintenance of a whole local community, the village. The allocation of privileges and obligations between the parts is such as to serve and permit the survival of the whole. Internal disturbance through fresh claims and sectional demands are as much to be resisted as impacts from outside. Coherence is maintained or restored by the preservation or re-settlement of status.

Although caste and its world have been under slow erosion—by improvements in communications and education—for a hundred years, their massive importance was only slightly touched. But the impact of caste on political life was restrained, first by the presence of alien rulers, second by the movement of nationalism, above all by the fact that even after Gandhi's arrival so much of the initiating, positive politics of India belonged to a fairly restricted *élite*. Now this has changed. From the traditional society, itself changing, caste moves out into politics. At the same time mass politics means new political invasions of traditional society. To these new encounters, caste brings as part of its way of life certain attitudes of special relevance to politics. Of these the central one concerns the nature of political authority. In the traditional idiom political authority is of course an extension of a certain general status; it has its natural, substantially hereditary seats. In most regions of India there appears to be a par-ticular local caste which is 'dominant'. In each village within the region the natural repositories of authority will be men of certain families within that caste. (Economic status seems to have some, rather variable, part to play in this matter of dominance.) Other castes will have their own leaders but they will be no more than spokesmen for partial groups. The political leadership of the whole little com-munity will be provided by those who have this task as one of their recognized functions, part of the contribution they are expected to render to the system of carefully graded privileges and obligations which they uphold and which upholds them. Political authority is thus taken as naturally determined and given, not a question of choice, election and wills. (Plato would have understood.)

The manner in which they will normally exercise authority is determined by the simple twofold political need of an Indian village: it requires leadership partly for the resolution and settlement of internal disputes, partly for the task of interceding with the outside world and its *Raj*. So the leaders must be good at reconciliation and the production of a 'consensus' and, secondly, they must be successful in 'securing favours' from the 'powers that be' outside.

The third language of saintly politics is to be found 'at the margin' of Indian politics. By this I certainly mean that it is in some quantitative sense relatively unimportant, spoken only by a few and occupying a definitely subsidiary place on the political page. But I would also be content to be taken to mean 'margin' to have something of the importance given to that term in economics: there may be few or none actually at the margin but the location of the point has an effect on all operators as a kind of reference mark. In other words, saintly politics is important as a language of comment rather than of description or practical behaviour. The outstanding figure of nation-wide importance in this idiom is Vinoba Bhave, the 'Saint on the March' who tours India on foot preaching the path of self-sacrifice and love and polity without power. His effective active followers may not be many but his own activities and pronouncements are reported week by week, almost day by day, in the press. The direct impact of Bhave is a matter of some uncertainty and dispute. The startling initial success of his call for donations of land for distribution to the landless prompted all political parties to pay tribute to him and accord him respectful recognition. Subsequently, doubts about the motives of land donors and a certain ineffectiveness in the distribution programme have lowered the temperature of enthusiasm. More recently, there has taken place the experiment of taking Bhave's help in dealing with the dacoit menace in the region south of Delhi; police action was called off while Bhave went in to talk to the brigand gang leaders; the present impression is that the dacoits were keen to benefit more from the withdrawal of police attention than from the message of Bhave.

But the direct effects of Bhave are less important than the indirect. This language has a widespread appeal to all sections in India. For many people it is identified with the political style of Gandhi. This is a bad over-simplification: for one thing this was only one of Gandhi's styles; for another, this idiom was already present in Indian society before Gandhi undertook its systematic and organized development. I do not know if in European history there are any even remote parallels to this kind of influence: possibly the sort of direction in which one might look would be that of the early Christian Church or some of the monastic orders. Be that as it may, the influence of 'saintly' policies in India cannot be ignored. Admittedly it affects men's actual behaviour very little; remarkably few men engaged in political activity within the other two idioms are striving to be saintly. Its influence is rather on the standards habitually used by the people at large for judging the performance of politicians. In men's minds there is an ideal of disinterested selflessness by contrast with which almost all normal conduct can seem very shabby. I do not imply that such a standard is applied continuously or to the exclusion of other standards. I would argue, however, that it contributes powerfully to several very prevalent attitudes to be found in Indian political life: to a certain withholding of full approval from even the most popular leaders; to a stronger feeling of distrust of and disgust with persons and institutions of authority; finally, to profoundly violent and desperate moods of cynicism and frustration. I repeat that I am not making 'saintly' politics a sole cause of these sentiments; I am only indicating how it can add, as it were, a certain bitterness and 'edge' to them. I would also (much more tentatively, for I do not know what social psychologists would say) suggest that the existence of this standard may if anything affect actual behaviour in a morally adverse manner: if the only really good life is one which seems to belong to a world beyond reach then a man might as well not strain too hard in that direction and indeed might as well be hung for a whole big black market sheep as for a little irregular lamb.

That I consider saintly politics worth listing as a third idiom does not imply that I see it as wholly unrelated to the other two. In curious ways which there is here no room to examine, it takes in much from both; indeed, in this lies much of its power. A Bhave talking of the corruption of party politics appeals at once to the modern notions of public spirit and civic conscience and the traditional ideas of non-competitive accepted authority working through a general 'consensus'. Similarly and even more conspicuously, a Narayan speaking of public 'participation' in a 'communitarian' democracy stirs the imagination of the advanced radical and the conservative traditionalist alike.

*   *   *

The tale of three idioms is one to be put to work, for it may help us to understand certain both general and particular aspects of Indian political life. Consider, for instance, this matter of the gap between profession and practice, the difference between the way things really get done and the way in which they are presented as being done. Of course, this kind of contrast happens everywhere: in England, for example, different sorts of 'old boy networks' are to be found smoothing the course of politics in city council, parliament and Whitehall alike. There is a cement of informality that holds together the formal bricks. But this is not the same as the mixing of entire political styles that happens in India. It is not simply that those people whom a foreigner is likely to question will reply in the 'Western' idiom for his benefit—though this certainly happens. It is also that such people will in any case habitually use that idiom when explaining things to each other. That is to say, Indian political life becomes explicit and self-conscious only through the 'Western' idiom, that is practically the only language in which the activity of description, giving an account of matters, will normally take place. But this does not prevent actual behaviour from following a different path. This situation is of course to be found in many spheres besides the strictly 'political'. 'Applications for scholarships will be considered by the Committee on the basis of recommendations submitted by the Head of the Department', but the natural tendency will be for the aspirant to tackle this problem in terms of 'favours' and 'influences'. Likewise with such matters political as the casting of votes, the selection of candidates and distribution of portfolios, and with such matters of administration as the siting of a new school or the granting of an industrial licence. One must be careful not to exaggerate and careful not to imply that in English local government or in American party organization everything is as in the textbooks. But I believe there is a substantial difference.

The gap between supposed and real patterns of behaviour is a much wider matter than corruption, but the two are yet closely related. Corruption—the fact itself but, even more important, the talk about it—occupies a great place in Indian politics. It is of two kinds. Much of what is called corruption is no more than behaviour conducted in terms of one idiom being looked at in terms of another. Anyone holding any kind of position of power may be inclined to regard that position in both modern and traditional terms. Even if he is himself peculiarly free from the grip of traditional categories and loyalties, he will be subjected to steady pressures framed in those terms—and it will be very difficult not to give in. Of course, the proportions in which modern and traditional are mixed will vary greatly: there may be 100 per cent modernism in the Planning Commission and 90 per cent traditionalism in a Mandal Congress Committee in Madhya Pradesh. But at most levels two mainly antagonistic sets of standards will be in competition for the power to control a man's conduct. Equally important, these two sets will also be employed—frequently by the same persons—for judging his conduct. The behaviour which the traditional language holds to be irresponsible is for the modern idiom responsible and that which the modern regards as irresponsible is for the other the very opposite.

This type of contrast can be greatly sharpened when the third idiom is present. This will happen more often than one might imagine. This is not simply because of the personal influence of Bhave or the traditional appeal of those ideas or even because of memories of the saintly aspect of Gandhi. It is also on account of the actual experience of many people in the nationalist movement. That movement did bring out of ordinary men and women a remarkable standard of behaviour. From a sense of dedication or merely from sheer excitement and exhilaration men forgot about themselves and thought only of the cause. There is perhaps a tendency today to exaggerate this in restrospective glances at the golden age, but there is a big element of truth in it. There is a natural unwillingness to accept that period as exceptional and therefore a strong inclination to be severely critical about the decline in standards.

The second kind of corruption is in a way the opposite of the first. The first is a demonstration of the power of the traditional idiom; the second is a sign of its weakness. When a man 'fixes' applications and licences in disregard of merit but in accordance with group loyalties he is obeying a law of social conduct more ancient than that of the upstart state. But when a man puts into his own pocket moneys intended for some organization, when he relentlessly exploits every situation for perfectly private gain, this is not obedience to the rule of any traditional society. No doubt in every society some men have been very selfish when opportunity was provided. But within a compact and tightly knit social unit of India's traditional kind, the checks on anti-social selfishness would be very strong indeed, the sanctions against it awesome. There can be little doubt that much present corruption in India is the work of men not long released from one set of firm social bonds, not yet submissive to a new set. Both corruptions can flourish side by side for two social processes are contemporaneous:

the intrusion of caste into the new fields (mainly of regional and even national politics) and the erosion of caste as a feature of social life as a whole. Corruption is at once what one political language calls the other and what happens when one is displacing the other.

Related to this is a further striking general feature of Indian political life—and again it is a feature rather of social life which politics shares: a certain caution and distrust in relations between people. In the Courts a man in India is innocent until he is proved guilty, but in social and political life the position tends to be reversed. One has noticed the wariness with which people encounter each other and the relative difficulty of establishing friendships except within 'community' groups. In politics this has its equivalent in the extraordinary extent to which the other man's motives are suspect, the difficulty of concerted action and so on. Myron Weiner has already discussed one aspect of this in his *Party Politics in India*:[1] the resistance to unification on the part of political groups with almost identical policies and the readiness in many groups to split and break away. He offered the explanation that in many cases party has become a substitute for a community group and that the members demand the snug and reassuring coherence of a unit in which there are no strangers or outsiders. A more general (though not incompatible) explanation would be that even in the sophisticated world of urban party politics men have not wholly shed the traditional attitudes. No one can be regarded as an individual, taken as he stands; he is always to be 'placed' in terms of the group to which he 'belongs'. This makes complete frankness and trust difficult. Shils has put the point very well when speaking of the Indian intellectual. 'If Indian intellectuals are "cut off from the people" the caste system must take some of the blame. . . . The alienation of the intellectual from Indian society is probably in fact less pronounced than is the alienation of most other Indians from Indian society.'[2] The intellectual's alienation may be in fact less pronounced but its impact is more agonizing for, as Shils goes on to say, the ideal of national unity is more real for the intellectual. He feels that something of this has been lost since the independence movement and he feels a resentment against the barriers that separate man from man—while himself remaining in some measure a victim of such attitudes.[3]

[1] Myron Weiner, *Party Politics in India* (1957), pp. 237 ff.
[2] Edward Shils, *The Intellectual between Tradition and Modernity: The Indian Situation* (1961), p. 70.
[3] *Ibid.*, pp. 70–1.

Thus man as man, man as clerk in an office, employee in a factory, even student in a college, is placed at a distance from his fellows; indeed, it is not easy to recognize the other as fellow. But this is not all. Present day India strikes many observers as a ruthless and unkind society—and this by way of contrast with the recent past. This may seem strange in view of the well-known efforts of the present régime to establish a welfare state and raise the living standards of the impoverished masses. Yet the impression has some basis. As the status society slowly crumbles, personal ambitions are released and new men press hard on the traditional holders of authority. Perhaps it is to be expected that men escaping from a world of set status may for a while swing violently to the opposite extreme of competitive struggle for all kinds of power. To caution and distrust of the other man there comes to be added disregard. This tendency, already present before independence, was somewhat held in check by the spirit of fellowship in the freedom movement; it has now been let loose.

It is, then, the meeting, the mixing, the confrontation of political idioms which dominates the Indian political scene and gives it distinctive tone. The 'pure' expressions of each language occupy certain areas but these are less significant than the areas of co-habitation. But what is happening in this great encounter? Does one language gain over the others?

The different views on this question have something to do with the professional interests of the observer. In particular social anthropologists and political scientists have seemed to be giving different answers, Indian politics becoming a battlefield in the process. The former has set out from his base in caste and kinship groups and found himself drawn towards the area of political behaviour; the latter, encamped in parliament and party, has had to reconnoitre the regions of social background. This is as it should be, for such movements only correspond to the changes actually taking place in Indian life.

The social anthropologist has put a strong and clear case. With the coming of independence (which incidentally made the serious study of caste possible and no longer an unpatriotic betrayal of the nationalist cause!), a wholly Indian administration and parliamentary democracy, caste and community have been able to move out of the villages and penetrate further towards the centre than ever before. The modern *élite* is no longer protected from the influence of traditional politics by the triple bulwarks of British administrative overseers (who mostly kept out of the caste network), the Indian national movement and a restricted electorate. The Constitution and the national leaders proclaim the goal of a casteless society and hardly a day passes without the vigorous condemnation by Nehru or one of his colleagues of the divisive forces of casteism, linguism, and the like. But these are the only terms in which the newly enfranchised masses know how to operate. And so, in the middle and lower reaches of the parties and the administration, realistic men learn that they must also talk that language if they are to be understood and if they are to be effective. What sounds good up in the Delhi Parliament or for the newspaper-reading public will cut no ice at the grass roots. Nor should it be imagined that caste has stopped at the city limits. It is true that the long run effects of urban life may lead to a weakening of its hold, but there appears to be sufficient evidence that in the shorter run caste not only continues to prevail in city life (caste members often settle in the same localities within the city; immigrants from rural areas keep very close economic and social ties with their village bases), but under urban conditions finds it desirable and possible to attain a higher level of organization than in rural India.

Work already done or in progress indicates clearly enough the pattern of sociological interpretation of Indian politics. Behind the voting figures there is revealed the work of intermediaries who secure the votes of their group for a given candidate. Behind the choice of candidates is discovered careful calculation of caste appeal. The whole shape of Mysore politics, which a political scientist might have been content to describe in terms of relations between parties and between the parliamentary and organizational wings of the major party, is shown to be determined by an age-old rivalry between two powerful castes in that region. Orissa's interesting political history of the last dozen years is likewise explained in terms of shifting caste positions and alignments. The working in practice of much of the movements of 'democratic decentralization' and community development is shown to be conditioned and/or distorted by traditional politics' powerful grip.

However, what the anthropologist may miss—and what political scientists have not been very effective in demonstrating—is that all this, although true and important, is only one part of a double process. For the modern idiom is also moving out of its base in the *élite* just as surely as the traditional idiom is emerging from its hidden habitat. Therefore the attempt to show how modern political institutions are open to manipulation and exploitation by traditional social forces should be accompanied by equivalent attention to the way in which such institutions by their existence constitute modern social forces.

*　　*　　*

Take, for instance, the Congress Party, probably the most important single political institution in India today. It certainly displays within itself most of the important features of Indian political life, while its present role and future development in great measure determine the course of Indian politics. (Yet it has not so far been made the subject of serious systematic study.)

In terms of our analysis, the Congress is a crucial meeting ground of the three languages of politics. Within the party are to be found many men who speak the modern idiom—most of them with skill and polish, some of them even with love. Most of the internal party debates would seem to be conducted in this language; for instance, the arguments between the 'right-wingers' (supposedly, for example, Desai, Pant) and the left (Menon and members of the one or two 'ginger groups') on the size of the public sector, the seriousness with which land reforms are to be tackled, the tone of voice to be adopted when speaking to China and the U.S. When commentators talk of the wide range of opinion held together by Nehru, it is a range within this one language which they have in mind. (The same range is to be found, though more obscurely, in the top administration.) The 'federal' tussles within the party are also for the most part in the modern idiom—the location of new steel mills and the choice of ports for development.

At the other end of the machine, so to speak, there is to be found a very different kind of person engaged in a very different kind of operation; the Mandal and District party leaders. Now I am aware that local party secretaries in England and ward bosses in the U.S. are concerned with rather different issues from those which preoccupy the parliamentary and senate leaders. The difference to which I refer in India is, however, a profounder one of the very manner and style of behaviour; the difference in social setting imposes quite different techniques and is associated with quite different values and standards. The Congress worker in 'rural' India (I use the quotes since the term has to be taken to include sections of cities too) has to operate in the traditional language. But who is the present-day Congress worker?

Most observers would agree that some change has taken place since independence in the character of the men who do Congress politics at the lower levels. Older party workers will often explain with regret and scorn how new men of the wrong kind have got into the organization. The voice of saintly politics is often heard in this strain. But the point has some validity. Of course, the motives which impelled a man to join and work for Congress in pre-independence days were more numerous and varied than the old-timers would have us believe, and 'national sentiment' no doubt covered a multitude of different characters. But the new men are indeed different.

Some investigators seem to have found two kinds of new men inside the Congress machine. First, there are the leaders of the new village establishment. Until the introduction of adult franchise, the politically active sections of rural India were generally men of higher castes than the peasants and for this reason even a mass party like Congress was manned by Brahmins and other high caste men out of proportion to their numbers. The politics of adult franchise has in many regions raised the influence of the non-Brahmin middle peasants who are at once numerous and—as compared with the hardly less numerous untouchables—economically substantial. Men from these groups seem to be more prominent in Congress than before. The opponents of the party cry out that Congress is courting and capturing the influential leaders of rural life. Of course it is. But it is equally true that such leaders have in their own ways been courting and capturing Congress. Village India, playing its own game of politics in relation to outside *Raj*, has been adjusting itself to Congress power. The men who for economic and electoral reasons count in any area naturally regard it as one of their functions to get to positions from which they can do what is expected of them by their clients and dependants.

Secondly, however, there may have arisen an even newer kind of local Congressman—the man who relies not on his local social status as a member of a dominant caste but solely on his political skill in the new politics. Whereas the first type would operate in the traditional idiom as a matter of course, this second brand of newcomer is really a modern who is simply able to exploit that idiom. (In addition to both these, there naturally continue to be many party workers who belong to those sections who, while numerically and even economically weak, provided social and intellectual leadership in the past.)

Thus Congress is one of the great meeting-places of the three languages of politics. That the party has in some measure gone traditional under the impact of mass electorate politics seems clear. But it must not be forgotten that a political party *as such*—its very organization, as well as the character of Congress national leadership and the fact of its governmental responsibilities—is a modernizing influence. So which language wins? The question remains—and must do so until we know more about Congress. But at least we know what we need to know: the procedures by which Congress' internal elections take place; the negotiations leading to the choice of Parliamentary and, even more important, State Legislature candidates; the relations between Pradesh Congress Committees and Congress State Ministries; the character of the agitations and campaigns on linguistic and communal (e.g. reservation of posts for scheduled castes) issues; the extent and character of party pressures on State Congress Governments in relation to land legislation. On each topic there would be at least two main features to examine. First, the extent to which community and caste considerations were present and influential; second, the extent to which the exercise and reception of authority was conducted in modern terms of the institutions and offices or in traditional terms of social status and customary respect. Lest it be thought that all this is in some derogatory sense academic, let it be said that the battles being conducted within the modern idiom as between 'right' and 'left', 'centralist' and 'statist' will be most significantly influenced by the outcome of the underlying conflict between the two languages. The traditional way points to the right and points away from the centre.

Consider also India's representative institutions. In this world too, as in the world of party, the two idioms meet (with the third idiom again keeping up, as it were, an influential running commentary on the proceedings). There is general agreement that the central Parliament in New Delhi is a powerful instrument of political education for members and public alike. The education it conveys is almost entirely in the modern idiom; this is certainly true of the debates on the floor of the House, in all the parliamentary committees and in some party committees; it is less certainly so in the case of certain other party committees and in regard to general lobby conversation. The members are powerfully influenced by its atmosphere and they are under that influence for by far the greater part of the year. The public that reads papers is also accustomed to watch it closely—so large is the space devoted by the press to its proceedings. The talk is all of issues and problems and programmes and the scale is emphatically all-India. As Asoka Mehta strikingly said recently, Parliament is the great unifier of the nation. This is true; it has taken over that role in large measure from the freedom movement. (I find the parallel with the Tudor Parliaments very close and instructive:

Nehru is the Queen in Parliament; in no other place does he 'stand so high in his estate royal'; and through Parliament the feudal powers in their country seats are kept relatively subdued and in order.)

Much less clear is the character of the State Legislative Assemblies. Students have already pointed out that the members of these bodies are drawn from layers much closer to those of traditional politics. Also they are in the Assemblies for quite a short part of the year; the rest of the time they will be in their home districts which are, increasingly, their constituencies. No one can visit the lobbies of a State Assembly without realizing quite vividly that the M.L.A. is 'in touch with' his constituents; the corridors are full of them, some still bearing the dust of the village tracks if not the earth of the fields themselves. The M.L.A. is thus another critical point in the drama of Indian politics: which language of politics does he speak? He is himself undergoing 'modern' education from his seniors on the front benches, but the 'courses' are shorter and of a fairly 'elementary' nature. Still he learns to think of his state (even if not yet of India) and to talk of power projects (even if the big decisions are taken in Delhi). At the other end there are the pressures from home and in the corridors —to remember that he comes from the Vidarbha part of Maharashtra, or that he is a Mahar or that he must please those who count in his district party. So evidently he becomes 'bilingual'. But we would still like to know in which language he does his thinking and his dreaming. And anyone anxious to secure the victory of the modern language over the traditional would do well to concentrate on the M.L.A. and should presumably try to strengthen the links that join him to circles where the modern idiom is spoken. The M.L.A. in one of the great 'gap-closers' in Indian politics but we do not yet know whether he is achieving this in ways favourable to the modern or to the traditional style.

Even State Ministers have to operate in the two languages. Indeed, one might say that the successful Chief Ministers are those who are equally skilled in both idioms. Chavan of Bombay may be a good example of this kind. But in at least one state, Madras, there was a fascinating division of labour between the Chief Minister, who speaks little or no English but manages the 'informal politics', and a colleague who handles the policy questions and converses with New Delhi.

*   *   *

The combination, the containment in peaceful interpenetration, of these diverse and in principle competitive languages of politics is the great achievement of political life in independent India. Vast social and economic changes are being accomplished steadily and without obvious drama and are being accommodated and digested by and within a political structure which is successfully flexible, 'politically multi-lingual'. The instruments of this achievement are, first, the two great legacies which India inherited from the days before 1947: the Government and the Movement, a stable administrative structure and a capacious political organization, both equipped with able leadership. To these must be added India's parliamentary institutions—in many respects a development of independence politics, yet owing much of their present success to earlier beginnings.

Yet the enterprise is not without its grave difficulties. Some of these may be indicated by turning attention to what is perhaps the really threatening force in Indian political life: the discontent of the educated middle classes. (None of the popularly supposed threats to democracy in India—a failure sufficiently to increase agricultural production, a slower rate of economic growth than China, etc.—has any political significance except in so far as it can operate through the opinions of this section of the population. And these opinions can be affected by many things besides economic statistics.) This discontent is as it were not in the direct line of fire between the modern and traditional idioms, but it is greatly influenced by factors arising out of that conflict.

The present mood of the educated mainly urban middle classes is dictated by those of its less successful members. There are many men (and an increasing number of women) who are in secure and satisfying employment in the services and in industrial and commercial enterprises—as technicians, administrators, educators and entrepreneurs. And it is of course true that they are relatively contented with their own lives. Yet it is striking to note the extent to which even such people will speak of India's political life in terms which seem to belong more appropriately to those of their fellows who are unemployed, mal-employed or insecurely employed. The general attitude is one of deep disgust with those in power and profound scepticism about the effectiveness or suitability of existing political institutions. The fact that much of the criticism is based on very great ignorance of what is actually going on does not lessen its significance. There is a conviction that all holders of political power —great and small alike—are abusing their positions for illegitimate ends. These may be personal or family or group. There are no men of 'public spirit' in public life, no disinterested politicians of pure motives.

In other words, this influential section of the public is engaged in a continuous complaint about political life in India. Too modern to be able to operate traditional politics, they are at the same time sufficiently sympathetic to certain idealized features of traditional society to be very ready to condemn modern ways of politics as unsuited to India's genius. They enjoy exposing the way in which institutions of modern politics are at the mercy of older systems and pressures. They learn easily the language of saintly politics—not necessarily directly, as preached by Bhave and Narayan, but as mediated to them through experience or impressions of the great days of the national movement. Eager to take part in politics, they find there is little room for them.

This explains in part the enthusiasm with which linguistic agitations are supported and even led by these elements. Their energies find release in these campaigns, for here an attractive common ground between traditional and modern politics is provided. The young student cannot hope to overcome his supposed alienation from the masses by raising and developing issues of, say, public economic policy. So he mainly neglects such questions. But if inter-group tensions develop, he will be there and so also will be the new caste leaders; the latter can rise to the level of such issues, while the student or clerk finds it no effort to come down to meet them, for part of him is already there. In the Assamese-Bengali killings, in the turbulent struggle for Maharashtra or Andhra, culture-gaps closed wonderfully; men from the worlds of both languages join hands. There may be an element of direct class interest involved in these cases—a belief that, for instance, the Bengalis are keeping you out of a decent job or the Gujeratis are not giving the others a chance. But these agitations, though evidently most satisfying emotionally—even recapturing the thrill of the freedom struggle—are, alas, mainly irrelevant to the main needs of the frustrated urban moderns. It is doubtful if they can for long give even emotional satisfaction.

Perhaps the central problem is that suitable channels for political action seem to be fewer than the demand for them. India's is an underdeveloped polity from the point of view of the needs of its educated middle class. It is shaped like a narrow pole rather than a solid pyramid. It is not exactly that there are no organizations and associations at a convenient level ('infra-structure'?), but rather that most of these are talking the wrong language. There are plenty of caste organizations, but few lively professional bodies or opinion-propagating societies. It may be that the middle-class feeling of wanting to 'participate' is abnormally developed (a hang-over from the national movement where all were excitingly employed, a sign of lack of absorption in their own jobs, a genuine misunderstanding of the meaning of democracy—some of all these things and no doubt more), but there is certainly no room on the narrow pole for all who seem to want a place there.

The structure of 'modern' political institutions is not only frustratingly narrow—limited to legislatures and parties. There is also the difficulty that that structure is itself dominated by one organization, the Congress Party. And there is very little that the middle classes can do about this in the short run. They might organize other parties, and indeed have of course done so—P.S.P., Jan Sangh Swatantra. But how can such parties make any impression on the solid base of the Congress which is located in the world of 'traditional' politics where Swatantra and P.S.P. alike hardly know how to walk? (The Communists have sometimes done better by exploiting caste blocs—as in Andhra and Kerala. Even Swatantra is learning, from some of its new-found allies of the 1962 elections.) In any case, in the world of 'traditional' politics, governments are not changed or chosen so much as used or evaded. The circle is a most vicious one: you can't be taken seriously by the local men who matter until you are the government, but you can't be the government until you have been taken seriously. It is interesting to reflect that nothing but adult franchise could have secured Congress rule with such certain stability; a more restricted franchise would have meant the conduct of politics in much more purely 'modern' terms, and that would have permitted a much greater 'openness of texture' and flexibility.

Thus, the vital educated middle classes are politically quite frustrated. They have no liking or trust or confidence in Congress, but they cannot budge it because the levers are not in their hands. So the 'modern' opposition remains puny, the 'traditional' 'opposition' works in other ways, and the student masses (the jargon seems correct in India's case) become a shade more cynical and despairing as each year passes. Of course, a dozen years of stable government in the wake of independence and partition is no mean blessing, as every administrator in India knows. Yet the disadvantages are now beginning to become substantial. The icepack is forming and the ship of state may soon be crushed. The most obvious dynamite available to break the ice and permit free political navigation is the withdrawal of Nehru. If that were to happen, Congress would less easily hold together. (No one else has such wide and varied appeal. No one else is so regulaaly forgiven. No one else has his ability and dedication. No one else could confuse the issues and blur the distinctions to the degree that Congress leadership demands.) In that case—and despite the temptation for all factions to stay under the Congress shelter—struggle could become more open. There would be awful dangers and great losses but there are days when these seem to be less terrifying than those entailed in getting frozen up.

TRADITION AND EXPERIMENT
IN FORMS OF GOVERNMENT

HUGH TINKER

*Reader in Government and Politics with reference to Asia
in the University of London*

As the movement for Indian political freedom gathered impetus in
the 1920's and 1930's, its objectives were only vaguely related to forms
of government. The Congress decision to boycott the Dyarchy
experiment reflected the negligible interest of Congress, led by
Gandhi, in experience in administration at the provincial or local
level: which was in striking contrast to the older generation of
Indian Liberals with their faith in the virtues of 'political education'
through work as Ministers and Municipal Councillors. In part, this
Congress attitude was a reaction against the British approach, consisting in juggling with constitutional formulae to evolve a system of
checks and balances which would conform to the *communitas com-
munitatum* which history, religious custom, and British policy had
created. To this constitutional conjuring, the Congress retaliated with
an unequivocal demand for freedom, culminating in Gandhi's call in
1942 to 'Quit India'. Gandhi, indeed, was responsible for a more
fundamental attitude of indifference or even hostility to constitutional
problems. His philosophy, drawn from Tolstoy and Kropotkin,
rejected the modern state as a foreign accretion upon the true India
which he saw as a federation of village republics, *Panchayat Raj.*
'That state will be the best which is governed the least', declared
Gandhi, and 'Society based on non-violence can only consist of groups
settled in villages in which voluntary co-operation is the condition of
dignified and peaceful existence. . . . The nearest approach to civilization based on non-violence is the erstwhile village republic of India.'
An interpretation of his political ideas was offered in *Gandhian
Constitution for Free India* (from which the above quotations come).[1]
The village shall elect its panchayat and sarpanch (president), and
about twenty villages shall be grouped in a taluka panchayat, consisting of these presidents. A District panchayat shall be formed from

[1] S. N. Agarwal, *Gandhian Constitution for Free India* (1946), pp. 39, 58.

the presidents of the taluka panchayats; these in turn contribute to Provincial panchayats, and these to a National panchayat. But the main fount of political, social and economic activity should remain the village panchayat. Great emphasis was placed on the need for unanimity in the choice of members, or alternatively in choice by lot: the purpose being to eliminate bitterness and faction from village life. In this *Gandhian Constitution*, many aspects of politics were simply passed over; as for example foreign relations, the role of the public services, and the machinery of law enforcement. This approach accorded with the traditional Hindu feeling that the nexus of caste and custom is infinitely more meaningful and binding than the panoply of imposed power which the state represented, from the Sultanate down to modern times. That element in Congress which looked to Nehru was most concerned with the problem of mobilizing the state to harness the means of production through Socialism: 'the failure of parliamentary democracy is not that it has gone too far, but that it did not go far enough . . . it did not provide for economic democracy.'[1] The Congress attitude to political institutions was expressed in a demand for a Constituent Assembly to determine the future structure of government (1934) and the formation of a National Planning Committee (1937) with Nehru as Chairman to co-ordinate the economic development of India.

The Muslim League, to an even greater degree, concentrated on the ultimate goal—independence—or liberation from Hindu rule. And while the Congress acquired some experience of administration in the Ministries of 1937–9, and then again after the 1945 elections, the League was able to form Ministries in 1946 only in two of the five provinces claimed for Pakistan (Bengal and Sind). Hence, the League's ideas on government were even less coherently formulated than those of the Congress.

The British Government's plan for the transfer of power entailed a transition period during which India and Pakistan functioned as Dominions under the 1935 Government of India Act. It was not, therefore, surprising that this 1935 Act became the framework of the two new countries' constitutions.

When the Constituent Assembly met in December 1946, expectations were still fixed on a loosely federated but united India. The terms of reference of the constitution-makers were defined in a Resolution on Aims and Objects, moved by Nehru, of which para. 3 states:

[1] Jawaharlal Nehru, *Autobiography* (1936), p. 530.

The said territories [British India and the Princely States] . . . shall possess and retain the status of autonomous units, together with residuary powers, and exercise all powers and functions of government and administration, save and except such powers and functions as are vested in or assigned to the Union.[1]

This was to be a loose federation, not unlike the United States under the Articles of Confederation. Even at this stage, Dr Ambedkar (soon to be Chairman of the Drafting Committee) called for 'a strong united Centre, much stronger than the Centre we had under the Act of 1935', while a solitary reference to Gandhi's *Panchayat Raj* was made by M. R. Masani, still in his Socialist-Marxist phase.[2]

After partition, with the need to mollify the Muslims removed, there was an overwhelming urge towards national unification, leading to the integration of the Princely States. Nehru and Patel played almost no part in the Assembly's proceedings, and the actual drafting of the constitution was left entirely to Sir B. N. Rau, the Constitutional Adviser. In March 1947 he circulated an elaborate questionnaire to all members of the Central and Provincial legislatures, and later to the Committee specially formed to report on the main principles of the constitution.[3] From this large-scale inquiry, Rau received exactly one reply.[4] Under these circumstances, he set out to write his own draft. Having been intimately connected with the introduction of the 1935 Act, it was natural that he should follow its provisions in detail. The pattern was only seriously questioned by the Assembly in regard to the basic electoral unit. Instead of election by universal franchise, some members urged that village panchayats should be charged with the electoral choice. The proposal did not meet with sympathy from Rau, and was rejected with scorn by Dr Ambedkar on the second reading of the draft constitution. He declared 'The love of the intellectual Indian for the village community is of course infinite if not pathetic', and added 'I hold that these village republics have been the ruination of India. . . . What is the village but a sink of localism, a den of ignorance, narrow-mindedness and communalism? I am glad that the Draft Constitution has discarded the village and adopted the

[1] *Constituent Assembly Debates*, vol. i, p. 56.
[2] *Ibid.*, pp. 91, 99.
[3] B. N. Rau, *India's Constitution in the Making* (1960), pp. 16–41. Items included: What should be the designation of the head of the Indian Union? How should he be chosen? Should the office rotate among the different communities in turn?
[4] *Ibid.*, p. 62.

individual as its unit.'[1] Otherwise, the labyrinthine debates of the Assembly seldom touched upon questions of government as such.

The most talked-over subjects were those of the minorities and their rights, language questions, and even such refinements as whether the United Provinces should be renamed Aryavarta or Gangavarta, or neither.

The constitution in its final form embodies certain fundamental rights and directive principles; Sir B. N. Rau refers to them as 'moral precepts',[2] and they were less cautiously defined by another leader as 'solemn promises and pious platitudes'.[3] Among these Directive Principles, the Gandhian state was buried away. Article 40 directs the setting up of village panchayats; Article 43 makes a brief reference to cottage industries; Article 47 requires the state to 'endeavour to bring about prohibition'; Article 48 urges a ban on cow slaughter. The remainder of the constitution 'is essentially the Act of 1935', as Dr P. S. Deshmukh observed.

When the constitution was finally adopted, two main schools of opinion declared themselves. One section—the smaller, and in general composed of the Liberals and moderates, former administrators and jurists—welcomed the constitution as a worthy instrument of government. This 'moderate' viewpoint was most plainly stated by Dr P. Subbarayan of Madras:

There are two things that the British have left behind for us; one is the efficiency of the civil service and the other is the rule of law. And I think both these points have . . . been incorporated in this constitution, because without an efficient civil service it will be impossible for the government to be carried on and for the continuity of policy to be kept. . . . Unless there is continuity there is bound to be chaos. . . . The second point . . . is the rule of law. . . . If there is anything I would like to cling to in the future of this country it is this rule of law. . . . I think we have provided in the constitution, in the powers vested both in the Supreme Court and the High Courts . . . for any citizen to have his right established as against the government of the day.[4]

To the Liberals, the principal lacuna in the constitution was the failure to give statutory force to the conviction (maintained since

---

[1] *Constituent Assembly Debates*, vol. vii, p. 39.
[2] Rau, *op. cit.*, p. 364.
[3] *Constituent Assembly Debates*, vol. xi, p. 753; Sardar Hukam Singh.
[4] *Ibid.*, p. 962.

the days of S. N. Banerjea and Pherozeshah Mehta) that there must be a complete separation of the judiciary from the executive. This relic of Mughal administration, perpetuated in the role of the District Magistrate, with his dual executive and judicial functions, had been regularly condemned in Congress resolutions. The constitution, to be sure, acknowledged this among the Directive Principles (Article 50); but, as Pandit Kunzru pointed out, the constitution-makers had drawn the teeth out of this proposition by dropping the original requirement that this separation should be carried out within three years.[1]

A much larger element deplored the whole constitution as a betrayal of Gandhian ideals and of the ancient spirit of India. From outside the Assembly, the Premier of Uttar Pradesh, Sampurnanand, declared:

Our constitution is a miserable failure. The spirit of Indian culture has not breathed on it: the Gandhism by which we swear so vehemently at home and abroad does not inspire it. It is just a piece of legislation like, say, the Motor Vehicles Act.[2]

Within the Assembly, members called their brainchild a 'cocktail', 'khichri' (kedgeree), and 'hybrid'. Others found in it evidence of the slave mentality: 'It is just like a bird which has lived in a cage all its life: when released it wants to go back to the cage'; 'The British quitted but physically; they left behind many things that they had created. . . . The constitution naturally reflects the *status quo*.'[3] This discontent (which was voiced unceasingly until the day the Assembly finally dispersed) concentrated on the need for decentralization. The original design was said to have been destroyed, and a highly centralized structure foisted upon the nation. Sampurnanand emphasized this feature:

The attempt at centralization of all power is hardly veiled and provincial governments have been sought to be reduced to the position of agents of the Centre. This is bad.

Gandhi, speakers reiterated, had taught quite otherwise:

The first and foremost advice which he gave . . . was that the constitutional structure of this country ought to be broad-based and pyramid-like. It should be built from the bottom and should taper right up to the top. What has been done is just the reverse.[4]

---

[1] *Constituent Assembly Debates*, vol. xi, p. 783.
[2] Address to University Convocation, Agra, November 19, 1949.
[3] *Constituent Assembly Debates*, vol. xi, p. 732.
[4] *Ibid.*, pp. 616–17; K. Hanumanthaiya.

What was needed was 'a Co-operative Commonwealth; as Bapu was good enough to call it, through the Kisan-Mazdoor-Buddhi jeevi-Kalakar raj'.[1]

As the specific answer to centralization, speaker after speaker urged the need for *Panchayat Raj*. Thus H. V. Kamath:

A time will arrive when India is stabilized and strong, and I hope we will then go back to the old plan of the Panchayat Raj or decentralized democracy, with village units self-sufficient in food, clothing and shelter and interdependent as regards other matters. I hope we will go back to that Panchayat Raj, Sir; to my mind the only system that will serve India and the world is what I may call spiritual communism.[2]

Some urged the total abolition of central government, like Ramnarayan Singh: 'Our country and our society does not need a government. . . . We need in our country Sevak Mandals, Societies of Servants, and not a government.'[3] Much of this thinking harked back to a legendary golden age; some was based in a concept of 'the Indian Revolution', which the constitution-makers had betrayed. All this feeling was ineffectual: but it was nonetheless deeply felt.

During the first years of independence, the political predominance of Nehru and Sardar Patel meant that their concepts of government were almost unchallengeable: national unity, modernization, and modified forms of State Socialism: these impelled the government machine. The considerable political forces searching for indigenous political patterns were held in check. But the demand for indigenous systems of government, and the resentment of the simulacrum of British administration which still prevailed in New Delhi, were only to be temporarily arrested.

The constitutional debate in Pakistan was infinitely more protracted than in India, and a constitution was not evolved until February 1956. Until then, the country was governed under the 1935 Government of India Act, somewhat amended and modified. The 1956 Constitution was never fully put into effect, and was totally obliterated by the military take-over of October 1958. In itself, therefore, this constitution was of transient significance, but the protracted constitutional debate requires understanding, reflecting, as it did, the confused political legacy which Mohammad Ali Jinnah left to Pakistan.

---

[1] *Constituent Assembly Debates*, p. 630; Professor N. G. Ranga.
[2] *Ibid.*, p. 690.   [3] *Ibid.*, p. 640.

From its inception, the leaders of the new nation were faced with two overriding questions: the role of Islam in the new state, and the relations between the East and West wings and the central government. Thus, the political debate to a large degree ran parallel to that in India. How far should the institutions of the new state be established on an indigenous ideology? Should the state proceed in the direction of centralization, or decentralization? But whereas the Gandhian doctrine was reasonably well defined, and its terms were not disputed even by those who (like Nehru) differed in their political philosophy, Jinnah left no accepted declaration of political faith, and his views were rapidly by-passed by those who sought to establish Pakistan as an Arab polity of the time of the Prophet.

Jinnah's concept of the new nation was enunciated in his inaugural speech to the Constituent Assembly of Pakistan, delivered on August 11, 1947. He urged his people to

Work together in a spirit that every one of you, no matter to what community he belong . . . no matter what is his caste, colour or creed, is first, second and last a citizen of this State with equal rights, privileges and obligations. . . . I cannot emphasize it too much. We should begin to work in that spirit and in course of time all these angularities of the majority and minority communities . . . will vanish. . . . You may belong to any religion or caste or creed—that has nothing to do with the State. We are starting with the fundamental principle that we are all citizens, and equal citizens of one State. . . . Today you might say with justice that [in Britain] Roman Catholics and Pro-testants do not exist: what exists now is that every man is a citizen, an equal citizen of Great Britain and they are all members of the nation. Now, I think that we should keep that in front of us as our ideal and you will find that in course of time Hindus would cease to be Hindus and Muslims would cease to be Muslims; not in the religious sense, because that is the personal faith of each individual; but in the political sense as citizens of the State.[1]

This vision of a secular state recommended itself to very few. Those who accepted its implications remained on the defensive, and the offensive was taken by the champions of an Islamic polity, of whom Maulana Abul Ala Maududi, founder of the *Jama'at-i-Islami*, was foremost. This party rejected the concept of a state based upon nationalism, and aimed at 'the establishment of the sovereignty of Allah throughout the world'. Pakistan was regarded by the Maulana

[1] *Constituent Assembly of Pakistan, Debates,* vol. i, no. 2, pp. 18–20.

as *kufr*, and all who took part in the operation of its government were sinners.[1] The equivocal attitude of the ruling Muslim League led to uneasy compromises such as the Objectives Resolution, adopted in February 1949, which subsequently became the preamble to the 1956 Constitution. The outspoken Munir Report (an inquiry into the fanatical riots against the Ahmadiyyah movement) characterized this Resolution as 'nothing but a hoax', pointing to the illogicality of commencing 'Sovereignty over the entire Universe belongs to Allah Almighty alone' . . . and then proceeding 'the Constituent Assembly . . . have resolved to frame for the sovereign independent State of Pakistan a constitution'. Justice Munir pointed out that 'An Islamic State . . . cannot be sovereign, because it will not be competent to abrogate, repeal or do away with any law in the *Qur'ān* or the *Sunna*. . . . In an Islamic State, sovereignty in its essentially juristic sense can only rest with Allah.' Thus, he argued, an Islamic state cannot be a democracy: even the legislature will not be responsible to the people, 'because *ijma'-i-ummat* in Islamic jurisprudence is restricted to *ulama* and *mutjahids* of acknowledged status and does not at all extend, as in democracy, to the populace'. The judge went on to declare that 'Legislature in its present sense is unknown to the Islamic system. There is in it no sanction for what may, in the modern sense, be called legislation.'[2] These paradoxes were not merely the contrivances of an acute legal brain. A basic principles committee wrestled with the dilemma from March 1949 to December 1952, when it was proposed that 'the head of the State, who should be a Muslim, should constitute a board of not more than five persons, well versed in Islamic laws, to advise the head of the State about the repugnancy of new laws to the *Qur'ān* and the *Sunna*'.[3] This proposal met with steady opposition from among the barrister-politicians, as introducing a vetoing power, owing responsibility to nobody. Eventually, the constitution evaded the issue, by including a provision (Article 198) for setting up a Commission to consider the question: this was never put into effect.

The second great dispute revolved round relations between East and West Pakistan. The former feared the domination of the West, specifically of the Punjabis. Attempts to make Urdu the sole national language were regarded as the symbol of this domination, being violently denounced in Bengal, and eventually two national languages were established: Urdu and Bengali (Article 214). A second conflict

[1] *Report of the Court of Inquiry constituted under Punjab Act II of 1954 to inquire into the Punjab disturbances of 1953* (1954), p. 243.
[2] *Ibid.*, p. 203.　　　　　　　　　　[3] *The Times*, December 23, 1952.

arose from the existence of one administrative unit in the East, the province of East Bengal, and a medley of administrative powers in the West, four provinces, several Princely States, and the semi-independent tribal areas. This array of forces was supposed to lend additional weight to the West wing in politics and government, accentuating the Western bias of political power and economic development. A movement for 'one unit' for West Pakistan gathered way, led especially by Mr Suhrawardy and his Awami League. A number of coalition governments came and went as pressures waxed and waned over this issue. The Establishment of West Pakistan Act of 1955 eventually brought about the integration of the provinces, states, and other areas of the Western wing into one unit.[1] The new system centralized provincial administration at Lahore, and there was considerable resentment among Pathans, Sindhis, and Baluchis at their subordination to Punjab, as they termed the new arrangement. These local divisions had their repercussions, contributing to the growing unrest and irresponsibility in national politics.

As was stated earlier, the tensions implicit in the situation in India were masked for a number of years by the dominance exercised by the centre. The powers of the President under Article 356 have been invoked in Punjab, in Andhra, and in Kerala: parliamentary government has been suspended, and a gubernatorial autocracy temporarily substituted.[2] An even greater centralizing, arbitrary authority (never contemplated by the constitution-makers) has been created by the Planning Commission, a body not envisaged in the 395 Articles and 9 Schedules of the constitution. The Planning Commission was set up in March 1950 by a Resolution of the Government of India, an administrative fiat. One authority calls it 'the Economic Cabinet, not merely for the Union but also for the States'.[3] Its relation to statutory forms of government remains undefined. The Prime Minister has been Chairman of the Commission from its inception (he is the sole remaining original member) and a Minister for Planning, responsible to parliament, was appointed in September 1951: these are the only

[1] The tribal areas of Baluchistan and the North West Frontier Province, and the States of Amb, Chitral, Dir, and Swat were expressly excluded from the legislative power of the West Pakistan Legislature, and the Governor-General was given specific supervisory functions over the Governor of West Pakistan in administering and legislating for these 'special areas'. 1955 Act, Section 3.

[2] President Prasad is said to have threatened to use his power of veto at least once to the central Cabinet: in October 1951, in connection with the Hindu Code Bill.

[3] Asok Chanda, *Indian Administration* (1958), p. 92.

channels whereby the Commission can be held responsible to the nation. The Deputy Chairman, Sir V. T. Krishnamachari, is a former Dewan of Baroda who is not an M.P.; and the *éminence grise* of the Commission, its Statistical Adviser, Professor P. C. Mahlenobis, is a *frondeur* in both academic and public life. The Commission has an authority parallel to that of the Cabinet, and soon after its inception the Finance Minister, Dr John Matthai, resigned on the grounds that the Commission was trenching upon the collective responsibility of the Ministers.[1] The Commission gave birth to a number of ancillary bodies, such as the Programme Evaluation Organization, the National Development Council, the Committee on Plan Projects, the Statistical Institute, and the various technical divisions. Most of these are empowered to investigate and recommend courses of policy which cover almost every aspect of the national life.[2] The consequences of one such investigation, the *Report of the Team for the Study of Community Projects*, will be considered in this paper.

The power of the Commission lies in its control over the distribution of economic resources between the states. For the Second Five Year Plan, the states proposed to spend over Rs. 2,100 crores; their ability to meet their own needs from revenue, loans, etc., amounted to Rs. 823 crores; some 60 per cent of their requirements had to be found from Central resources. Bombay was able to provide for about two-thirds of its planned expenditure internally, and Madras for about 55 per cent: all other states were heavily dependent on the Centre.[3] Besides allocating subventions, the Planning Commission also determined forms of developments and its dictates were absolute in the field of industrialization. However, the states had some means of asserting themselves in that, apart from a few major projects directly under Central direction, the great mass of projects were being implemented by the states: the Centre might propose, the states could dispose. Despite appeals from the Prime Minister to all State Ministries to keep strictly within their allocations, all the states have

---

[1] Resignation Statement, May 31, 1950.

[2] For a full description of the Planning Commission's ramifications see *The Organisation of the Government of India*, Indian Institute of Public Administration, Bombay, 1958, pp. 342–53. Studies made by one of the Technical Divisions, that for Education, have ranged over school feeding, and a schools health service; Hindi, and Regional languages; National Archives, National Theatres, National Cadet Corps, Social Service Camps, etc.: any division can investigate almost anything.

[3] *Second Five Year Plan* (1956), pp. 85, 106–7.

regularly exceeded their budgets; some, like Bihar, by gigantic amounts. The unpopularity of the Planning Commission among the states is likely to lead to intensive pressure for its abolition when Mr Nehru finally ceases to be Prime Minister.

Apart from this extra-constitutional organization there were few innovations in the political institutions of independent India. Parliamentary government at the Centre and at the state level functioned, so far as procedure went, exactly as at Westminster. Such novelties as the Assurances Committee (an attempt to make ministers and officials answerable to the M.P.s) and the Delegated Legislation Committee (formed to supervise all orders and rules made by ministers under their statutory powers) were completely in the spirit of the Mother of Parliaments. The civil service continued to play a unique part in national life. The First Five Year Plan forecast that the 'first effect . . . of development will be to increase the district officer's work and responsibilities still further', and this has certainly occurred.[1] The separation of judicial from executive functions, anticipated in the constitution, has taken place only to a very limited extent. For example, of the fifty districts of Uttar Pradesh, in seventeen an Additional District Magistrate (Judicial) has been appointed: but he is supervised by the Commissioner (a senior executive officer) and he is still liable to be called upon by the District Magistrate for riot duty (an executive function).

In the sphere of local self-government, the trend has been back towards autocracy. In state after state, the District Boards have been abolished or superseded. 'The gradual erosion of District Boards from the social polity' has been partly due to their inability and unwillingness to expand their incomes in a period of rising prices and rising expectations. Even existing taxes were not fully realized. Another cause was the emergence of new and more potent authorities. In almost every state, District Planning Committees were constituted, sapping the powers of the District Boards.[2] Another factor is what one writer calls 'intolerance towards political minorities'.[3] Congress governments have resented the success of the Communist Party in bringing local bodies under control. The party directed a considerable part of its effort towards winning local elections. The party Draft

---

[1] *First Five Year Plan* (1952), p. 131.

[2] *Report of the Team for the Study of Community Projects and National Extension Service* (the 'Balvantray Report') (1957), vol. ii, pp. 10–12.

[3] V. Venkata Rao, *A Hundred Years of Local Self-Government in the Andhra and Madras States* (1960), p. 484.

Resolution of 1953 harks back to the political education principles of Gokhale and Pherozeshah Mehta:

Our comrades have been returned in large numbers to many Municipalities, Local Boards and Panchayats. A correct understanding of our tasks in the municipal and local bodies is even more urgent than [in] the legislatures. The Municipalities are positive centres of some amount of power directly in the hands of the people's representatives, unlike the legislatures, where the legislative and executive functions being separated and the organs of the executive being totally outside the pressure of the people's representatives, no positive tasks of execution as such can be done by the legislators. It is not so in the municipal and local bodies. . . . The British rulers also, in order to buy over the liberal bourgeoisie and to give a safety valve called these institutions 'Local Self Government'. As a result, the municipal and local bodies have come to possess some amount of importance and power in the local life of the people. . . . However poor and meagre be the powers, these small centres [have] . . . power to do good to the life of the people. Our representatives must learn the art of running them properly. They are surely not speech-broadcasting houses only. Local Self Government must become the platform of strengthening the people's solidarity. . . . We have to see . . . that our cadres in these bodies do get serious education in the running of these bodies.[1]

Communist successes included the domination of the cities of Calcutta, Bombay, Madras and Delhi at different periods of the '50's. Their rise to power was frequently caused by extraneous issues, such as the demand for a separate Maharashtrian State, which led to the election of a Communist Mayor of Bombay.

Along with the erosion of the powers of municipalities and District Boards went the limitation of the powers of the city corporations: the bodies where a civic spirit had, perhaps, shown most vigour. The office of Municipal Commissioner as permanent head of the city administration, with a wide and well-defined range of authority, was extended from the City of Bombay to Calcutta, Madras, Ahmedabad, and Poona. A tendency was apparent for the absorption of suburban municipalities in an all-embracing authority for the conurbation: a 'Greater Bombay' (1951-2) and 'Greater Poona' (1952) were constituted, with a new Delhi Corporation (1958) covering the old city

[1] V. B. Karnik (ed.), *Indian Communist Party Documents*, 1930–1956 (1957), pp. 121–2.

and the new residential areas, though not New Delhi. These developments were intended to provide some counterpoise of central authority to political truculence and independence.[1]

Against the decline of the institutions of local self-government founded on the British pattern must be set the attempt to establish village panchayats throughout the country. The legislation under which they came into being reveals different objectives. Some states were attempting to find a new kind of organization which would go some way towards realizing the Gandhian ideal. Others were more concerned to establish an authority which would form a suitable unit of administration. In the first instance, panchayats were established for every rural community, however small, on the grounds that the village or hamlet is the 'little society', the microcosm of the Indian community. Thus, in Uttar Pradesh, there is a panchayat for every hamlet with a minimum population of 250 souls. The whole village is given its part to play in the *Gaon Sabha* or village meeting, which all adults are entitled to attend. The *Gaon Sabha* meets twice a year, after harvest; it elects a Chairman, the *Pradhan*, and a council, the *Gaon Panchayat*; it also helps to choose a judicial tribunal, the *Nyaya Panchayat*. The village's budget must be submitted to the *Gaon Sabha*, which can debate all the business transacted by the Panchayat, and if it wishes remove the *Pradhan* or other members from office. An example of the other form of panchayat is to be found in Madras. Under the 1950 Act, there are two classes of panchayat. The first class is confined to towns with a population of 5,000 and above, with an annual income of Rs.10,000. These panchayats employ an Executive Officer, and are municipalities in all but name. The second class consists of smaller units: villages with less than 500 inhabitants are grouped into unions. The 'small panchayat' group comprises Uttar Pradesh, Madhya Pradesh, Punjab, and Bombay; the 'large panchayat' states are Madras, Andhra, Orissa, Bihar, Rajasthan, Kerala, and Himachal Pradesh: West Bengal, Mysore, and Assam 'have not made any appreciable progress in establishing panchayats'.[2] By 1956, there were 123,670 panchayats for about 280,000 villages: over half the total number of villages in the country.

[1] According to the central Minister for Community Development: 'We destroyed Local Self Government Institutions because, we say, they had grown to be seats of decadence, faction, inefficiency and maladministration. We nurtured the illusion . . . that it was much easier to administer the country through Government servants.' S. K. Dey, *Community Development* (1960), vol. ii, p. 184.

[2] *Fifth Evaluation Report*, Planning Commission (1958), p. 17.

POLITICS AND SOCIETY IN INDIA

These figures do not imply that panchayats are actually functioning in half the villages of India: it has been estimated that 'not more than 10 per cent of the total number are functioning effectively'. Their poor performance reflects the circumstances of rural life. Faction dominates most Indian villages, and 'the number of panchayats which are torn by factions or in which squabbles are rampant is large. In fact in some states they are in a majority! 'Panchayat elections have resulted in creating or aggravating factional rivalries in about one-third of the villages in which there is a contest'; 'separatism arising out of caste distinction' is said to be on the increase. 'Often the panchayats consisted mostly of the wealthy and influential persons. It has been observed that in spite of the provisions contained in the Panchayats Acts for . . . reservation of seats for Scheduled Castes/ Tribes and Harijans, in general panchayats cannot be said to command the loyalty of all sections of the community . . .; in practice the economically weaker sections have as yet little voice in the affairs of panchayats. In some cases they are in debt to the Sarpanch who is often a man of substance.'[1]

It seems probable that, in many villages, the statutory panchayat exists merely as a 'front' organization, and that the real locus of power remains in the hands of influential villagers who function as go-betweens or patrons in village negotiations, bargains, and disputes. A series of studies of power and leadership in different parts of rural India is prefaced by this observation:

While in all these villages the traditional caste panchayats continue to meet and to carry weight, in none of them does the government or judicial panchayat have prestige. The long identification of government officials with an alien or unsympathetic government has apparently not been disturbed by the events of independence. . . . In some villages, the village leaders of recognized stature have consented to assume offices in the government panchayat. But such membership is not the source of their leadership.[2]

In the middle 1950's the political scene in India was clouded by dissatisfaction. In the sphere of parliamentary government there was discontent with the increasing centralization of administration, and with the functioning of western-style democracy, for which the

[1] Balvantray Report, vol. ii, pp. 1–12.
[2] R. L. Park and I. Tinker (eds.), *Leadership and Political Institutions in India* (1959), p. 393.

phrase 'Fifty-one Per Cent Democracy' was becoming fashionable. This view was given point after the 1956 General Election when, in seven of the thirteen states of the Union, Congress governments retained power on a minority vote.[1] Copy-book imitation of western political institutions had fallen short of expectations: but so had the new village panchayats, which signally failed to create the *Panchayat Raj* of Gandhian belief. Everywhere, political theorists and practitioners began to talk of the need for rethinking.

India's search for new forms of political expression did not extend to the desperate lengths of Pakistan's renunciation of copy-book parliamentary democracy by the military coup of 1958.

After Jinnah and Liaqat Ali Khan were removed from the reins of power, the stability of the whole system, no less, was the supreme issue of government. The penetrating Munir Report concluded with an enigmatic reflection upon the relation between politics and religion under a system of government established in the name of democracy:

We are prompted . . . to enquire whether, in our present state of political development, the administrative problem of law and order cannot be divorced from a democratic bedfellow called a Ministerial Government, which is so remorselessly haunted by political nightmares. But if democracy means the subordination of law and order to political ends—then Allah knoweth best and we end the report.[2]

The Muslim League's pretensions to form a 'Freedom Movement' were shattered by total defeat in the East Pakistan elections of 1954, and it was succeeded by parties of fragmentation. The only firm hand ready to steady the ship of state on its erratic course was that of the Governor-General. Pakistan's constitutional evolution was influenced (though probably not intentionally) by Jinnah's assuming the office of Governor-General with its legacy of Mughal and Viceregal power, while the office of Prime Minister was overshadowed and, after the assassination of Liaqat Ali Khan, diminished in authority. Ghulam Mohammad, Governor-General from 1951, regarded his office as the ultimate reserve of power: he dismissed Nazimuddin from the premiership in 1953 for his pusillanimous hesitation during the Ahmadiyyah riots, even though he still enjoyed a majority in the

---

[1] The Congress share of the popular vote was as follows: West Bengal, 49·2 per cent; Bombay, 48·6 per cent; Madras, 46·5 per cent; Uttar Pradesh, 46·3 per cent; Bihar, 44·5 per cent; Orissa, 40 per cent; Kerala, 37·5 per cent.

[2] *Report of the Court of Inquiry . . . ,* p. 387.

Constituent Assembly. When the latter attempted to restrain him it was dissolved in October 1954.[1]

The cloak of juridical sanction was afforded to this action by the Supreme Court, but increasingly the concept of the supremacy of law and the omnicompetence of the constitutional lawyers was giving way to the ancient sanction of military might. Ghulam Mohammad was succeeded as Governor-General (and subsequently President) by Major-General Iskander Mirza, a tough and wily former Frontier political officer. The Constituent Assembly, reconvened by direction of the Supreme Court, attempted to bind the Head of the Executive by exactly defining his powers and by declaring that 'the President shall act in accordance with the advice of the Cabinet' (Article 37). However, within three months of the promulgation of the new constitution it had been suspended in East Pakistan by Presidential fiat, on a report from the Governor that 'a situation has arisen in which the government of the province cannot be carried on in accordance with the provisions of the constitution'.[2] Thereafter, Mr Suhrawardy was able for a time to re-establish the role of the politician as prime minister: but the forces of faction and division were not stayed. In March 1957 it was the turn of West Pakistan to witness the constitution suspended, as the only alternative to chaos. Finally, on October 7, 1958, President Mirza declared martial law and formally abrogated the constitution. General Ayub Khan, the Commander-in-Chief, was summoned to take over the management of the country. He declared: 'My authority is revolution; I have no sanction in law or constitution.'[3] The General chose his words well. Ideologically, the new régime was the reverse of 'revolutionary'; its political and social ethos marked a return to the heyday of Lord Curzon. Yet it was truly revolutionary in utterly renouncing the dogma held by generations of nationalist leaders that all that was needed by the nations of Asia was to be freed from Colonialism, and to adopt parliaments, and party systems, in order to enjoy a state of political bliss; and in rejecting the belief that these institutions could be brought into existence by the activities of learned legal draftsmen, spinning their clauses, articles and schedules.

At first, the military régime's energies were devoted to practical reforms: to fighting inflation and the rackets, to solving the scandal

[1] Under the 1935 Government of India Act, the Governor-General had the power to dissolve the legislature (Section 19), but this power had been omitted under the Governor-General's Ordinance 22 of 1947.

[2] *The Times*, May 28, 1956.   [3] *Pakistan Times*, October 10, 1958.

of refugees waiting ten years for housing. But the military leaders were conscious that these activities merely provided a holding operation. There must, eventually, be a planned advance: but in which direction, and under whose leadership? Almost all the leading politicians had been required to retire from public life for a six-year period, and those few (like Mr Suhrawardy) who refused to don the penitent's garb voluntarily, were haled before Special Courts where their public life was scrutinized in minute and damaging detail.[1] The lawyer-politicians then, were debarred from leadership: the great landlords, who had dominated West Pakistan politics, were deprived of much of their power by measures of land reform. The civil servants, also, were suspect for their connivance with the discredited politicians. The intellectuals and the students were served notice that the noisy protests of former days would no longer be tolerated. From whence might come the new forces of leadership for a rejuvenated Pakistan?

General Ayub's solution harked back to that of nineteenth century British administrators: he sought to evolve a system of representation based upon the 'natural leaders' of society. These 'natural leaders' were looked for among the men of influence and standing among a predominantly rural, traditional society. In West Pakistan these might be the 'squire' or *chaudhri*, the retired army officer, the prosperous peasantry. In East Pakistan these 'natural leaders' were sometimes prominent villagers (known as *Sardar, Morol,* or *Matbar*), but more often were leaders by profession, like the village schoolmaster, the *mulla, maulvi* or *pir*, the local holy man; and occasionally a conscientious, resident land-holder. This leadership was to be deployed by means of a pyramid of councils, based upon the Union Council, directly elected by the people, and leading up to provincial councils at the apex. This tier upon tier of indirectly elected bodies is not dissimilar to the system in operation between 1892 and 1909, when the members of provincial legislatures were partially chosen by electoral colleges provided by the Municipal Councils and District Boards; these non-official members of the provincial legislatures in turn selected four of their number to become members of the Viceroy's Legislative Council. The philosophy of the new order was also similar to that of the Ripon school of local self-government enthusiasts: it was hoped that through actual experience of the working of public services at a local level, leaders could be trained to manage national affairs. In the Ripon period this was often called 'political education'; President Ayub named his new experiment

---

[1] Proceedings were taken under the Elective Bodies (Disqualification) Order.

'Basic Democracy': democracy 'of the type that people can understand and work'.[1]

The new bodies were constituted under the Basic Democracies Order of October 1959. The foundation, the Union Council, inherited an established unit of administration, the Union Board in East Pakistan; comprising a group of villages with a combined population of about 10,000. In West Pakistan there was no such precedent: previously there had been a very limited number of village councils, with the District Boards above, and no unit of self-government in between. The Union Council is mainly elected by the village folk, but some nominated members are appointed by the District Officer. All members are non-officials. Town Committees are similarly established for the smaller towns, replacing former minor municipalities. Chairmen are elected by the members of the Union Councils, and they in turn are ex-officio members of the next tier, the *Thana* Council (East) or *Tahsil* Council (West). The chairman and some members of these bodies are district officials. Then comes the District Council: the chairmen of the sub-district councils are ex-officio members, but as these are officials, the link which is supposed to join together village and nation is broken at this level. A number of non-officials are appointed to the District Councils—chairmen of municipalities, and selected chairmen of Union Councils. These non-officials may not exceed the number of officials.

The district and sub-district councils are, at present, co-ordinating bodies, extensions of the machinery of district and departmental administration. Potentially, under the terms of the Basic Democracies Order, they are capable of becoming representative, and even responsible bodies; but their early functioning provides little indication of the direction in which they are likely to move. Most attention has been focused upon the Union Councils as the fundamental organs in which the pattern of growth will emerge: to these bodies and to their members, the generic term 'Basic Democracies' and 'Basic Democrats' has been applied.

In East Pakistan the members of the new Union Councils are, in the main, similar to (in many cases, identical with) the members of the former Union Boards. They come from the rural middle class, those who are indeed 'middle men' between the village folk and the town. By far the largest group are the lawyers; together with contractors, holders of licences and concessions, and other traders; together with a few landlords. In the West, the social origins of the

[1] *The Times*, October 27, 1959.

members are more diverse, and more specifically rural. Traditional views of leadership have almost entirely excluded the landless men and the more lowly castes and tribes from the councils, but many peasants lacking formal education have been elected.[1] The predominant element is provided by the 'yeoman' farmer. The proportion of graduates among members in the West is said to be 10 per cent in the town committees, and 2 per cent in the rural councils: figures which have some relation to the educational background of the electorate.

The functions allotted to the new councils are far-reaching, and their potential financial resources are also considerable: but these are allotted on a permissive, not a compulsory basis, and in consequence the councils in their early days have continued to levy much the same taxes as the old Union Boards in the East, and have necessarily been limited to the same restricted exercise of their functions. In the West, some councils are reported to have shown more enterprise. The councils (especially their chairmen and secretaries) are to be stimulated and instructed by the junior district staff, the Circle Officers in the East and tahsildars in the West. But it is unlikely that a new spirit will rapidly appear. It has long been accepted among the middle class or more prosperous element who have predominated in local bodies, that local self-government means low (indeed, nominal) taxation, and poor (or nominal) public services.[2] In this situation, the Basic Democracies are somewhat covetous of the resources invested in Community Development.

Community Development—or Village A.I.D. as it was first called—preceded Basic Democracy in the field, and in many ways anticipated its purpose. But whereas the latter is intentionally concerned with tutelage or guidance in citizenship, the former is directed to setting the people free from control. The ethos of Community Development in Pakistan, as elsewhere, was to galvanize rural society into productive activity by stimulating the peasants to help them-

---

[1] Among the 39,000 Basic Democrats elected in West Pakistan, 11,636 are said to be illiterate: East Pakistan has elected only 888 illiterates. *Annual Report on Basic Democracies, 1959–1960* (n.d.), p. 11.

[2] At the district level, the District Councils have taken over the finances and functions of the old District Boards. Thus in Khulna, the income of the District Board in 1930 was Rs. 8 lakhs; in 1958 it was Rs. 8·5 lakhs. But because of the fall in money values, in 1930 terms, the income had dwindled to Rs. 1·75 lakhs. 'No exhortation is going to change these basic factors in local government administration', adds the *Outline Report* of a Seminar held at the East Pakistan Academy for Village Development, Comilla, August 1960 (p. 37).

selves, and to encourage them to discover their own 'felt needs'. In Pakistan, as elsewhere, the seed of paradox is buried in this philosophy. But despite the shortcomings revealed in the application of Community Development, the senior officials concerned were able, more clearly than their colleagues in 'the regular line' to discern the dilemma of the newly independent country where a minority seeks radical change and the majority acquiesces in the custom of the past.

Early analyses, while dwelling upon the past dependence of the people upon authority—'Government will provide'—assumed that a new relationship would naturally evolve as the new Community Development methods made their impact upon the people: 'A unique experiment is now being made in the history of administration when orders are not issued from the top but people's representatives are allowed to discuss their problems freely and draw out a list of priorities.'[1] An 'awakening' of popular activity was confidently anticipated once village participation was invited. Further experience indicated that this transformation would not come easily. Community Development was accepted by the village folk as yet another measure of government patronage and direction: a process which might be manipulated, but could not be assimilated by the governed.

In the colonial countries which have attained independence during and after World War II people continue to treat the Government as something alien. Hostility and hatred against the foreign rule have been transferred to the successor Governments.

In most of the underdeveloped countries the Government servant is treated like a small autocrat. . . . He is feared. People obey him, but mostly because they fear some harm will come from him. Government service as such makes one unfit for acceptance by the village society as their leader.

So writes the Chief Administrator of the Community Development Programme in Pakistan.[2] In these circumstances, there is always the temptation to the Village Worker and his superiors to revert to the methods of benevolent autocracy. Moreover, as the Chief Administrator has discerned:

It is one of the inner contradictions of the Community Development Programme that the people directing the programme represent the

[1] *Village AID in West Pakistan* (1957), p. 23.
[2] Masih-uz-Zaman, *Community Development and its Audience* (1960), pp. 15, 17.

interests and classes which stand to lose their status, privilege and power if the programme succeeds. Today political and economic power is concentrated in the hands of the westernized *élite* and specially the Government servants. Democratization of the society is bound to reduce this power and the advantages that accrue from it. It is, therefore, not surprising that the Community Development workers sometimes fail to practise what they teach.[1]

Thanks to this kind of shrewd self-analysis from the highest levels of the organization, and a readiness to adjust copy-book techniques to local needs, Village A.I.D. was able to initiate and foster a modicum of rural reconstruction. Village Councils were formed in many areas, and the leaders of these councils joined together in Block Advisory Committees. A considerable amount of economic improvement resulted from Village A.I.D.; rather less success was achieved in social uplift, and the 'self-help' aspect was least pronounced. One senior official, in acknowledging the shortcomings of the programme, put the blame mainly on the failure of other departments to co-operate: 'The directive letters issued by the Prime Minister to the Chief Ministers of the Provinces, and by the Chief Secretary to the heads of departments fell flat. The nation building departments never committed themselves to carry out a co-ordinated programme at the village level.'[2]

When the Basic Democracies were initiated, the decision was taken to marry the Village A.I.D. organization with the new structure with the intention of obtaining just that co-ordination which had been lacking. The Village A.I.D. Administration became the National Development Organisation, and with Basic Democracy was the concern of a new Ministry of National Reconstruction and Information. In the new situation, Village A.I.D. was assigned the role of technical advice and service. The two provincial academies at Comilla and Peshawar had the task of giving training and 'orientation' to officials concerned with Basic Democracy. The Basic Democracies were expected to absorb the consultative councils set up by Village A.I.D.; thus, its village councils were made co-extensive with the wards of the new Union Councils, and the elected councillor became chairman, though he might have had little contact with community development problems. Moves were made to integrate the community

---

[1] Masih-uz-Zaman, *Community Development and its Audience* (1960), p. 19.
[2] *Outline Report*, Seminar, East Pakistan Academy for Village Development, Comilla, 1960, p. 19. Speech by Manzoor Elahi, C.S.P.

development budget with the budgets of the Basic Democracies. The whole process was marked by extensive, though unacknowledged, manœuvring for position between the heads of the established community development organization and the new officials of Basic Democracy. Each party uneasily suspected that the other was trying to 'swallow' him. Basic Democracy, with its inadequate funds, looked hungrily at the allocation to community development, and also to its plant and equipment (including its sizeable supply of jeeps: this being the principal administrative status symbol in southern Asia today). However, the most probable outcome of this see-saw between the two forms of local action, between the 'tutelary' and the 'voluntary' principles, seems to be the re-emphasis of the power of the traditional district and provincial administration.

The purpose of community development and Basic Democracy is defined as economic expansion: 'From minor welfare work they were being called upon to take part in the national development effort. The most important feature of this effort was the co-ordination of the local development programme with the national development plan. The local effort instead of being an effort in isolation was now to become a part of the integrated whole.'[1] The emphasis of administration has shifted from Law and Order to Economic Development: but the ethos of the traditional administration of the *hakim* remains. For example, in September 1960, the Governor of East Pakistan called for the complete eradication of the water hyacinth (now regarded as a choking weed) from the paddy fields of the province within sixty days! Alamgir, the Mughal despot, might be puzzled by the nature of this decree: the terms in which it was ordained would be wholly familiar to him.

At the time of writing (May 1961) the new constitution has been submitted to the President, but its proposals have not been announced. It appears probable that it will provide for a national assembly which will have power to ratify legislation, but which will not (unlike parliaments established on the Westminster model) have authority to concern itself with the business of government. This will continue to be the preserve of the President, the official administration, and the Basic Democracies. There will be a complete 'separation of powers' on the Montesquieu pattern.

Pakistan's present search for forms of government suitable for a people who (according to President Ayub) are 'not yet ready' for democracy has given the quietus to the agitation for an Islamic state,

[1] *Outline Report*, p. 11.

so hotly debated in earlier years. The President appears to regard Islam as at best a private matter of conscience and morality (like Jinnah) and at worst a reactionary influence: 'the cobwebs of superstition and stagnation'.[1] It is true that the new capital will be called Islamabad, and that encouragement is given to the promotion of pure religion. But the *ulama* are not appeased, and their discontent with the present régime is not disguised.

In sum, the effect of the military revolution has been to revert to the politics of Curzon's India: efficiency, rationalization, development, but no real popular government. The régime still has to tread the path from autocracy to democracy, so baffling in the last days of Imperialism. It still has to evolve a polity that will reconcile modern political aspirations and traditional attitudes. The inconsistencies in a mixed system of official control and popular consultation still remain to be resolved.

The epidemic of military *coups d'état* in 1958 had dual repercussions upon thinking Indians. There was a somewhat self-righteous reaction, 'It can't happen here', a feeling that India was unique, as the Speaker of the Lok Sabha implied when stating 'In our country, as the last remaining democracy in Asia and the biggest democracy in the world, we have our duties to perform . . . in the cause of democracy'.[2] But there was an opposite reaction, an uneasy sense that parliaments and political liberties were not enough; that a deeper social security must be created. These feelings seem to underlie a typical expression of Nehru's 'thinking aloud' to a symposium convened in the Parliament building at New Delhi to consider 'Problems and Prospects of Democracy in Asian Countries'. He asks: what is democracy? His search leads to this conclusion:

Democracy is something deeper than a political form of government —voting, election, etc. In the ultimate analysis, it is a manner of thinking, a manner of action, a manner of behaviour to your neighbour. . . . If the inner content is absent and you are just given an outer shell, well, it may not be successful. I do not know whether I am prepared to say that the same type of democratic institution is suited to every country. . . . In the final analysis, you come back not to political terms, not to economic terms, but to some human terms; or, if you like, spiritual terms. We want to produce a good life, a good

---

[1] *The Times*, November 12, 1960.
[2] *Future of Asian Democracy*, Indian Bureau of Parliamentary Studies, New Delhi, 1959, p. 13.

individual. . . . We go back to the individual being given that opportunity [to realize himself] and also the institutions and forms of government being so organized as to encourage this aspect.[1]

To reach this position, Nehru was compelled to acknowledge that political democracy is inadequate; social equality is an essential component: 'Political freedom under economic pressure is very limited freedom'; and yet 'I do not see any real progress unless the individual progresses, and I do not see any individual progress unless a large measure of freedom for him is given to progress'.[2] Between the Marxist and the Liberal within Nehru there is no reconciliation.

Recognizing that this dilemma poses a problem for authority and government, the Prime Minister does not attempt an answer to his own questions, confessing 'I have not the faintest notion as to what it will lead to'.

The most generally accepted recipe for Indian democracy is the elevation of the ancient Indian ideal of social harmony, or unity, into a present-day political principle. Thus, the Speaker of the Lok Sabha, the first parliamentarian:

In a parliamentary democracy, unanimity must be aimed at; it may not be practicable. But unanimity must be the goal. . . . My own feeling is, each man whether he is in the opposition or in the Government is as much a representative of his constituency as any other man. . . . It only happens that on the Government side a larger number of representatives join together. . . . [To ignore the opposition member] merely on the strength of numbers leads to frustration, and very often if he does not succeed in Parliament he breaks the law outside. So, in a parliamentary democracy, the party in power should carry the opposition with them as much as possible. . . . Before important matters are brought before Parliament, the Government must consult the opposition also. Some people believe that . . . democracy can exist only under the capitalist society. Can there not be democracy coupled with socialism? . . . I would go even further. If it pleases my friends the communists, we will have democratic communism in this country. There is no harm in that.

We have to follow a policy which is evolved according to our own pattern and which is consistent with our own historic tradition and the feelings of our own people.[3]

[1] *Future of Asian Democracy*, Indian Bureau of Parliamentary Studies, New Delhi, 1959, p. 8.
[2] *Ibid.*, p. 5.
[3] *Ibid.*, pp. 89–90.

This approach is shared by some Communist leaders, such as P. C. Joshi:

In Parliament we are fighting too much as parties; let us have forms of consultation. Our Chief Minister [of Kerala] Namboodiripad said that. The British form of political ding-dong does not suit us. I submit the future of parliamentary democracy in India depends on how all patriotic and democratic elements in our country fulfil the tasks facing the Indian nation. . . . Can we unite and evolve policies and achieve these things?[1]

Even a democratic Socialist finds difficulty in sustaining the role of creative opposition. Asoka Mehta, the P.S.P. leader declares: 'Opposition to become strong often utilizes the deeply felt loyalties of religion, language, tribe or caste. . . . Opposition if confined to the political plane remains anæmic.'[2] In consequence, Mehta has to concede that 'the main function of the Opposition is to exercise vigilance'. In this situation, he finds that 'the executive gets exalted, the legislature deflated'.[3] The continuing dominance of the executive, or the administration, in both India and Pakistan is a political feature previously emphasized. Apprehension that the power of the executive has increased rather than declined since independence has led many to hark back to the Gandhian ideal. One of the most coherent expressions of this spirit is the Sarvodaya movement, whose aims are presented in a penetrating work of social and political analysis by Jayaprakash Narayan: *A Plea for Reconstruction of Indian Polity.*[4]

This is not the place to attempt a general summary of the Jayaprakash thesis, but its political implications must be noted. He sees 'the problem of devising the right kind of polity' as 'part of the larger problem of social reconstruction'. 'The problem of present-day civilization is social integration. . . . The problem is to re-create the human community.'[5] His social reconstruction will be founded in a rural co-operative society. He insists that neither society nor the state

---

[1] *Future of Asian Democracy*, Indian Bureau of Parliamentary Studies, New Delhi, 1959, p. 87.

[2] *The Opposition in the New States*, by Asoka Mehta, p. 5. Discussion Paper presented to the Rhodes International Seminar, October 1958 (Congress for Cultural Freedom).

[3] *Ibid.*, p. 3.

[4] Printed in Draft form (for private circulation) in 1959. This Draft by no means represents the final conclusions of Jayaprakash, and is stated to have been prepared 'in haste'.

[5] *Ibid.*, pp. 36–7.

can be an aggregation of individuals: the community, not the individual, remains the basic social unit for India. His goal is *gram dharma*: 'the function of *dharma* is to hold together harmoniously the social order' we are told; it is law rooted in social custom, that is, social ethics. This cannot be revived by means of legislation; it must 'arise from life itself'.[1] Jayaprakash contrasts his 'communitarian' society with the present 'centralism', which he believes is an inherent element of parliamentary democracy. He deplores the forces of faction and sectional interest which are generated: 'Parties create dissensions where unity is called for, exaggerate differences where they should be minimized.' He finds that 'A natural outcome of centralization of power and administration is bureaucracy'.[2]

The solution propounded by Jayaprakash draws heavily upon Gandhian teaching: a federation of village republics: but the village is not regarded as self-sufficient, and the sense of community is expected to broaden out to include neighbouring villages. He expects these associated villages (which he calls the 'regional community') to provide the main focus for the communitarian society: 'as we proceed from the inner to the outer circles of communal life and organization, there is less and less to do for the outer communities; so that when we reach the circle of the National Community it has only a few matters to attend to, such as: defence, foreign relations, currency, interprovincial co-ordination and legislation.'[3] The present vast responsibilities of the Centre in the economic and social field would be dissolved: 'Planning would begin from the primary community and therefrom fan outwards. In our scheme of things the regional plan, i.e. the plan of the regional community, would be the pivotal plan. This would mean that the regional plan—and not the village plan which would be too small for the purpose—would be the *unit* out of which the whole national plan would have to be constructed.'[4]

Many of the details of the political philosophy of Jayaprakash echo traditional Hindu values; the spirit of community is expressed in the search for unanimity; when members of panchayats are selected, the method of choice should be 'by general agreement or by drawing lots' (the latter method being adopted in the Bhoodan movement for distribution of lands). The executive at the higher levels would function by means of committee: the District Council, the provincial Pranta Sabha, and the national Rashtra Sabha. There would be no prime

---

[1] *A Plea for Reconstruction of Indian Polity*, pp. 23–4.
[2] *Ibid.*, pp. 52, 54.   [3] *Ibid.*, pp. 43–4.   [4] *Ibid.*, p. 58

minister or ministers; the decisions of the executive committees would be implemented by officials appointed by these different committees at their different levels; the all-India services would virtually disappear. Clearly it is necessary to accept the Jayaprakash thesis *in toto* or not at all. The concept of the basis of democracy as the community— not the individual—is vital. Even on his own terms, certain features are inadequate. The plan does not really provide for the cities, absorbing population at an ever increasing rate (despite the concept of 'agroindustrial society', and the provision for federations of cities). The plan offers no place to the dynamic element in present-day India; the entrepreneurs, industrialists, and progressive farmers. The total emphasis on community means an emphasis on all the static, reactionary elements in India; and acceptance of their values must mean the dismissal of any possibility of short-cuts to economic growth and transformation. Moreover, the uncritical evocation of the 'little village republics' of the past, so beloved by Indian dreamers and schemers (Ch. 3) bases the thesis not in reality and experience but in a bogus antiquarian myth, and weakens confidence in the forward-looking aspects of Jayaprakash's thinking. Even so, *A Plea for Reconstruction of Indian Polity* is indeed a proposal for reconstruction, not for Utopian revolution. It evokes the historic balance of the Hindu polity, with its overall concept of universal emperor, *Cakravartin*, and its infrastructure of Rajas and Patels and other accepted local rulers: the immanent vision of Indian unity, and the actual reality of local autonomy. Many observers dismiss Jayaprakash as a theoretician, out of touch with reality. It is therefore striking that the most important practical proposal for administrative decentralization and local self-help bears a distinct resemblance to the *Plea for Reconstruction*: the proposal made by the hard-headed Gujarati business man and politician, Balvantray G. Mehta and his colleagues in their *Report of the Team for the Study of Community Projects*.[1]

This Report was mentioned earlier in this paper as one of the products of the activities of the National Planning Commission. It is somewhat ironical that this most powerful plea for local self-government should originate under the auspices of the focal power for centralization.

The Balvantray Report (as it is known) forms an indictment of the formalistic or theoretical application of Community Development.[2]

[1] Committee on Plan Projects, New Delhi, 1957, 3 vols.
[2] The findings are analysed in some detail in the writer's 'Authority and Community in Village India', *Pacific Affairs*, December 1959.

The Indian village of today is revealed as a web of conflicting interests and rivalries. The panchayat is found to have only a nominal existence in most places. The machinery for popular consultation, established under the Community Development programme is revealed as ineffective or even non-existent, and the 'participation' of the people, both in *shramdan* (work-gift) and in donations is shown to be frequently secured only by pressure and even compulsion on the part of the district staff. Altogether, the traditional village attitude of looking to Government to provide for their needs is found to have undergone little change.

However, the Report discerned some grounds for optimism: 'A few panchayats have been successful in a small measure in mobilizing voluntary labour for community work. In such villages a new leadership is emerging, indicative of a new attitude to local welfare and local development and a realization of the value of local institutions.'[1] On this somewhat slender foundation, the Report proposed what was specifically described as 'an act of faith—faith in democracy'.[2] This was a radical plan for devolution and popular self-government. It was recommended that the main responsibility for economic and social uplift should be entrusted to a local representative body at the level of the Development Block (an area of about one hundred villages) to be called the *Panchayat Samiti*. Within each Block the villages would be grouped together in 'circles', equivalent to the jurisdiction of the *Gram Sevak* (Village Level Worker). Each circle would cover a population of not more than four thousand, and about twenty circles would make up the Block. The members of the village panchayats of a circle would each elect one of their number to be a member of the *Panchayat Samiti*.[3] The Samiti is to be responsible for the development of agriculture, and local industries; for public health, welfare work, and the administration of primary schools.[4] It is to have the right to levy a broad range of taxes, tolls, and fees, as well as a sizeable proportion of the land revenue.

At the district level there is to be a *Zila Parishad*, of which the members will be the presidents of the *Panchayat Samitis* (initially,

---

[1] Balvantray Report, vol. i, p. 44.

[2] *Ibid.*, p. 21.

[3] Beside the twenty-odd circle representatives, the Samiti would co-opt two women; and where 5 per cent or more of the Block population belong to the Scheduled Castes or Scheduled Tribes, they also would send co-opted representatives to the Samiti.

[4] A detailed list of the powers of village panchayats, *panchayat samitis*, and *zila parishads*, is given in the Balvantray Report, vol. iii (pt. i), pp. 167–9.

the Block Development Officer, but later a non-official), members of the state legislature and of Parliament whose constituencies lie in the district, and the departmental heads of the 'nation-building' departments in the district. This new body will replace the former District Board, the District School Board, and other organs; but its role is supposed to be that of a co-ordinating authority; the *Parishad* is expressly denied executive functions; 'that way lies danger to the initiative, and therefore the effectiveness of the panchayat samitis'.[1] The intention is to vest authority in a 'single representative and vigorous democratic institution': the Report emphasizes that:

It is not theory or dogma which is impelling us to make these recommendations but practical considerations. Democracy has to function through certain executive machinery, but the democratic government operating over large areas through its executive machinery cannot adequately appreciate local needs and circumstances. It is, therefore, necessary that there should be a devolution of power and a decentralization of machinery and that such power be exercised and such machinery controlled and directed by popular representatives of the local area.[2]

The Balvantray proposals were accepted by the governments of all the states, except those of Bombay and West Bengal. Legislation followed during 1958 and 1959; the old District Boards were abolished, and provision made for a three-tier system of panchayats, for the Village, the Block, and the District. The first state to introduce the new system—known as *Panchayati Raj*—was Rajasthan, in October 1959; followed by Madras, Andhra, Mysore, Kerala, and Assam.

First reports give a tentative indication of the pattern that is emerging within *Panchayati Raj*. The first elections did not fulfil the hopes for a new spirit of 'unanimity'. Even the realistic Balvantray Report anticipated that panchayats would be elected on a basis of 'the general consent of the people', and regarded as 'an opportunity for service . . . rather than as a means for obtaining power'.[3] But the political parties have seized upon the *samiti* and *parishad* elections, recognizing that they represented an important potential reservoir of power. In Rajasthan, the Congress captured many of the new councils and installed party men in key posts. Many of the new chairmen of *samitis* and *parishads* were co-opted from politics. As in the Basic Democracies in Pakistan, a new form of local government did not,

[1] Balvantray Report, vol. i, p. 20.
[2] *Ibid.*, pp. 6, 7.
[3] *Ibid.*, p. 18.

of itself, produce the anticipated new types of leader. In Rajasthan, at the village level, new development projects must be approved by a two-thirds majority of the members; this provision was intended to fulfil the concept of unanimity, but in practice in the prevailing atmosphere of village faction, it is more likely to lead to deadlock and delay in village development.[1] The Rajasthan legislation also empowers the District Officer to suspend resolutions and orders of the *samitis*, while the state government can actually reverse them. There has been a considerable struggle between the 'executive' and the 'representative' elements in the new bodies; and as in Rajasthan the administration has been in the melting-pot, following the liquidation of princely rule, it is not in a strong position to withstand pressure. Elsewhere, the grip of the executive will not be shaken so readily. In Madras, for example, the new District Development Council (the equivalent of the *Zila Parishad*) has the Collector as its President, while the members from the state legislature and from Parliament are not accorded the right to vote. In consequence, the politicians' enthusiasm to take part in the new Councils has been considerably tempered, and the district administration continues, much as before.

Will this cycle of local self-government meet with the same stubborn refusal of Indian rural society, and Indian district administration to adapt towards a new relationship: followed by the same tendency to greater official control and centralization which occurred after the failure of the panchayat experiment in the early 1950's? Or will this 'act of faith' in transferring power to the samitis have the singular significance of the 'leap in the dark' in England in 1868, when electoral power was first given to the working class—will this be the moment (unsuspected, as now) when political power in India begins to pass from the urban middle class to the rural masses?

The parliamentary system was adopted in India mainly because the Westernized professional and upper middle classes accepted it as the proper, democratic form of government. In Pakistan, the lack of any effective demand for parliamentary government from the miniscule Westernized middle class led to its early demise. Will the same eclipse follow the transfer of the political initiative from the hands of the Indian urban upper middle class to the rural masses? In Pakistan, the failure of the parliamentary system has led to a return

[1] P. K. Chaudhuri, 'Decentralisation or Delegation of Power? The Rajasthan Panchayat Samitis and Zila Parishad Act, 1959', *Economic Weekly*, October 3, 1959.

to autocratic government. The effort to galvanize the mass of the people into a dynamic relationship with their government has been launched: but the controlling hand of authority seems (initially) as dominant as ever. In India, the civil service is effectively subordinated to ministerial direction: but at lower levels the relationship of representative to executive is less easily defined. Autocracy is giving way to democracy. But in this 'transfer of power' the new form of government proves unable to establish a partnership between the representative element and the official element. The latter inherits the accumulated authority of tradition, together with new powers created by the new responsibilities assumed by the modern state in welfare and economic development. The representative element fails to attain a countervailing importance in public life. The leading politicians, as Ministers, become part of the executive. The non-ministerial politicians occupy an amorphous middle position between the executive and the public as 'fixers', manipulators of the administrative machine: or else play an entirely neutralizing role, on the *satyagraha* pattern, bringing government into disrepute or even into nullity.

Moreover, the whole political debate fails to secure agreement on the basic foundations of democracy. In the West, democratic government (and indeed the whole ethos of modern society) hinges upon the individual as the unit of decision; upon free political choice, free (in great part) from the trammels of family, religion, domicile, and occupation.[1] This establishes a direct relationship between the individual and the state: for in choosing its representatives, the electorate gives a vote of confidence to a party, and determines which shall form the Government. It is clear that in southern Asia, the 'freedom' of the individual voter is illusory. Caste, religion, language, and other forces condition his vote. So the attempt is made to fuse these divisive forces into a general sense of community. The prevailing communitarian concept of democracy places emphasis upon the corporate will, and the ties that bind village with village. This emphasis upon the corporate expression of the popular will, when interpreted in the form of institutions, appears to be inseparable from a system of indirect election and representation. Whereas parliamentary democracy envisages the individual voter directly choosing his parliamentary representative (and thereby his central government) the new system merges the individual into the village, village into

---

[1] Everything is relative: Sir Ivor Jennings devotes a large part of his *Appeal to the People* (1960) to showing that these factors do exercise their influence upon the British voter.

neighbourhood, and so upward, tier upon tier. The little community of the village blends into the great community of the nation: but interposed are many layers of councils, and individual political decision and accountability are deliberately erased.

How far will this communitarian system help evolve a partnership between the executive (the bureaucracy) and the representatives of the people? First experience, both of *Panchayati Raj* and of Basic Democracy, suggests that one side will tend to dominate the other: they will not easily coalesce. So long as the substance of power rests in the hands of the executive, largely controlled from above (by the state or central government)—so long will any attempt to encourage local self-government (including the new samitis and parishads) be subject to a magnetic pull from above. Until the tradition of superior authority diminishes, the effective locus of power cannot be located at the level of village or neighbourhood: in this regard the Jayaprakash *Reconstruction* is more practical than the present *Panchayati Raj* or the Basic Democracies scheme.[1]

[1] In a statement to Parliament on May 13, 1961, S. K. Dey, Minister for Community Development, announced that Jayaprakash Narayan had been appointed chairman of a Study Team on Community Development. With regard to *Panchayati Raj*, the Minister commented 'It is hoped, in future, some sort of functional representation will be provided to Zila Parishads, both in the State legislature and, maybe, indirectly in the Parliament.'

INDEX

For Product Safety Concerns and Information please contact our EU
representative GPSR@taylorandfrancis.com
Taylor & Francis Verlag GmbH, Kaufingerstraße 24, 80331 München, Germany